IMAGES
of Rail

Washington & Old Dominion Railroad Revisited

On the Cover: Perhaps the most photographed derailment on the Washington & Old Dominion Railroad (W&OD), diesel-electric freight locomotive No. 55 stumbled over a broken rail while switching hopper cars at East Falls Church on May 30, 1951. Railfans were taking a farewell trip on passenger car No. 45, anticipating the cessation of passenger operations the following day. John F. Burns, one of the railfans, photographed the activity. (Courtesy of John F. Burns.)

IMAGES
of Rail

Washington & Old Dominion Railroad Revisited

David A. Guillaudeu and Paul E. McCray

ARCADIA
PUBLISHING

ISBN 978-1-4671-1638-1

Published by Arcadia Publishing
Charleston, South Carolina

Printed in the United States of America

Library of Congress Control Number: 2015954748

For all general information, please contact Arcadia Publishing:
Telephone 843-853-2070
Fax 843-853-0044
E-mail sales@arcadiapublishing.com
For customer service and orders:
Toll-Free 1-888-313-2665

Visit us on the Internet at www.arcadiapublishing.com

This book is dedicated to the employees of the railroad who built, operated, and maintained such a fascinating railroad, especially the late Doug Lee; and to John F. Burns.

Contents

Acknowledgments		6
Introduction		7
1.	Rosslyn	9
2.	Great Falls	23
3.	Leesburg	35
4.	Purcellville	59
5.	Mills	69
6.	Locomotive Details	85
7.	Maintaining the Right of Way	101
8.	W&OD Railroad Regional Trail	117

Acknowledgments

Thank you to the following folks who helped make this volume possible with their assistance, information, and shared memories (in alphabetical order): Jay Adams, A. Smith Bowman Distillery; Mary Ahrens, A. Smith Bowman Distillery; David Alden, Railway & Locomotive Historical Society; Douglas Bailey, engineer, Iowa Traction Railway; W. Burton Barber, W&OD engineer right of way and structures; Jason Brownell, Bruce Brownell Inc.; Mark Buckingham, Wolfe House and Building Movers; John F. Burns, railfan; George Combs, Special Collections, Alexandria City Library; Beckham Dickerson, architect, Kamstra-Dickerson Associates Inc.; Coby Ellison, curator of collections, St. Louis Museum of Transportation; Alyssa Fisher, intern, Aldie Mill Historic Park, Northern Virginia Regional Park Authority (NOVA Parks); Tracy Gillespie, site manager, Aldie Mill Historic Park, NOVA Parks; Herbert H. Harwood, railfan; Michael R. Johns, general manager, Iowa Traction Railway; Doug Lee, W&OD engineer and conductor; David Marcham, W&OD employee; Charles Mauro, local Herndon historian; John Richards, conductor, Iowa Traction Railway; Lisa Rogers, co-owner, Loudoun County Milling Company; Wynne C. Saffer, son, C.C. Saffer & Brother Mill; Eugene Scheel, local historian; Neil Steinberg, photographer, Photoworks, Leesburg, Virginia; Joseph Weyraugh, railfan; Jonathan Wingate, Burlington Junction Railway; Clarice Wyse, president, Toledo, Lake Erie & Western Railway and Museum Inc., Grand Rapids, Ohio; and Eric E. Zicht, professional engineer and land surveyor, Zicht & Associates PLC.

Photographs where only the photographer's name is given are from author David A. Guillaudeu's collection. Where no photographer or collection is credited, the photograph was taken by author David A. Guillaudeu. Throughout the text, when the word "author" is used, it refers to David A. Guillaudeu.

Years given in the map captions for aerial photographs refer to the dates the name is known to be accurate for. In most cases, these are the dates of the Sanborn Fire Insurance Company maps that were used as references.

INTRODUCTION

Early Virginia colonial landowners bought their lands for shillings per acre. The way to make money was to then develop the land and sell it for hundreds of pounds per acre. As the country was new, the landowners needed a reason for entrepreneurs to develop the land. Trading was one such means—purchasing farm products and selling them to city dwellers and exporting them. In early colonial times, tobacco was the cash crop. As the soil wore out, wheat became one of the main products, along with flour. The same early landowners also had their sights set on the Ohio River valley. To promote trade and look to the future, they needed a port location that was as close to the sources of products to be exported as possible, as well as a location from which the Ohio River valley could be easily reached. Several locations were considered, but in the end, the Alexandria area was chosen for its natural port on the Potomac River that could handle oceangoing vessels. The headwaters of the Potomac were a short portage trip from the Ohio River. On the way to the Ohio, the Potomac River met up with the Shenandoah River, where products from the valley's rich agricultural fields could be shipped.

To support traffic through the port, the Little River Turnpike and the Alexandria-Leesburg Pike were built as pathways of commerce into Virginia's interior. Meanwhile, the Chesapeake & Ohio Canal was built from Washington toward Cumberland, Maryland. The Alexandria Canal, completed in December 1843, connected Alexandria to the Chesapeake & Ohio Canal at Georgetown, District of Columbia. It was operated from 1843 until the Civil War. Its main commerce was in coal mined in western Maryland.

After its retrocession to Virginia from the District of Columbia in 1846, Alexandria undertook the construction of several railroads. Chief among these early railroads was the Orange & Alexandria Railroad and the Alexandria, Loudoun & Hampshire Railroad. The Orange & Alexandria Railroad tapped the fertile farm fields of central Virginia, bringing in flour and grain.

Lewis McKenzie, an Alexandria businessman, had projected that sales of coal might reach 15 million tons. He realized that the Alexandria Canal was not efficient enough to carry this much coal and that the only transportation available that could do so was a railroad. He gathered some friends and petitioned the Virginia General Assembly for a charter to build a railroad to the coalfields of Hampshire County, Virginia, near Paddytown (now Keyser, West Virginia). After the Civil War, the Alexandria, Loudoun & Hampshire Railroad realigned its sights on the Ohio River and the coal mines in the area. It renamed itself the Washington & Ohio Railroad.

Briefly, the Alexandria, Loudoun & Hampshire Railroad began construction in 1857, ran its first paying train service to Vienna in 1859, and began scheduled operations to Leesburg on March 4, 1860. The Civil War stopped new construction and saw the destruction of much railroad property. It took the railroad until 1867 to resume service to Leesburg. Then, the railroad, broadening its horizons and intending to reach the Ohio River, renamed itself the Washington & Western Railroad. By this time, the Baltimore & Ohio Railroad had reached Harpers Ferry and connected with the Winchester & Potomac Railroad, which served Shenandoah Valley farmers. Construction halted at Round Hill in 1874 until the Snickersville citizens were able to successfully petition the Southern Railway, which then owned the tracks, to extend the railroad four more miles to their town. Southern Railway agreed on the condition that the town be renamed, and Bluemont was selected. The Southern Railway began operations to Bluemont on July 4, 1900.

Meanwhile, other investors had obtained a charter for the Great Falls & Old Dominion Railroad (GF&OD) in 1900. In 1901, John R. McLean and Stephen B. Elkins purchased the GF&OD and completed its construction to the Great Falls of the Potomac River. Construction was completed on July 3, 1906, and service began the next day, on the Fourth of July. McLean and Elkins created a scenic resort at Great Falls that became a great success. They decided to expand their operations in Northern Virginia and took out a lease on the Southern Railway's Bluemont Branch. They connected the branch with the Great Falls line via four short miles of double track called the Spout Run Division. In 1912, the combined trackage was placed under a new corporate name, Washington & Old Dominion (W&OD) Railway, which became the W&OD Railroad in 1935. The Chesapeake & Ohio Railway (C&O) purchased the W&OD Railroad in 1956, anticipating the construction of a coal-fired power plant north of the community of Cascades north of Ashburn in Loudoun County. The C&O sought abandonment after the power plant was sited in Maryland and the C&O could not obtain favorable zoning in Fairfax County for additional railroad customers.

Images of Rail: *Washington & Old Dominion Railroad Revisited* was written to provide more details on a cross-section of railroad topics. Many previous articles and books have provided overviews of the history, the different pieces of equipment, and the operations of the railroad. The intent with this volume is to take a more detailed look at several different topics and not to try to cover a full range of topics. Time has passed on, and the industrial areas of the towns the railroad served have been irrevocably changed such that it is difficult to envision where the railroad ran or what the town was like during its railroad days. By presenting pictures from one end to the other of Rosslyn, Leesburg, and Purcellville, the authors capture the past essence of these places. Feed and grain mills were present in many of the towns the railroad served. They received grain and fertilizer and shipped other grain and feed out. In looking at the mills and a few other line-side industries, the effects of the railroad on the local economy can be seen.

The first volume covered the passenger equipment and the Evans Auto-Railer in some detail, with a passing mention of other pieces of equipment. This volume provides details on three more pieces of equipment: the Forney steam locomotive, the Baldwin-Westinghouse electric freight locomotive, and the Burro Crane Inc. Model 30 crane. Three Forney locomotives were purchased from the Manhattan Elevated Railway and used for a short time on the GF&OD. Two Baldwin-Westinghouse electric freight locomotives provided the backbone of the W&OD's freight service during the interurban era (when the trains ran on electricity drawn from overhead wires). The chapter on locomotives presents cab interior photographs of steam, electric, and diesel-electric locomotives spanning the operating years of the GF&OD and W&OD (1906–1968). The first volume showed how W. Burton Barber's crews replaced two bridges. This volume looks at how his crews handled washouts, placed equipment back on the track, and utilized the Burro crane. In the last chapter, Paul McCray describes the history of one of the lasting legacies of the W&OD: the NOVA Parks W&OD Railroad Regional Park and its trail.

Just for fun, find the hidden bird's nest.

One

Rosslyn

Once the Potomac River leaves the confines of its banks at Rosslyn, it spreads out tremendously, making any bridge farther south a much longer affair than one at Rosslyn. Thus, Georgetown in the District of Columbia was the closest point on the Chesapeake & Ohio Canal to Alexandria, and Rosslyn became the northernmost community in Virginia that the canal passed through.

Once the bridge was there and John R. McLean and Stephen B. Elkins decided to operate a railroad from Washington, DC, to Great Falls, Rosslyn became the natural location for the railroad's operating facilities. Rosslyn was the center of GF&OD operations from 1906 to 1912 and then W&OD operations from 1912 until 1962, when the Spout Run Division was abandoned. While Georgetown had been the northern terminus of the railroad from its inception, the closing of the Aqueduct Bridge due to deterioration caused the railroad to move its northern terminus to Rosslyn. Rosslyn was the main passenger terminal for the remainder of the railroad's passenger carrying years. Rosslyn was also the station where passengers could change to trolleys bound for the District of Columbia via the Capital Traction Company (1923–1933), the Capital Transit Company (1933–1951), or Alexandria, or Mount Vernon via the Washington-Virginia Railway (1923–1927) and the Mount Vernon, Alexandria & Washington Railway (1927–1932). According to John F. Burns, Capital Traction Company built the passenger terminal in return for the W&OD's right to cross the Potomac River.

The next two pages present maps of the W&OD Railroad showing the route of the railroad against today's roads. After some aerial photographs, the chapter continues its presentation of the railroad facilities at Rosslyn. The pictures are organized to show the railroad from its east end to its west end. While the track arrangement at the east end changed through the years as the rails were cut back from Washington to Rosslyn during the passenger service days and then cut back again to North Nash Street, the remainder of the yard was fairly stable until abandonment.

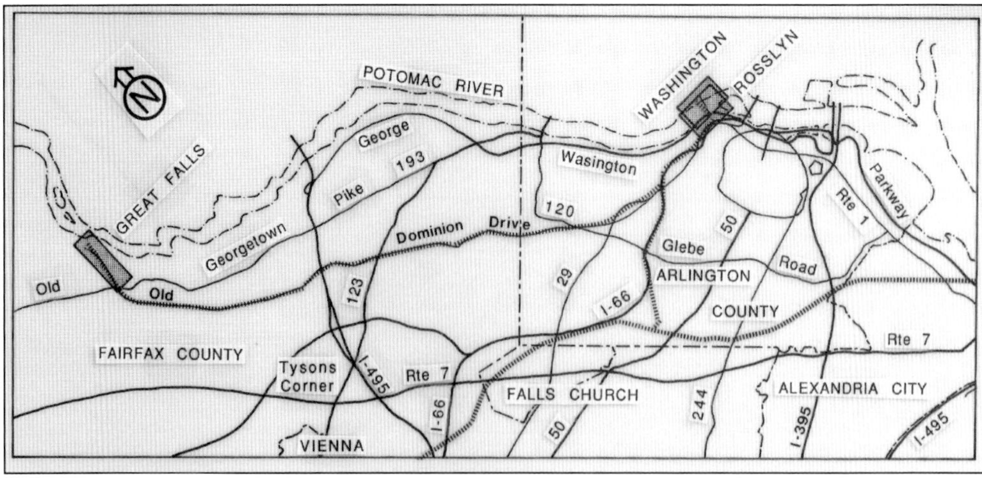

This map shows the major roads along the south side of the Potomac River from Washington, DC, to Great Falls. The gray rectangles represent station areas. The right of way of the Great Falls & Old Dominion Railroad became Old Dominion Drive. The Counties of Fairfax and Arlington were fortunate to obtain the right of way, as it provides the major road passing through this area.

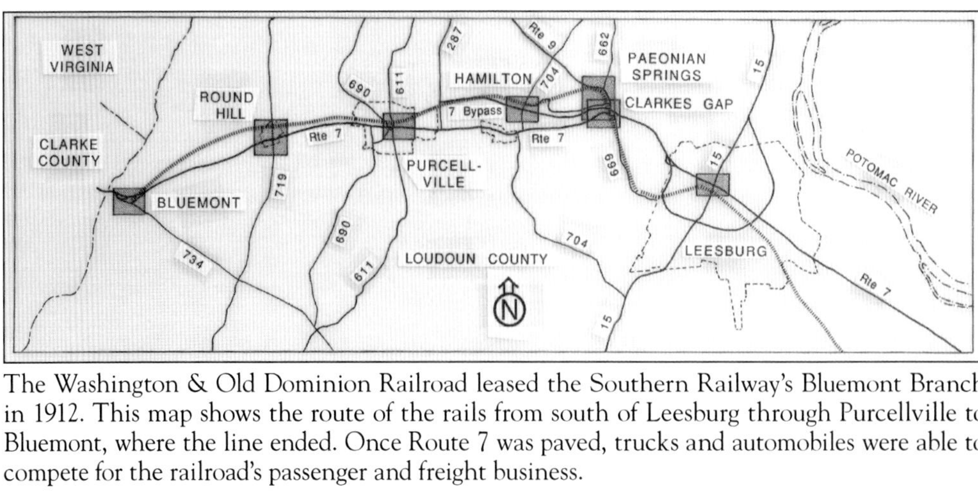

The Washington & Old Dominion Railroad leased the Southern Railway's Bluemont Branch in 1912. This map shows the route of the rails from south of Leesburg through Purcellville to Bluemont, where the line ended. Once Route 7 was paved, trucks and automobiles were able to compete for the railroad's passenger and freight business.

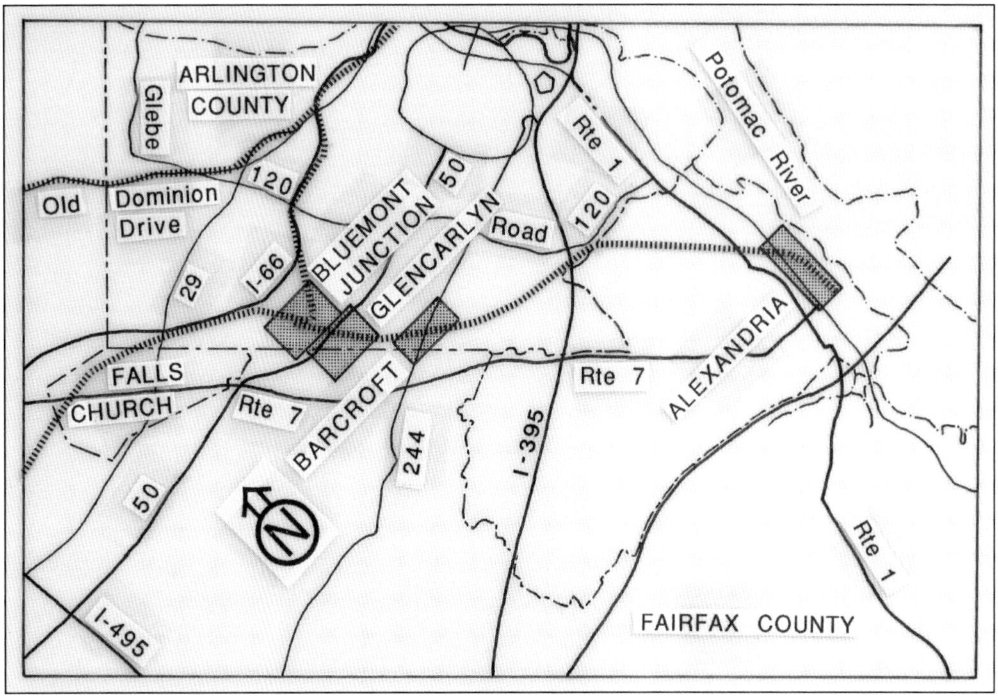

The Bluemont Branch of the Southern Railway ran from Alexandria to its namesake roughly following the path of Four Mile Run from Glebe Road to Falls Church. The W&OD Railway built the Spout Run Division between Bluemont Junction and Thrifton (near present day Lyon Village on Lee Highway, or Route 29). Thrifton is where the line to Great Falls met the Spout Run Division rails.

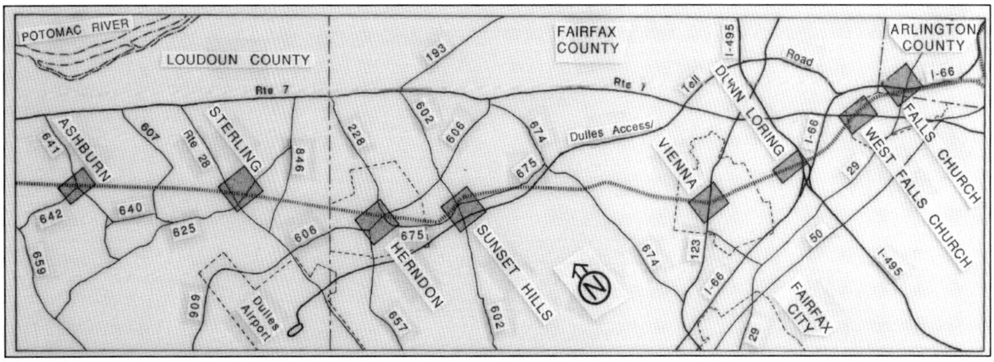

This map shows the middle towns and stations along the railroad. Camp Alger was located at Dunn Loring during the Spanish-American War. The A. Smith Bowman Distillery was located at Sunset Hills. The Cherrydale Cement Block Company's third plant was located on the east side of Herndon. Construction of Dulles International Airport led to the suburbanization of eastern Loudoun County and the loss of farms and railroad customers.

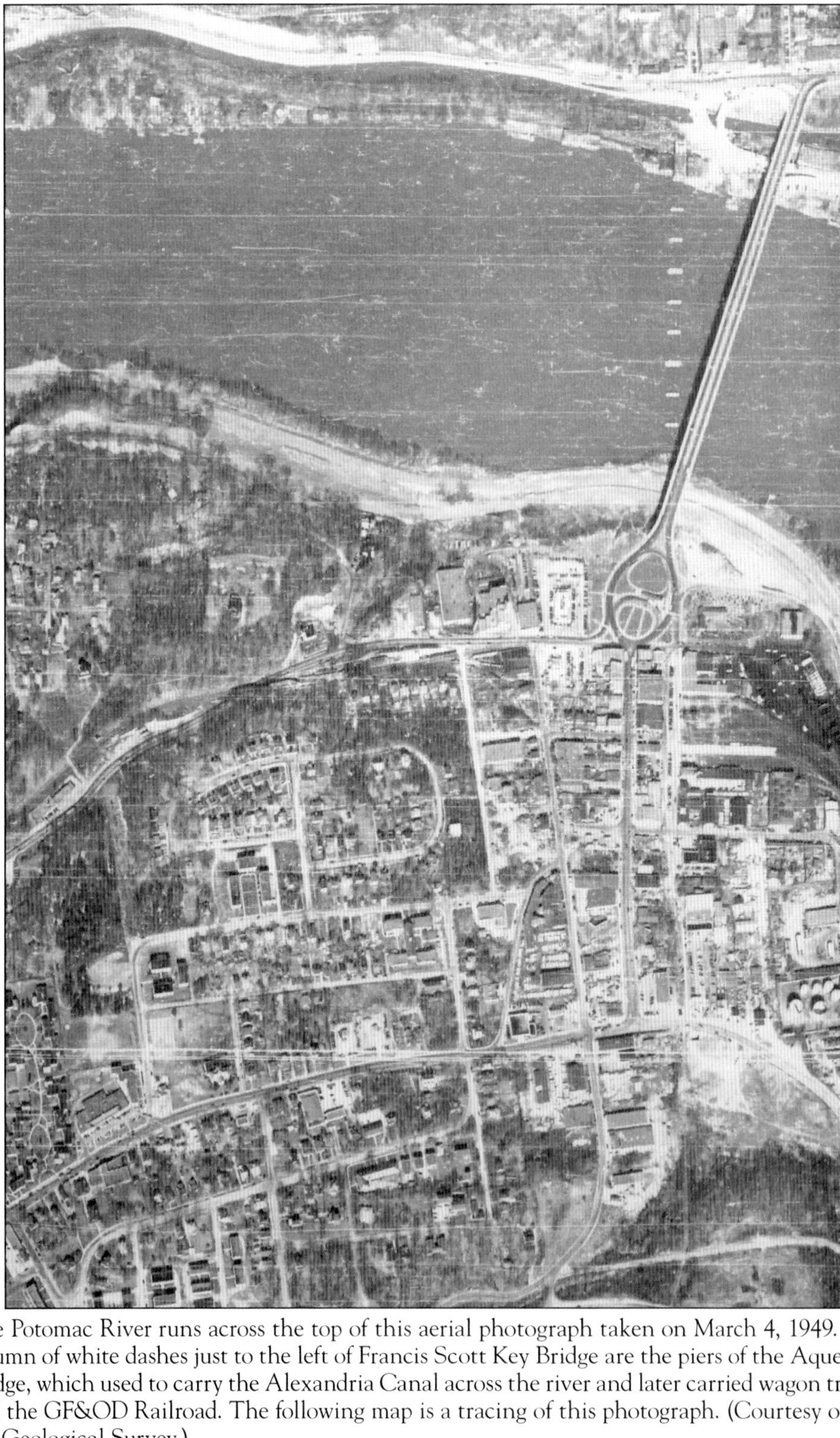

The Potomac River runs across the top of this aerial photograph taken on March 4, 1949. The column of white dashes just to the left of Francis Scott Key Bridge are the piers of the Aqueduct Bridge, which used to carry the Alexandria Canal across the river and later carried wagon traffic and the GF&OD Railroad. The following map is a tracing of this photograph. (Courtesy of the US Geological Survey.)

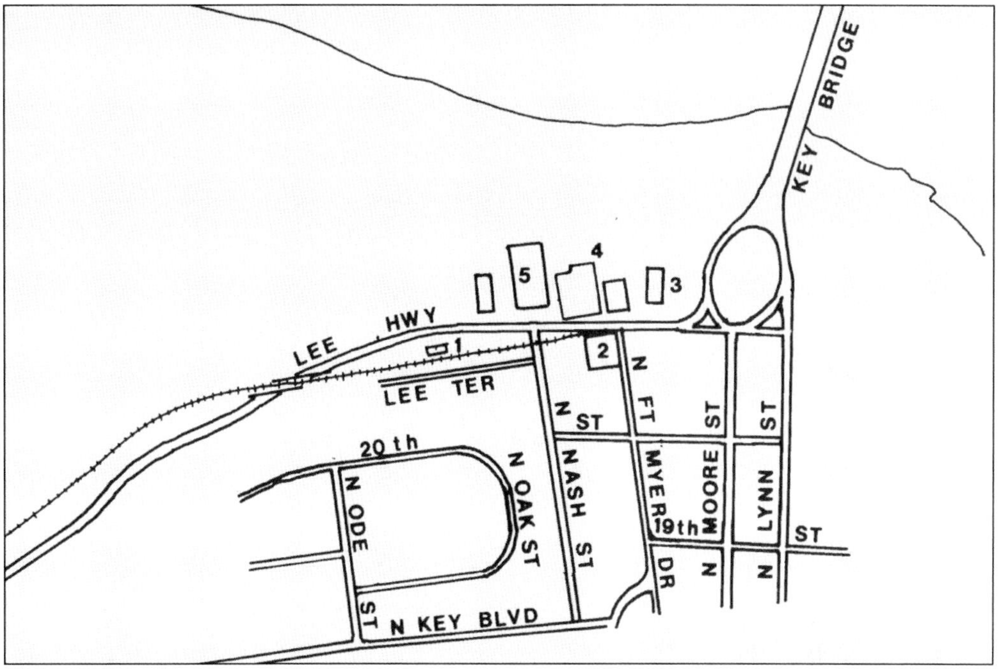

The railroad's facilities were located primarily on the south side of Lee Highway. Tracks ran east along Lee Highway to the Rosslyn passenger terminal. The numbered points are: (1) W&OD freight house. (2) Rosslyn car and locomotive shop. (3) W&OD Rosslyn passenger terminal, located about where the Key Bridge Marriott stands. (4) Fowler Carbonic Company. (5) Industrial building constructed after 1936.

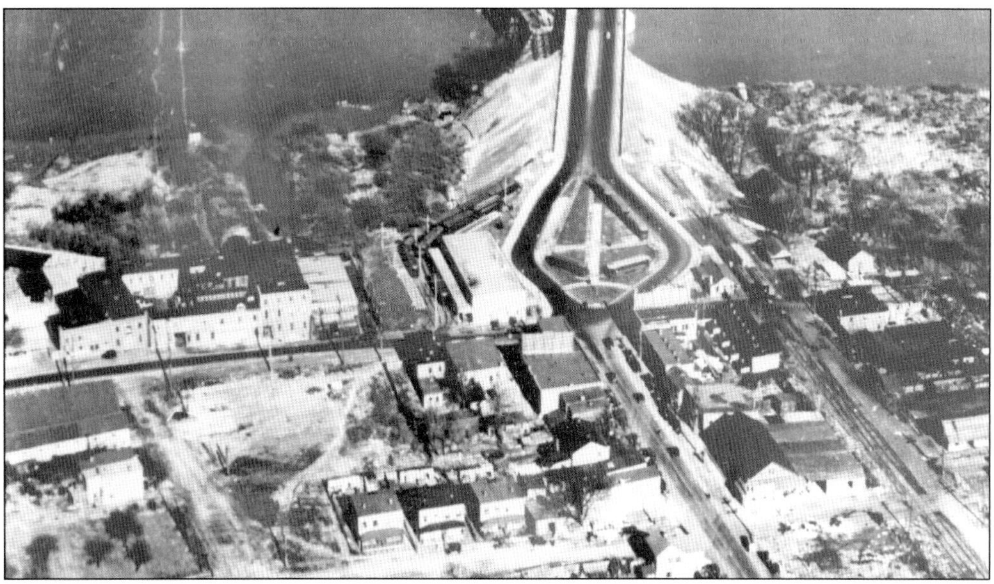

This aerial photograph was taken during the construction of the Francis Scott Key Bridge, about 1923. The Rosslyn passenger terminal is located on the west (left) side of Capital Traction Company's trolley loop at the south end of Key Bridge. The complex of buildings to the left of the terminal and right of the Fowler plant housed the Rosslyn Packing Company in 1921. (Courtesy of the National Archives.)

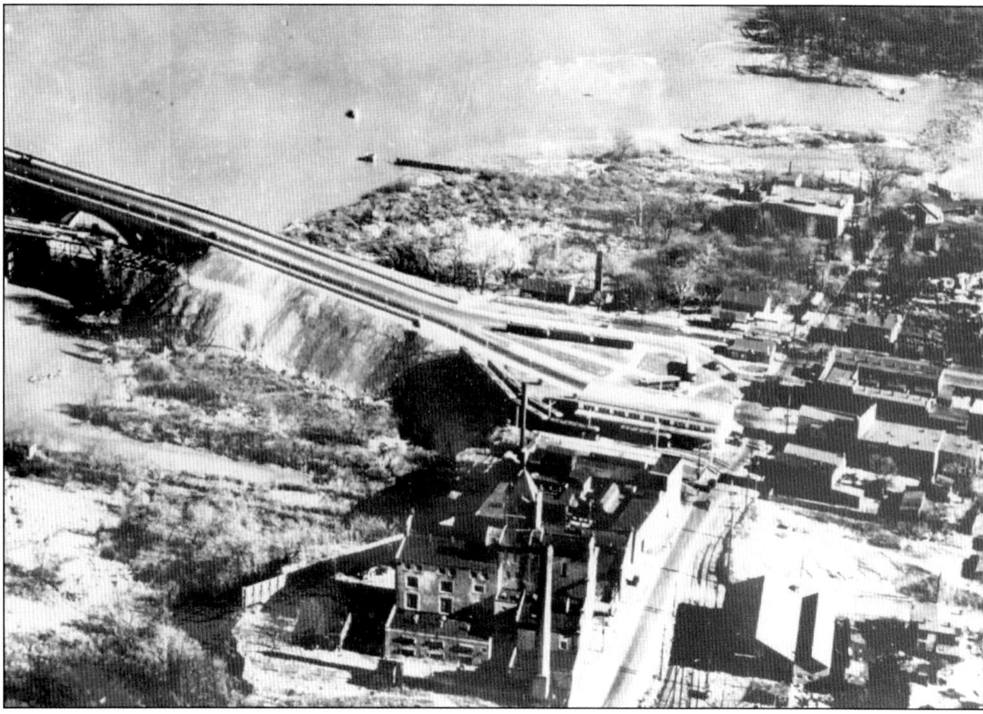

This view looks east from above present-day Spout Run Parkway. The Rosslyn terminal of the W&OD Railroad is at center. Rosslyn terminal had a fruit stand where passengers could buy apples, snacks, candy, and newspapers. Across Lee Highway from the roundhouse is the John E. Fowler Carbonic Corporation complex, which manufactured syrups for soft drinks. (Courtesy of the National Archives.)

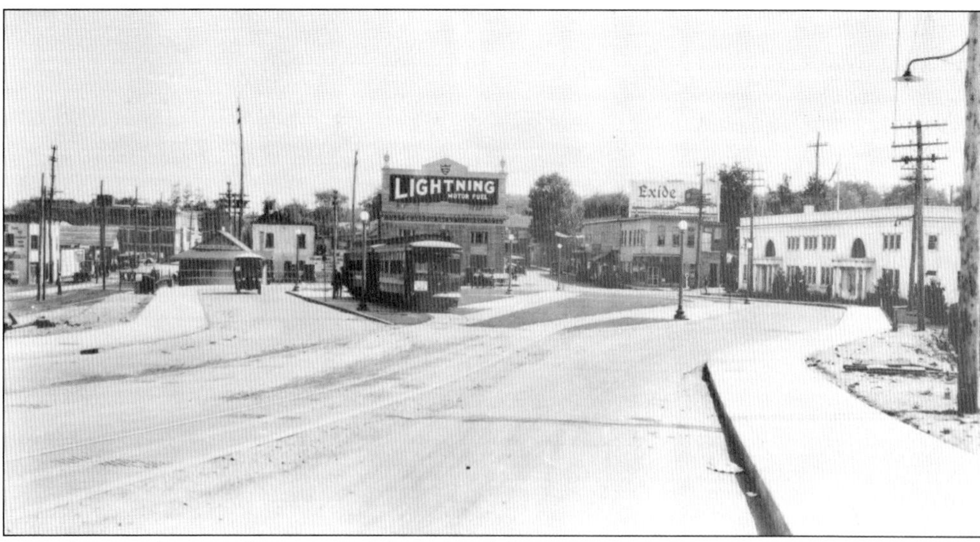

An unknown photographer captured the railroad days of Rosslyn about 1925. From left to right are the Rosslyn station of the Washington-Virginia Railway Company, two trolley cars of the Capital Traction Company headed north onto the Francis Scott Key Bridge, and the Rosslyn terminal of the W&OD. The Rosslyn terminal included a Capital Traction ticket office, easing the way for passengers traveling on into Washington. (Courtesy of the Library of Congress.)

John A. Fielding took this photograph of the track side of the Rosslyn terminal while standing on the south side of Lee Highway looking northeast around 1930. Car No. 5 was one of the original GF&OD passenger cars built by the Cincinnati Car Company in 1906. The sign over the door to the right of the trolley car reads "Colored Waiting Room."

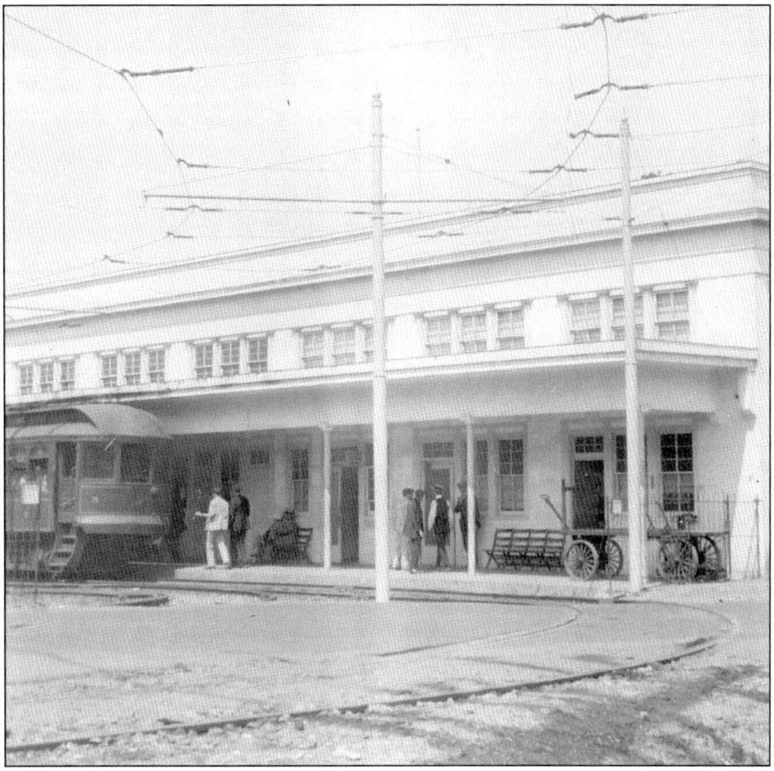

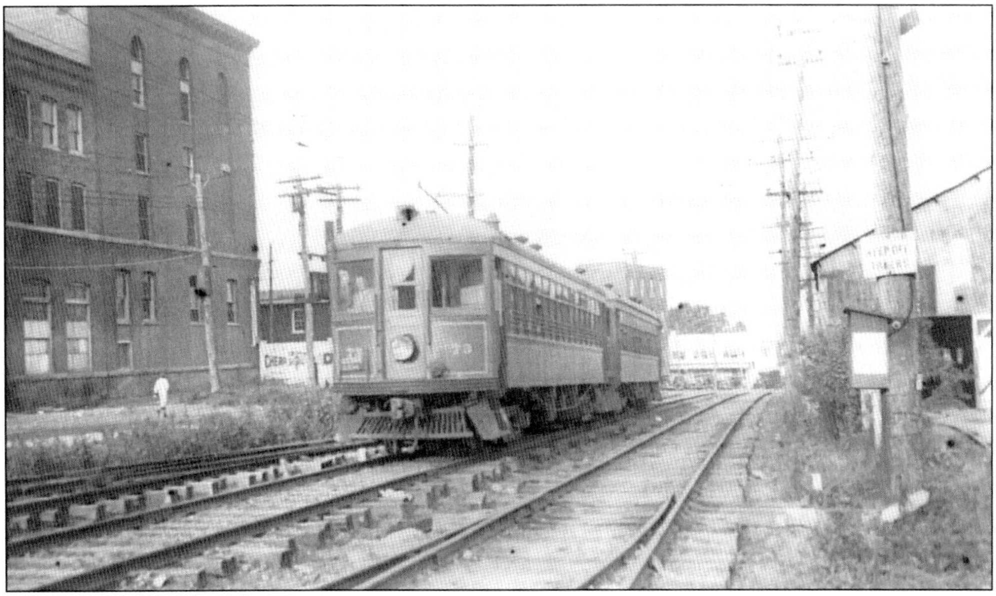

Lead car No. 73 was built by the Southern Car Company in 1912. This photograph is unusual because it was taken in the 1930s looking east down Lee Highway before the Rosslyn terminal was torn down and the right hand track was cut back to end at Fort Myer Drive. The Fowler Carbonic Company plant is at left. (Courtesy of NOVA Parks.)

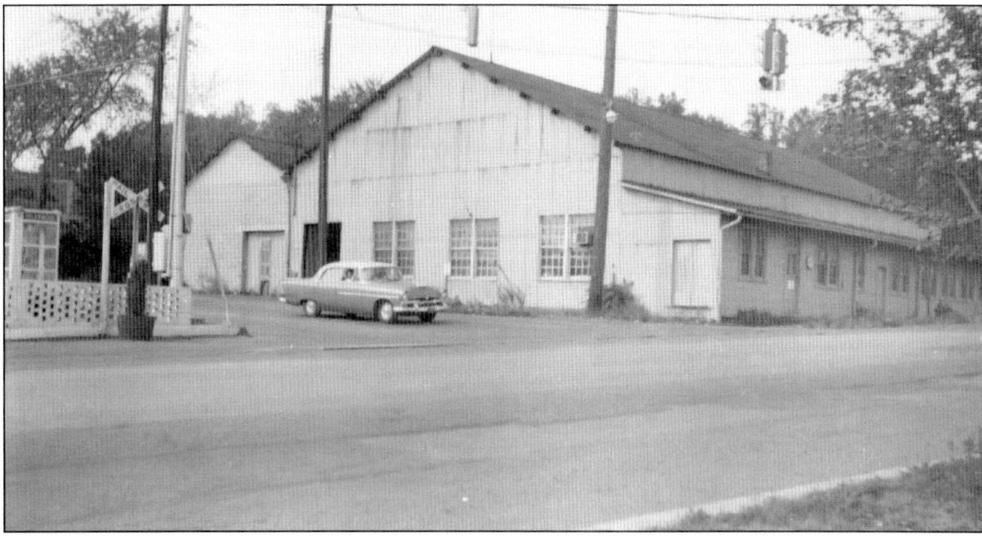

LeRoy O. King Jr. photographed the east end and north side of the Rosslyn roundhouse about 1961. The large portion of the roundhouse is the old Georgetown train shed, re-erected as the car repair bay. The lean-to at right housed the passenger waiting room from 1939 to 1941. (Courtesy of LeRoy O. King Jr.)

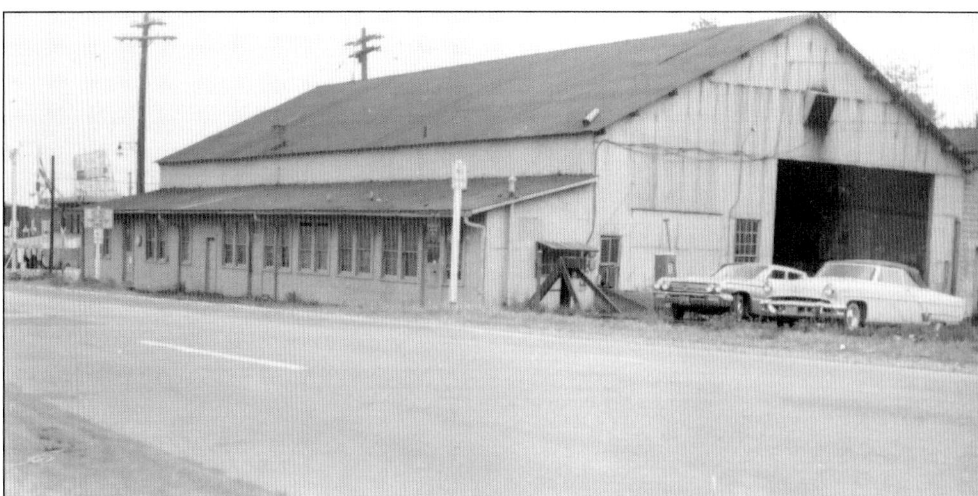

LeRoy O. King Jr. photographed the west end and north side of the Rosslyn roundhouse about 1961. Lee Highway runs through the foreground. The roundhouse contained locker rooms, restrooms, a machine shop, and a blacksmith shop in addition to the engine bay. Equipment included a 36-inch metal lathe and a fire-driven drop forge. (Courtesy of LeRoy O. King Jr.)

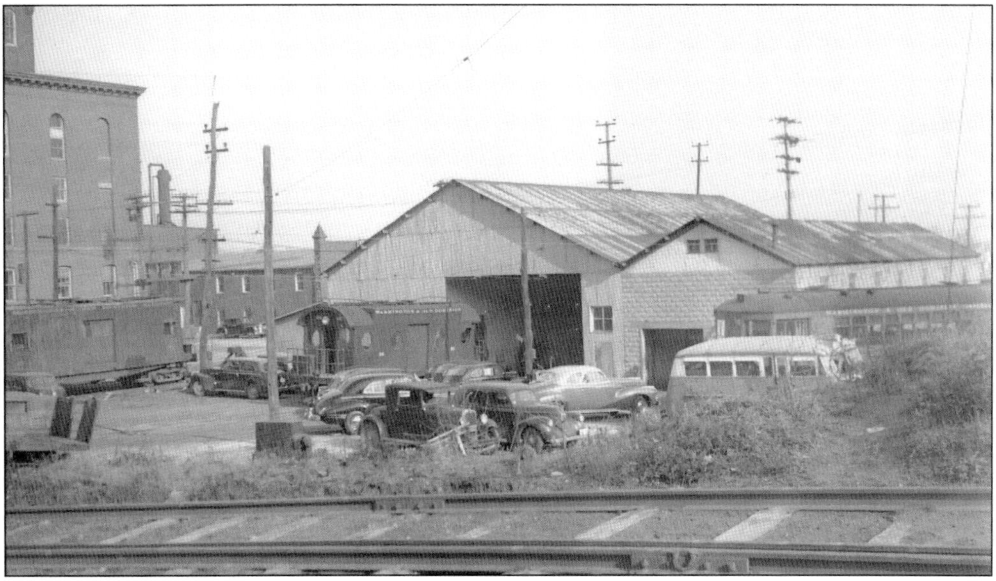

Robert Crockett captured home shop-built electric locomotives No. 25 and No. 26 in February 1941. An Evans Auto-Railer bus is parked in the lot, and a Southern Car Company combination passenger-baggage car is on the track beside the roundhouse. The U-shaped cable welded to the two rails in the foreground is a bonding wire, a part of the electrical power system. (Courtesy of NOVA Parks.)

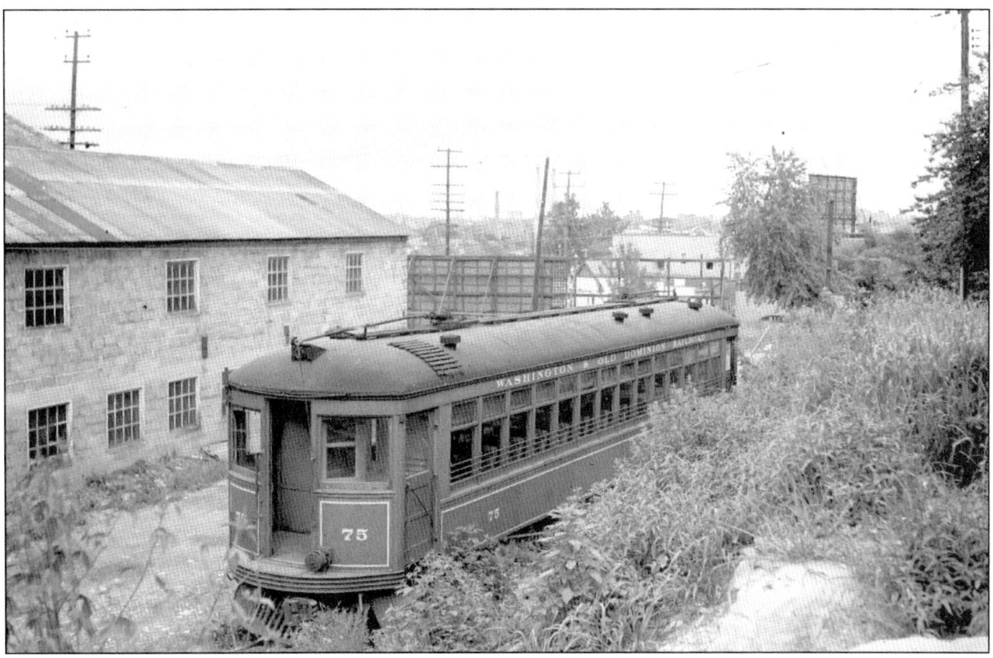

John F. Burns photographed car No. 75, built by Southern Car Company in 1912, on the track on the south side of the roundhouse on August 10, 1940. The portion of the roundhouse seen here was used for less-than-carload freight.

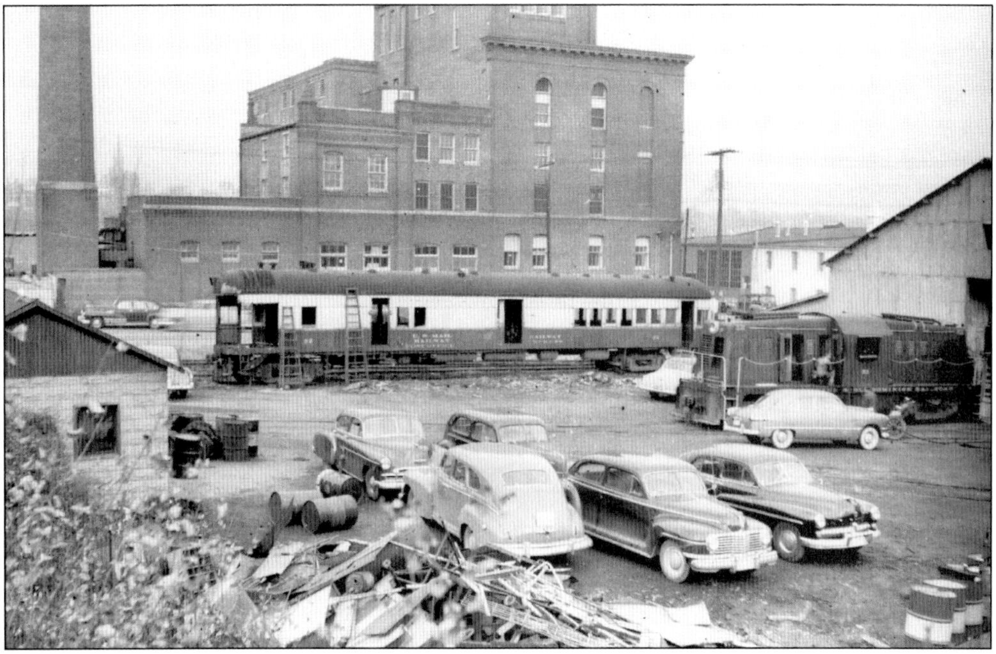

When John F. Burns photographed the scrapping of mail-baggage-passenger diesel-electric car No. 52 on November 15, 1951, the engine had been removed. The whole Lee Highway side of the Fowler Carbonic Company plant is visible at the rear. Diesel-electric locomotive No. 53 had recently been acquired from the US Army. A luggage rack from No. 52 can be seen in the foreground.

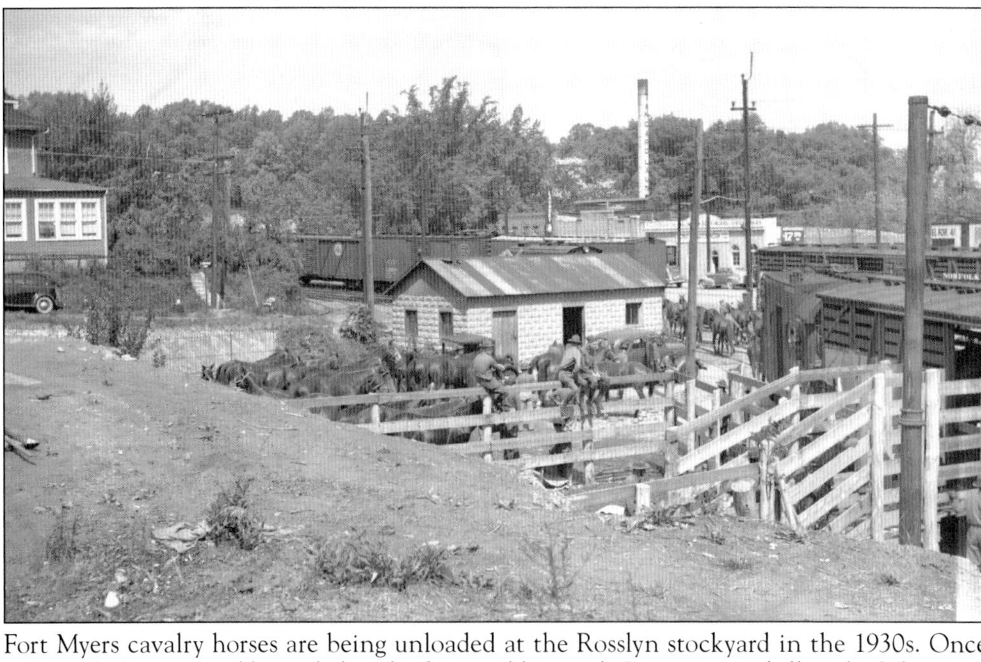

Fort Myers cavalry horses are being unloaded at the Rosslyn stockyard in the 1930s. Once unloaded, they were ridden or led to the fort's stables. Nash Street runs uphill to the left center. The Standard Laundry smokestack rises above the barely visible roof of a Baldwin-Westinghouse locomotive. Cattle might have been unloaded here for the Rosslyn Packing Company. (Courtesy of NOVA Parks.)

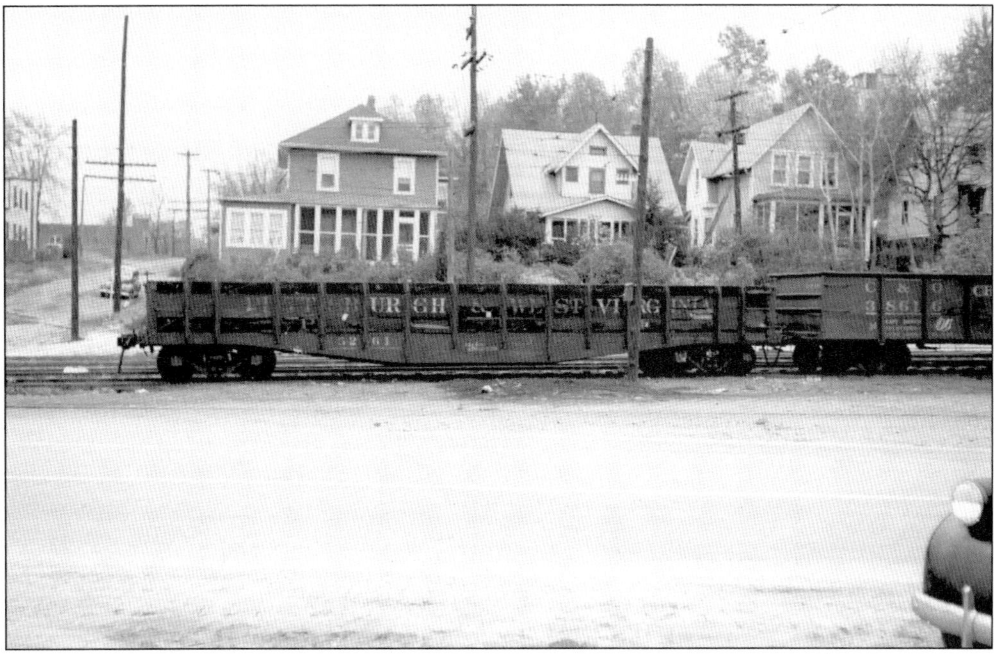

John F. Burns photographed a number of freight cars in Rosslyn in the 1930s and 1940s. Here, he captured Pittsburgh & West Virginia Railroad gondola car No. 5261 in the yard on November 4, 1939. The track running across and then south (uphill) on North Nash Street can be seen to the left of the gondola car. The houses are located on what was Lee Terrace.

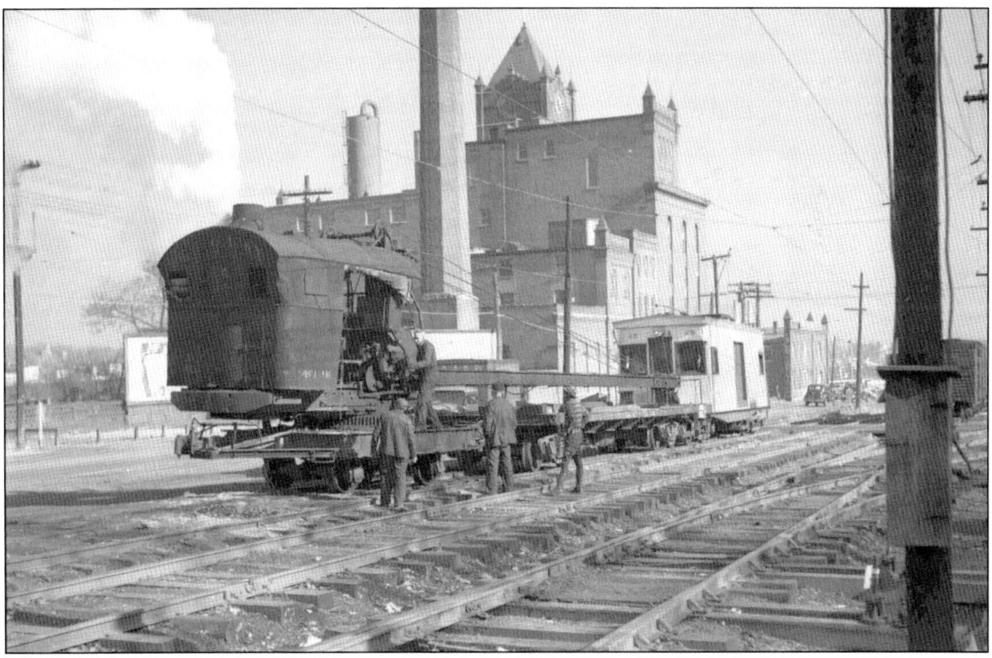

Carl Crosen, the man standing on the steam crane's base, is conferring with his shop crew. W&OD locomotive No. 25 is on the other end of the flatcar. This "idler" car provides room for the crane's boom to lay down below the electric overhead wires and a way for a locomotive to move the crane. This photograph was taken by John F. Burns on January 3, 1942.

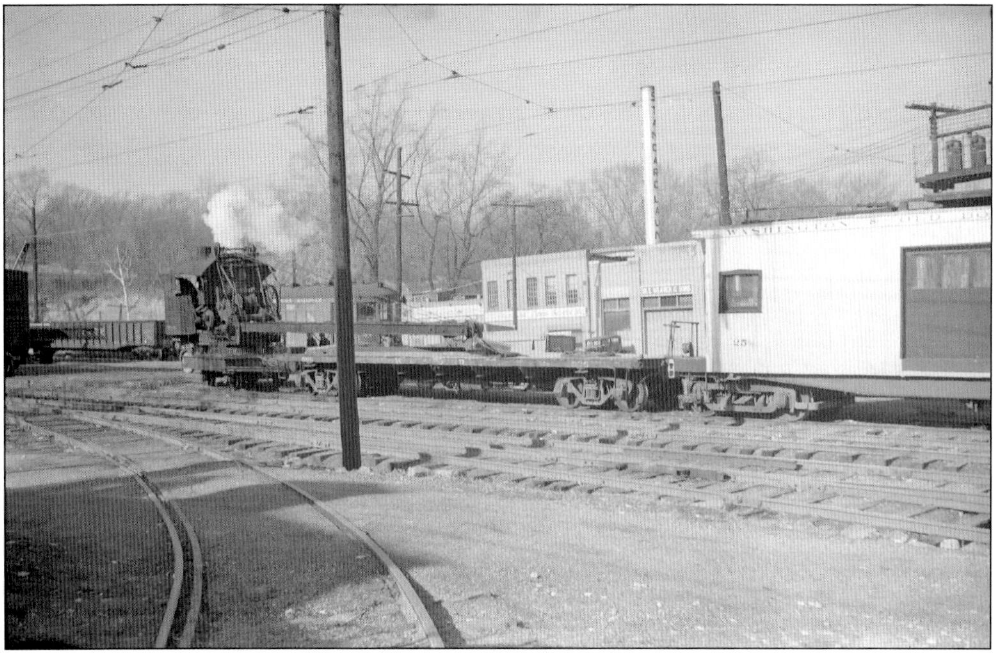

Two signs on the buildings at the back read "Standard Linen Service Inc." and "W.T. Weaver & Sons." Railway Post Office car No. 44 is standing on the back track next to Lee Highway. The sharp bend in the track turning south onto North Nash Street necessitated a guard rail to keep the equipment on the track. This photograph was taken by John F. Burns on January 3, 1942.

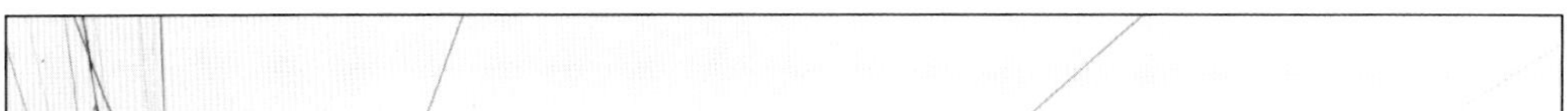

Leonard W. Rice photographed the west end of the Rosslyn yard standing a little west of North Nash Street in April 1943. The W&OD Railroad had recently purchased the two-car diesel electric passenger train sitting on the back track (in the railroad's parlance) to reinstate passenger service between Rosslyn and Leesburg. A Railway Express Agency truck is at right and a mail truck is at center.

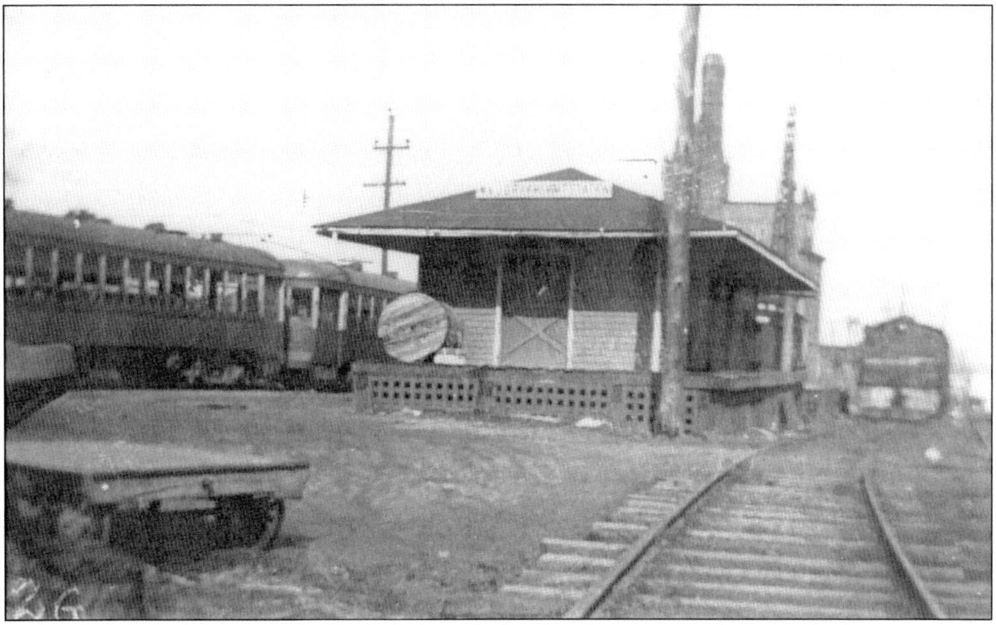

This is a rare view of the west end of the Rosslyn freight station. The view looks east toward Rosslyn. At this time, the building was used for storage. The 125-foot-high smokestack of the Fowler Carbonic Corporation stands between the near pole and the boom of the steam crane. (Courtesy of NOVA Parks.)

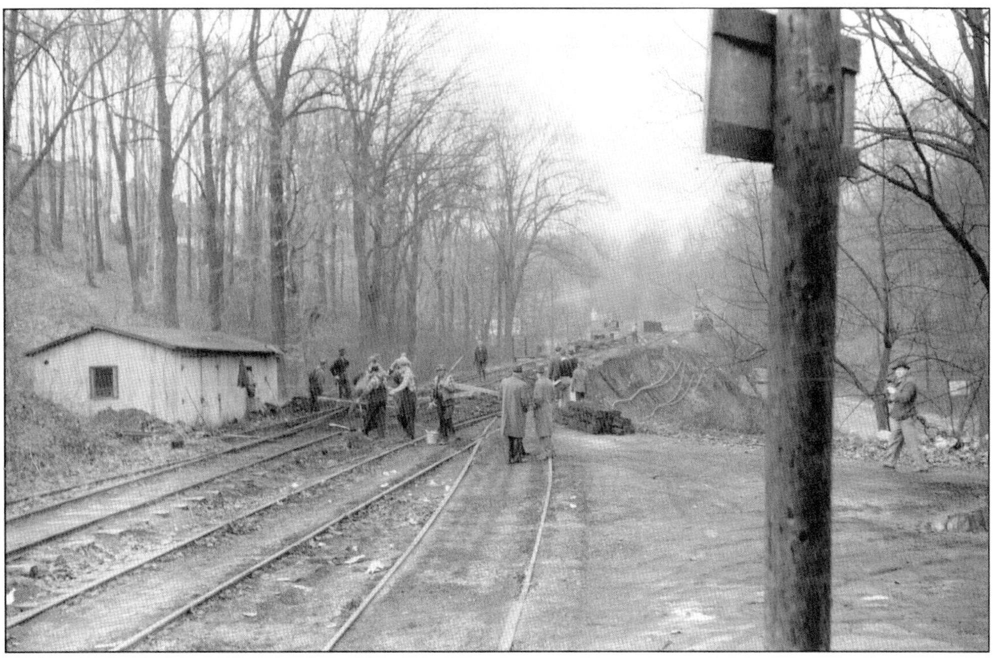

A cave-in just east of the bridge over Lee Highway, whose through girders are visible at the rear, occurred on Friday, January 7, 1949. Photographers came out to view the track gang crews repairing the embankment. The view looks uphill toward Lyon Village and Cherrydale. Car No. 45 is visible at the rear above the right bridge girder. This photograph was taken by John F. Burns on January 8, 1949.

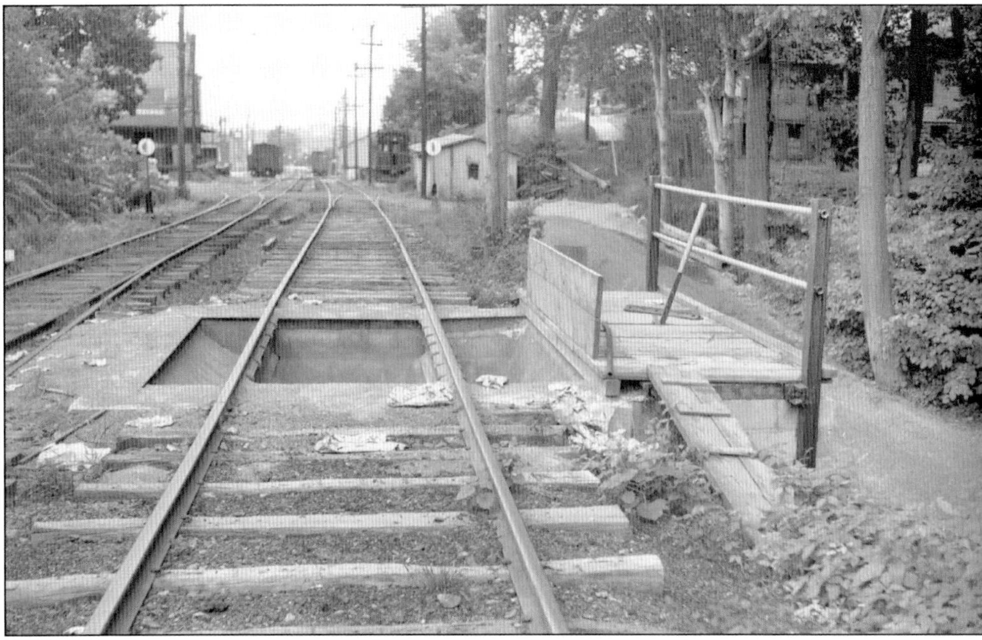

John F. Burns recorded this gravel hopper with its unloading lever at the west end of the Rosslyn yard on August 24, 1940. Locomotive No. 26 is just to the left of the building at right. The original freight station is at left. With this view, it is easy to imagine operating the controls of a passenger car coming into Rosslyn.

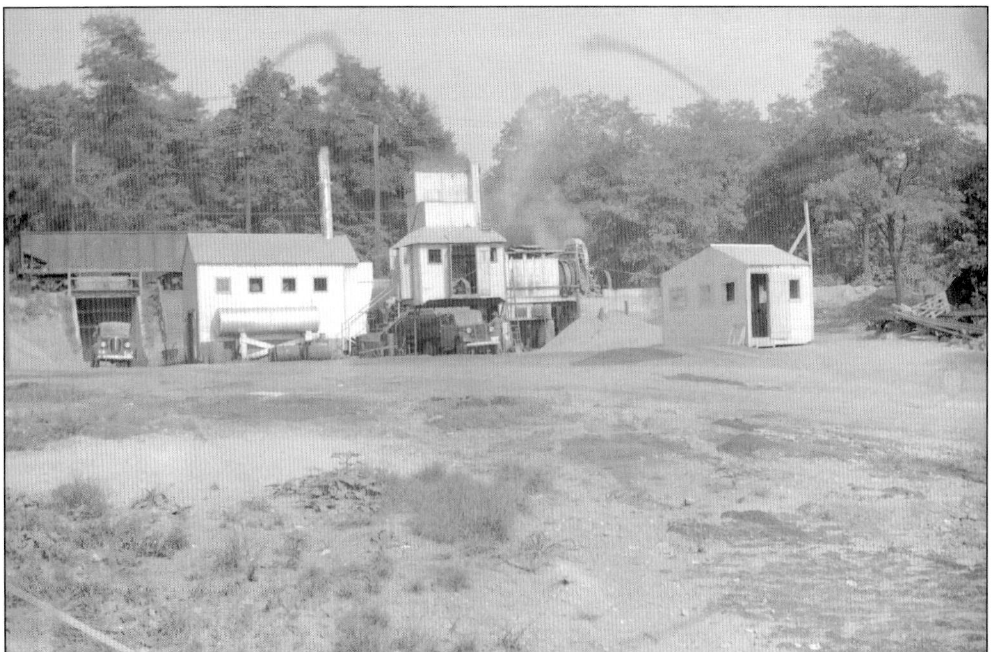

An unknown photographer captured a hopper car at the facility pictured above. This facility was probably run by the Arlington Stone Company. The company frequently received four loads of stone a day from Trap Rock. Based on other photographs, this one was taken in the late 1930s to 1940s. The facility was shut down shortly thereafter. (Courtesy of NOVA Parks.)

Two

Great Falls

According to National Park Service files at Great Falls Park, Patowmack means "trading place" in the Algonquin Indian language. Chesapeake Bay Indians met mountain Indians on the river's banks on both sides of the falls. Mountain Indians brought animal skins and flint to trade for shells (for wampum), sea grasses, and fish brought by the Chesapeake Bay Indians.

McLean and Elkins, as wealthy men with an interest in railroads, purchased the GF&OD from the original owners in 1901, then undertook the construction of the GF&OD to make money transporting people. To increase ridership, they built a scenic resort at Great Falls. Riders could hear music from the carousel as they approached the park. At the beginning of the 20th century, when the weather was cold, construction crews were behind schedule, and they had to blast the soil during the winter and early spring of 1906 in order to build the right of way, because the soil was as solid as a rock.

Frank L. Ball called the trolley lines the greatest thing that ever happened to Arlington. With the trolleys, citizens no longer had to slog through mud or brave wet weather. A side benefit to early residents along the line was the sale of surplus electricity by the railroad. Of course, the lights dimmed and stoves lost power during the morning and evening rush hours. At holidays, Great Falls passengers could be seen hanging on the car steps and anything they could grab onto. Occasionally, portable substation No. 1 was placed at Vanderwerken station near Little Falls Road. Then the trolleys would zip up the hill.

The Great Falls line had 39 passenger stops along its route. While some shelters are shown on the following pages and others were shown in the first volume, not all stops had shelters. Development of the line allowed workers to become commuters from homes in the country to jobs downtown.

The Interstate Commerce Commission in its 1918 valuation report lists a surprising number of facilities at Great Falls. These included a freight platform, a watchman's house, three water stations to supply park facilities, the passenger station, an ice house, a tool house, a ladies' toilet, a men's toilet, a pump house with a Westinghouse electric motor, and dining and dancing pavilions.

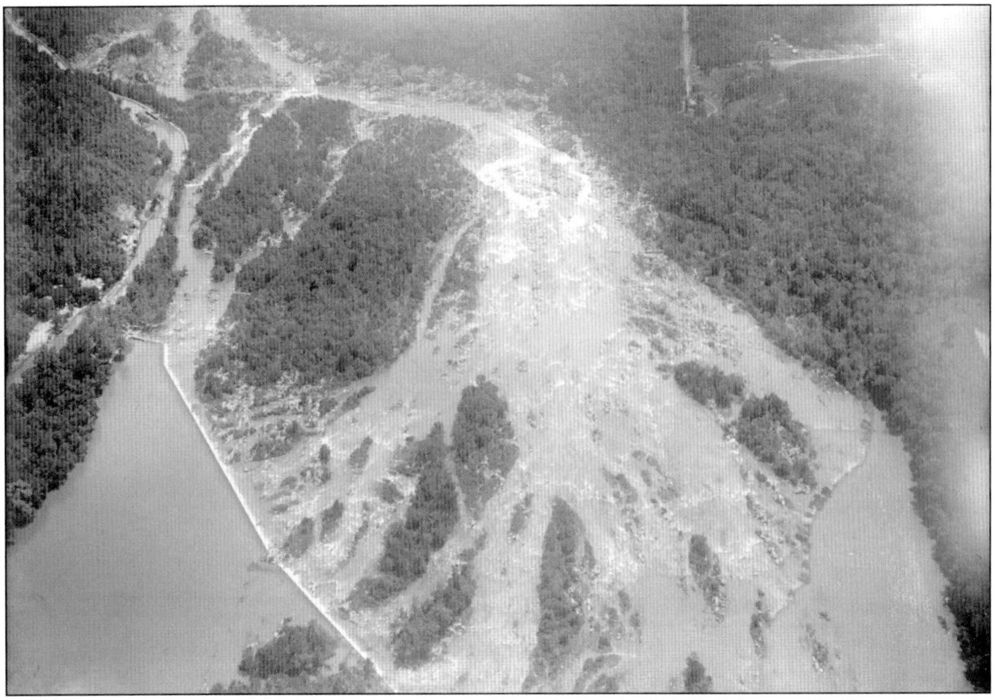

This 1919 aerial photograph by Harris & Ewing may be the only one of Great Falls taken while the Chesapeake & Ohio Canal was operating. The gray rectangle in the woods just above the river at top center is the roof of the 95-by-40-foot dancing pavilion. (Courtesy of the Library of Congress, Harris & Ewing Collection.)

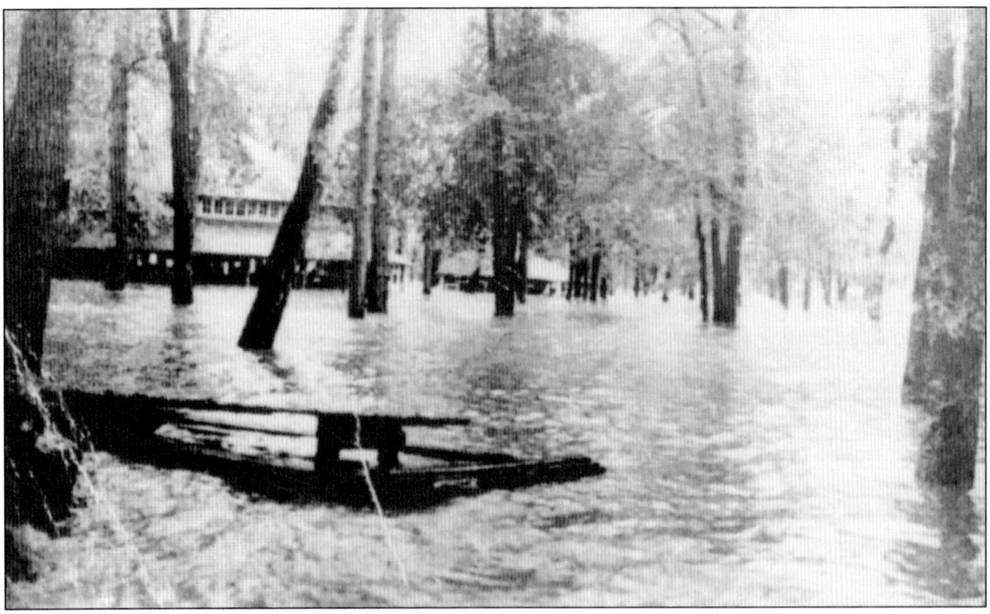

Floods, such as this one in 1936, destroyed Great Falls carousels and restaurants. The large structure might be the restaurant. The other might be the remains of the dining pavilion. Helen and Russell Orrison recalled that the floodwaters reached to the bottom of the steps leading to the station seen on page 30. (Courtesy of the Fairfax County Public Library Photographic Archive.)

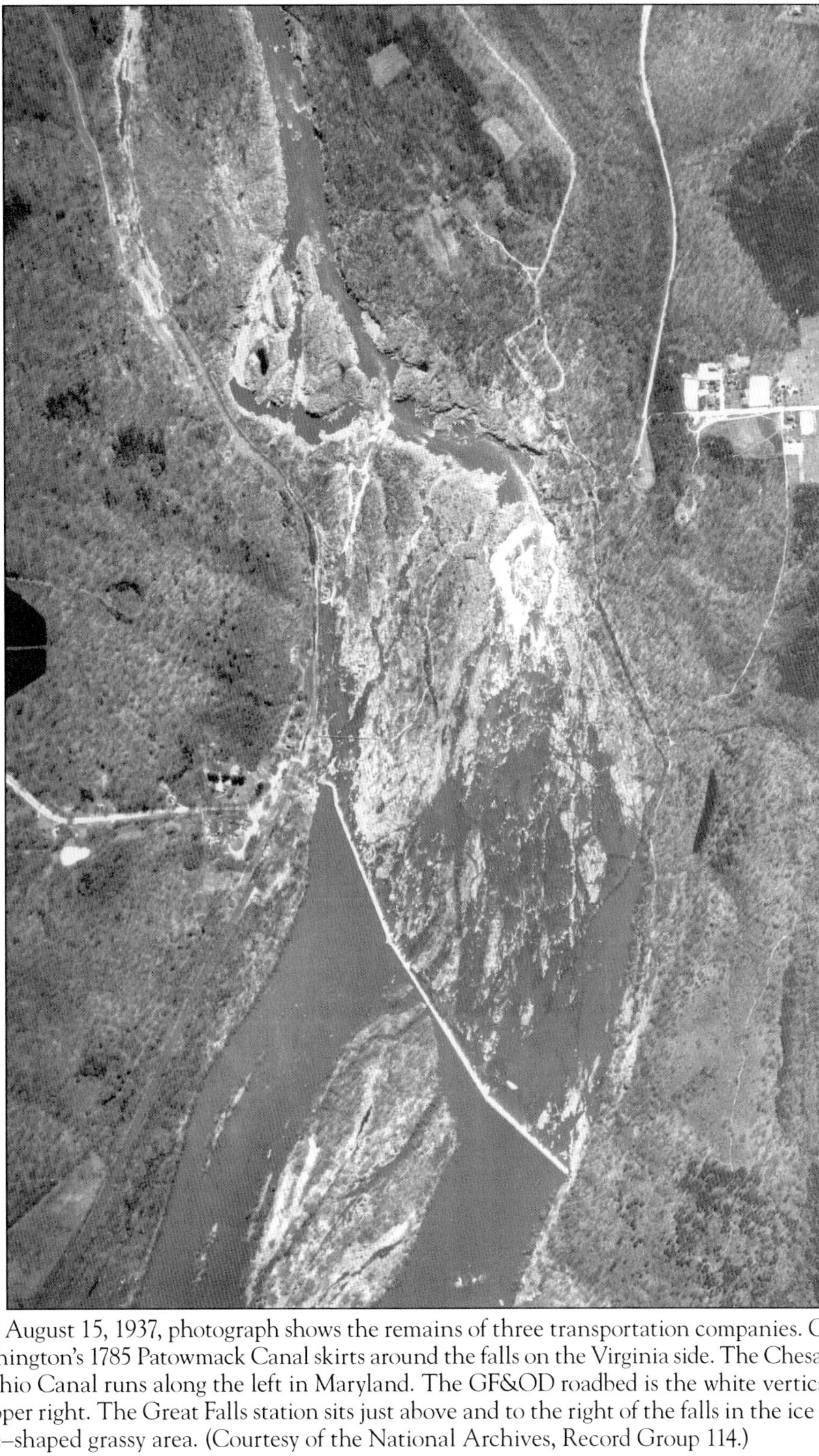

This August 15, 1937, photograph shows the remains of three transportation companies. George Washington's 1785 Patowmack Canal skirts around the falls on the Virginia side. The Chesapeake & Ohio Canal runs along the left in Maryland. The GF&OD roadbed is the white vertical line at upper right. The Great Falls station sits just above and to the right of the falls in the ice cream cone–shaped grassy area. (Courtesy of the National Archives, Record Group 114.)

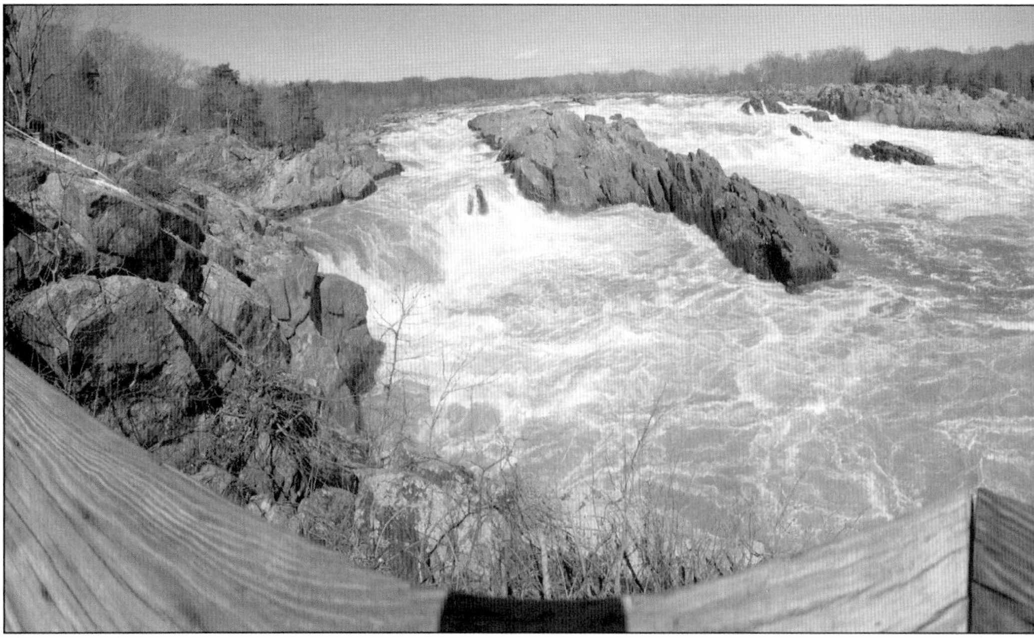

Fascination with the Great Falls by Europeans began when George Washington was overseeing the construction of the Patowmack Canal around the Great Falls. Pictures show visitors during the Civil War era. This panoramic view is comprised of photographs taken on February 27, 2014. Except for a few obvious items, such as the wood railings, there is very little difference between

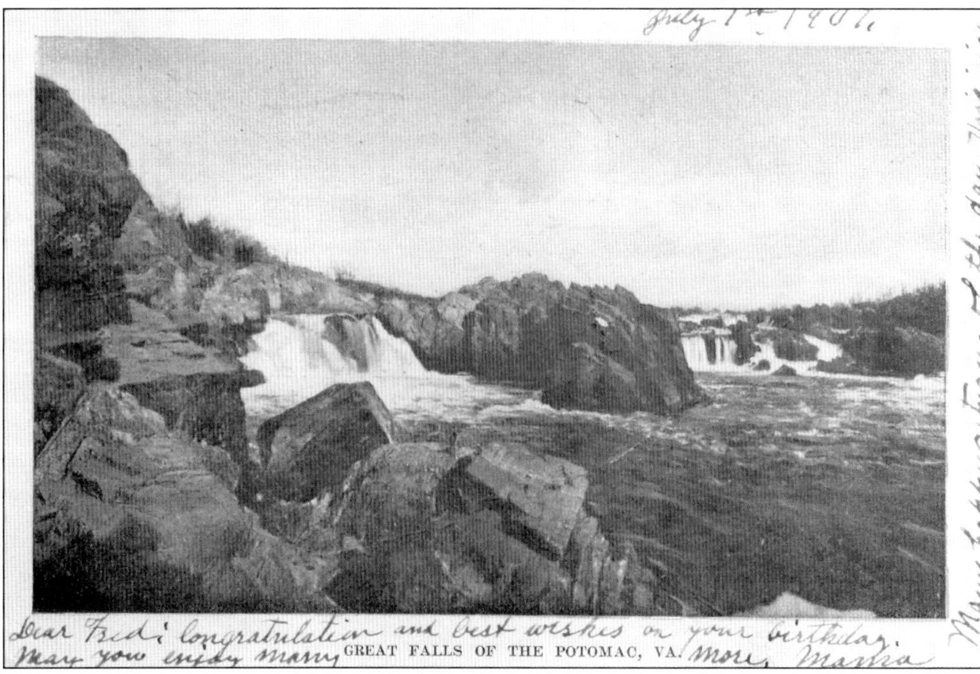

This postcard picture was taken not far from the panoramic view above, just closer to the river when the water flow was lower. This is one of the postcards the GF&OD used to advertise its park. Others advertised George Washington's Patowmack Canal. The back of this postcard advertises the falls as the largest south of the Niagara River falls.

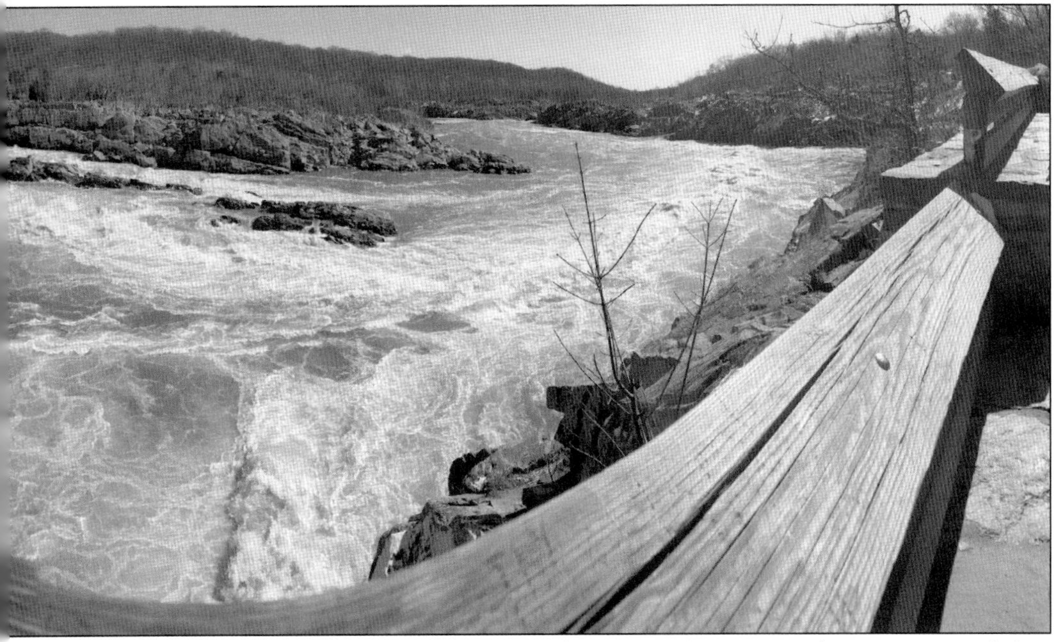

this view and the postcard below mailed on July 1, 1907. Amateur geologists can spend days around the falls. The group of rocks in the middle of the river at left center are severely folded 500-million-year-old mica schist.

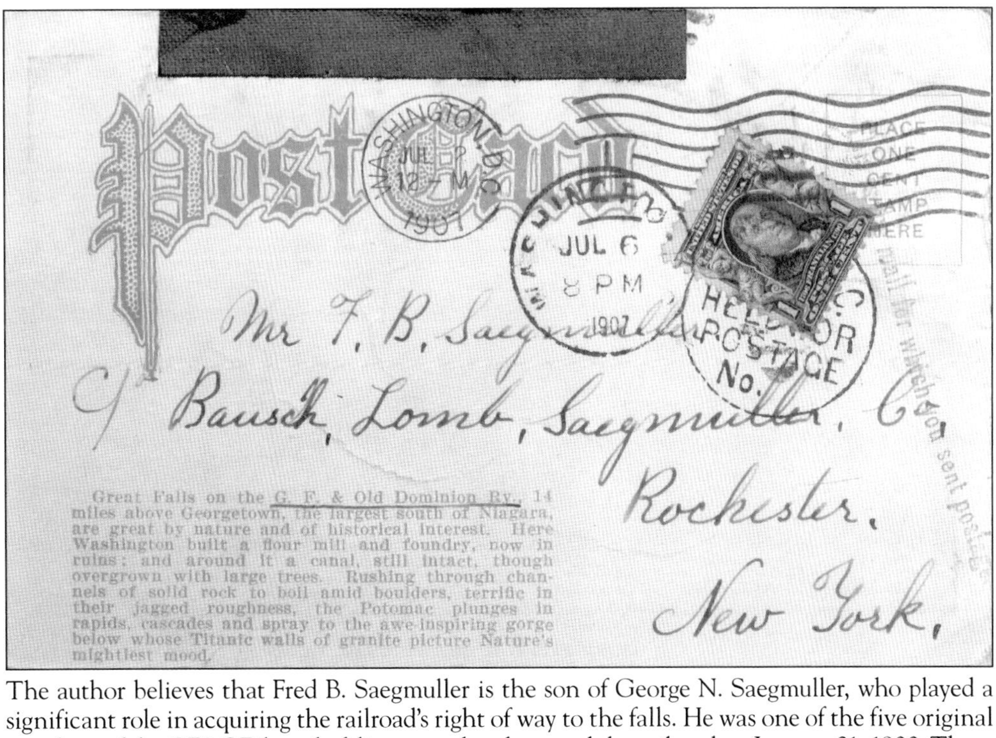

The author believes that Fred B. Saegmuller is the son of George N. Saegmuller, who played a significant role in acquiring the railroad's right of way to the falls. He was one of the five original members of the GF&OD board of directors who chartered the railroad on January 21, 1900. Three of the directors married Vanderwerken sisters, and Saegmuller's wife was a cousin of theirs.

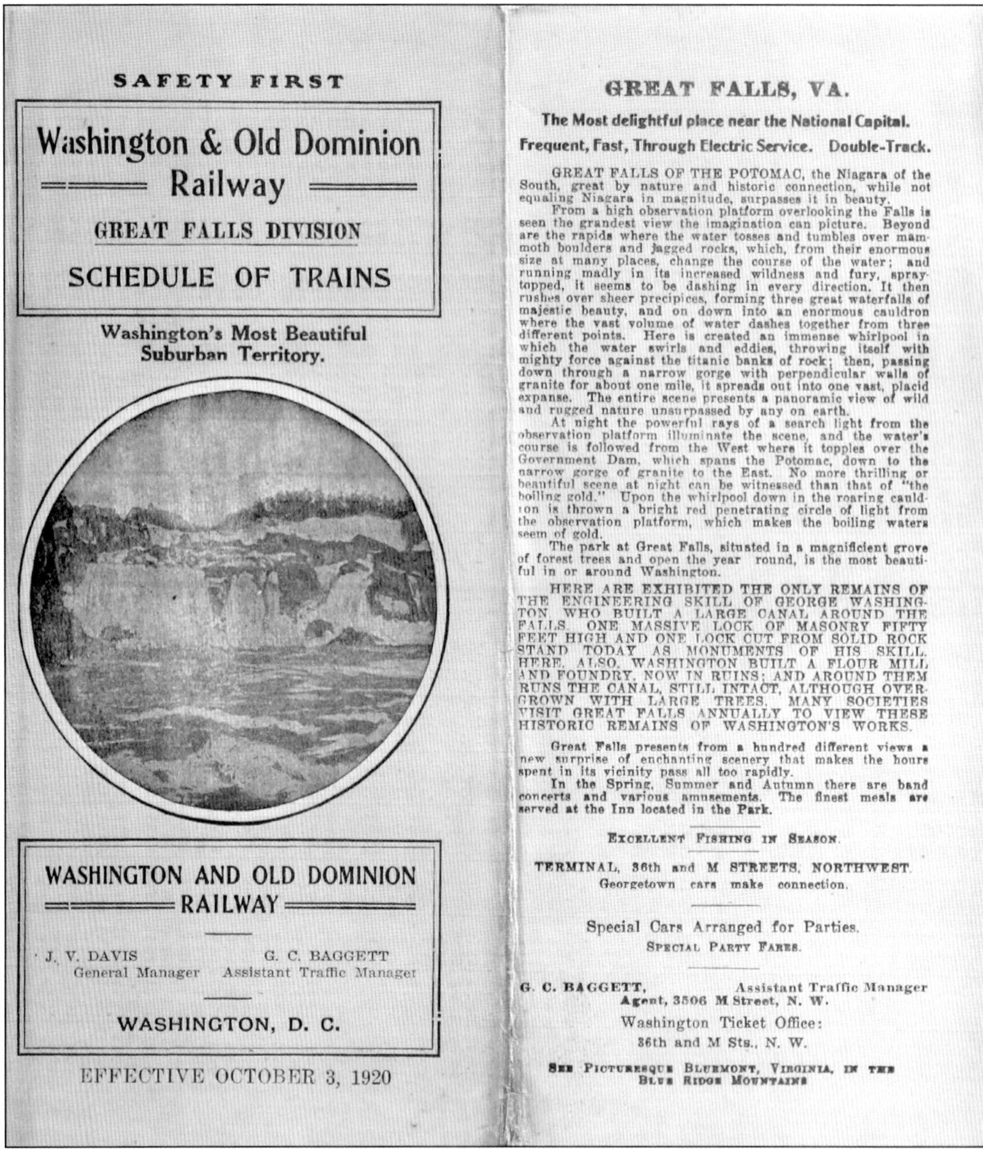

SAFETY FIRST

Washington & Old Dominion Railway

GREAT FALLS DIVISION

SCHEDULE OF TRAINS

Washington's Most Beautiful Suburban Territory.

WASHINGTON AND OLD DOMINION RAILWAY

J. V. DAVIS
General Manager

G. C. BAGGETT
Assistant Traffic Manager

WASHINGTON, D. C.

EFFECTIVE OCTOBER 3, 1920

GREAT FALLS, VA.

The Most delightful place near the National Capital.

Frequent, Fast, Through Electric Service. Double-Track.

GREAT FALLS OF THE POTOMAC, the Niagara of the South, great by nature and historic connection, while not equaling Niagara in magnitude, surpasses it in beauty.

From a high observation platform overlooking the Falls is seen the grandest view the imagination can picture. Beyond are the rapids where the water tosses and tumbles over mammoth boulders and jagged rocks, which, from their enormous size at many places, change the course of the water; and running madly in its increased wildness and fury, spray-topped, it seems to be dashing in every direction. It then rushes over sheer precipices, forming three great waterfalls of majestic beauty, and on down into an enormous cauldron where the vast volume of water dashes together from three different points. Here is created an immense whirlpool in which the water swirls and eddies, throwing itself with mighty force against the titanic banks of rock; then, passing down through a narrow gorge with perpendicular walls of granite for about one mile, it spreads out into one vast, placid expanse. The entire scene presents a panoramic view of wild and rugged nature unsurpassed by any on earth.

At night the powerful rays of a search light from the observation platform illuminate the scene, and the water's course is followed from the West where it topples over the Government Dam, which spans the Potomac, down to the narrow gorge of granite to the East. No more thrilling or beautiful scene at night can be witnessed than that of "the boiling gold." Upon the whirlpool down in the roaring cauldron is thrown a bright red penetrating circle of light from the observation platform, which makes the boiling waters seem of gold.

The park at Great Falls, situated in a magnificient grove of forest trees and open the year round, is the most beautiful in or around Washington.

HERE ARE EXHIBITED THE ONLY REMAINS OF THE ENGINEERING SKILL OF GEORGE WASHINGTON WHO BUILT A LARGE CANAL AROUND THE FALLS. ONE MASSIVE LOCK OF MASONRY FIFTY FEET HIGH AND ONE LOCK CUT FROM SOLID ROCK STAND TODAY AS MONUMENTS OF HIS SKILL. HERE, ALSO, WASHINGTON BUILT A FLOUR MILL AND FOUNDRY, NOW IN RUINS; AND AROUND THEM RUNS THE CANAL, STILL INTACT, ALTHOUGH OVERGROWN WITH LARGE TREES. MANY SOCIETIES VISIT GREAT FALLS ANNUALLY TO VIEW THESE HISTORIC REMAINS OF WASHINGTON'S WORKS.

Great Falls presents from a hundred different views a new surprise of enchanting scenery that makes the hours spent in its vicinity pass all too rapidly.

In the Spring, Summer and Autumn there are band concerts and various amusements. The finest meals are served at the Inn located in the Park.

EXCELLENT FISHING IN SEASON.

TERMINAL, 36th and M STREETS, NORTHWEST.
Georgetown cars make connection.

Special Cars Arranged for Parties.
SPECIAL PARTY FARES.

G. C. BAGGETT, Assistant Traffic Manager
Agent, 3506 M Street, N. W.
Washington Ticket Office:
36th and M Sts., N. W.

SEE PICTURESQUE BLUEMONT, VIRGINIA, IN THE BLUE RIDGE MOUNTAINS

The GF&OD advertised the falls on the backs of its timetables and on postcards. This timetable is dated October 3, 1920. The railroad played searchlights over the falls at night from the tower shown on the next page. (Courtesy of W&OD Railway.)

This postcard, published by J.P. Bell Company of Lynchburg, Virginia, shows the wooden tower at the falls. The obverse reads "High up on the rocks at Great Falls, Va, 15 miles from Washington, D.C., on the Washington & Old Dominion Railway, stands the scenic tower from which a commanding view of Nature's grandeur may be obtained in all directions." (Courtesy of the Fairfax County Public Library Photographic Archive.)

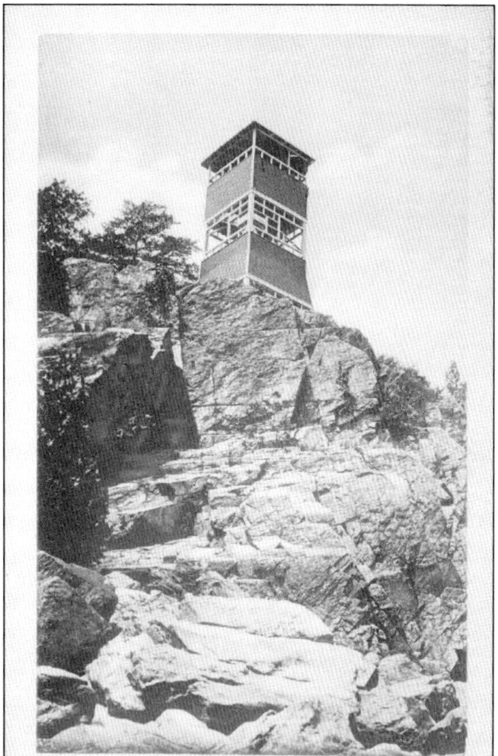

Scenic Tower at Great Falls, Va., on W. & O. D. Ry.

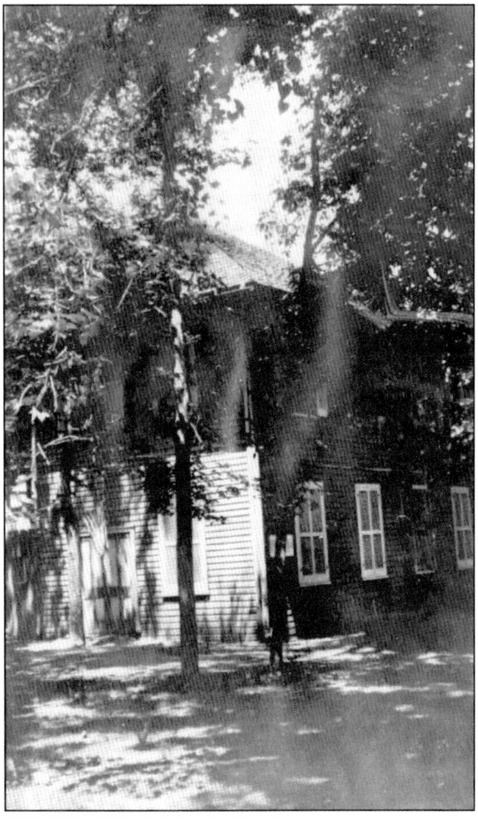

The Interstate Commerce Commission conducted a valuation survey in 1918 during World War I. This photograph from that survey captured the stage end of the dancing pavilion on June 17. The hip roof of the dancing pavilion, built by Myron Horton of Franklin Park, can be seen in the aerial photograph on page 24. (Courtesy of the Interstate Commerce Commission.)

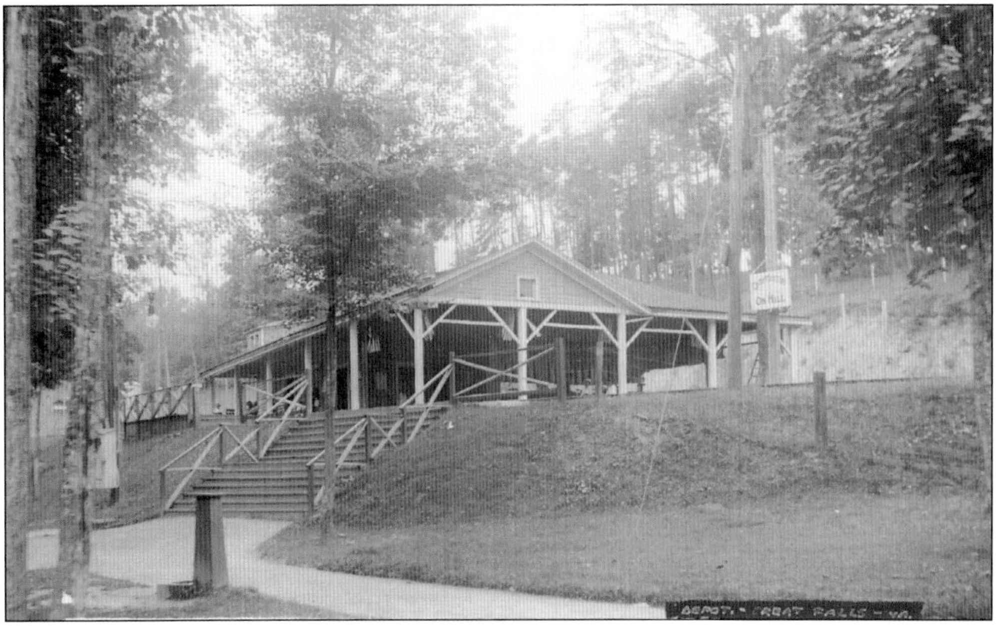

The sign on the post advertises a camp meeting on the hill. This photograph was probably taken in the 1920s and shows the river side of the station. Wide stairs indicate use by heavy crowds. American flags hang under the eaves, so perhaps the camp meeting occurred around July 4. (Courtesy of NOVA Parks.)

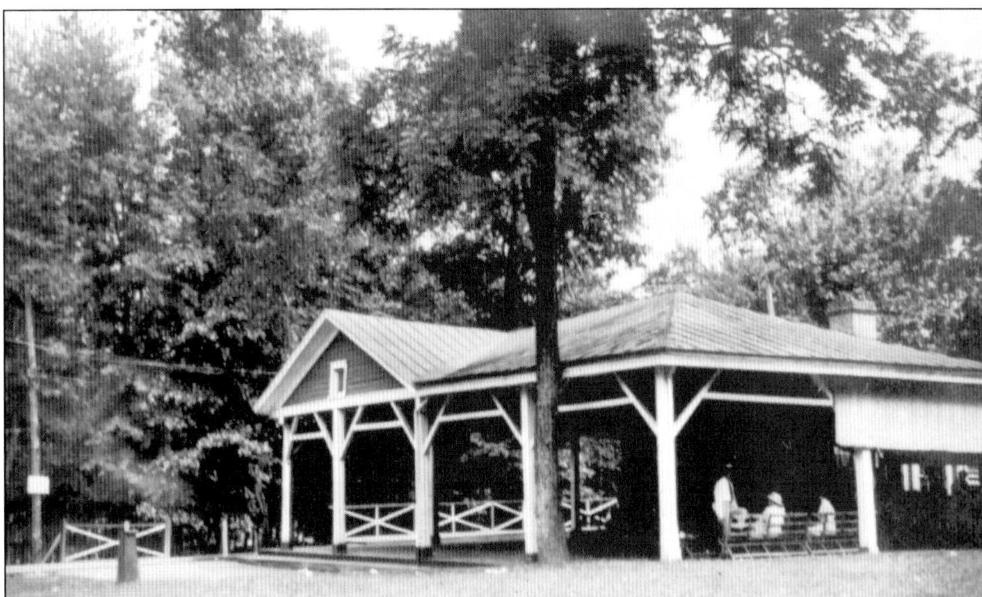

The Interstate Commerce Commission valuation team photographed the west end of the Great Falls station on June 17, 1918. Awnings and shelters were constructed in the park right after it opened in response to the inconvenience storms caused in July 1906. (Courtesy of the Interstate Commerce Commission.)

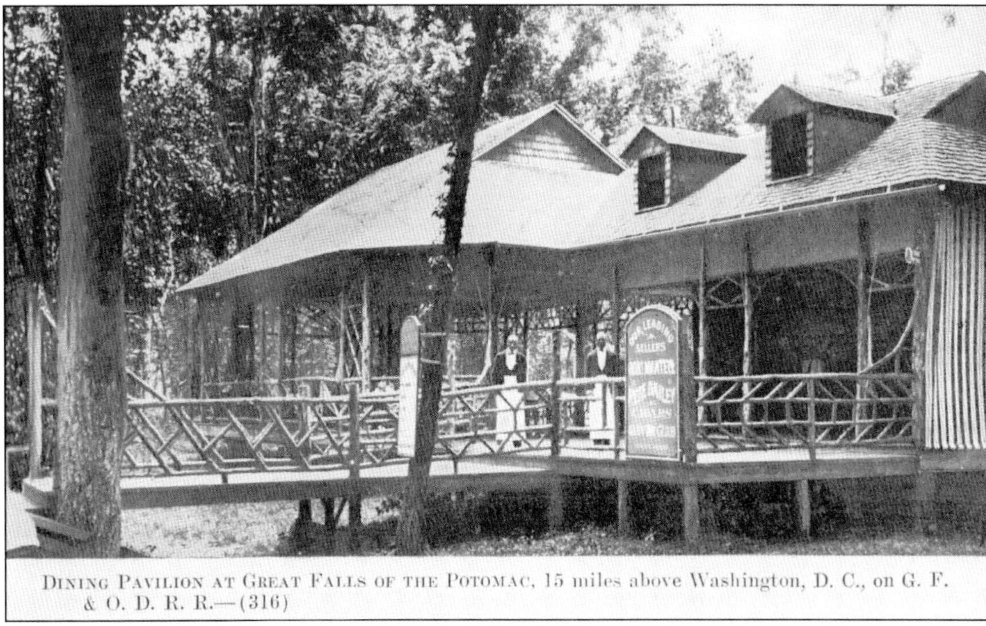

Though still standing at the time of the valuation survey in 1918, the 50-by-39-foot dining pavilion was not being used and had been replaced by a restaurant. The sign in this pre-1912 postcard reads "Our Leading Sellers, Robt Mantell, Pete Dailey Cigars, Glover Club." (Courtesy of the Fairfax County Public Library Photographic Archive.)

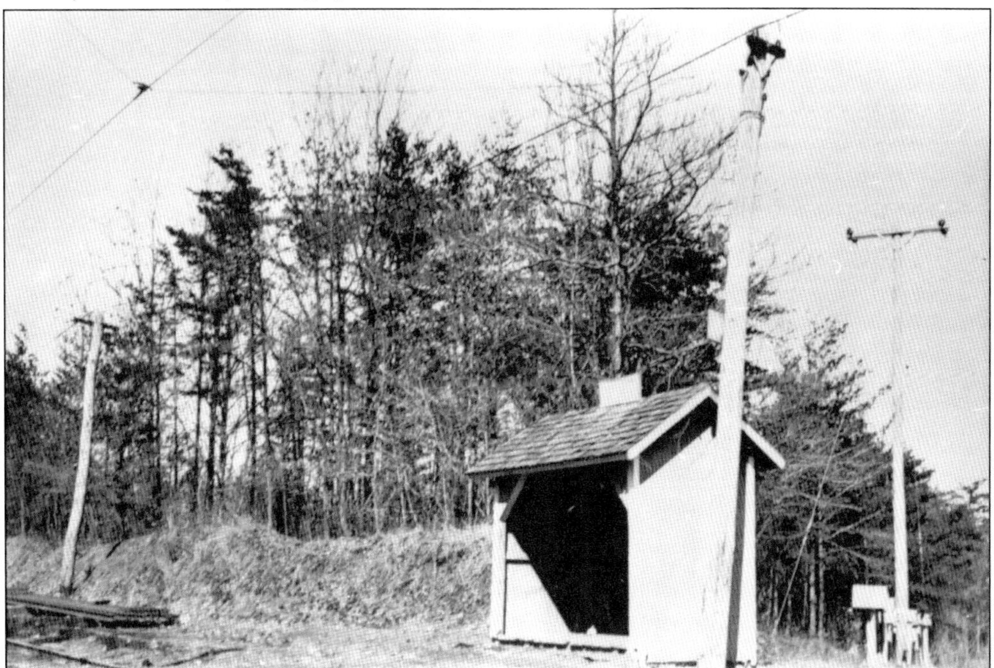

The W&OD Railway took a number of photographs of its facilities. The Elkins shelter was located on the north side of Georgetown Pike, on the east side of the tracks, 12.9 miles west of Rosslyn. Georgetown Pike was built to connect the town of Leesburg with the community of Georgetown in the years before the railroad. (Courtesy of Herbert H. Harwood.)

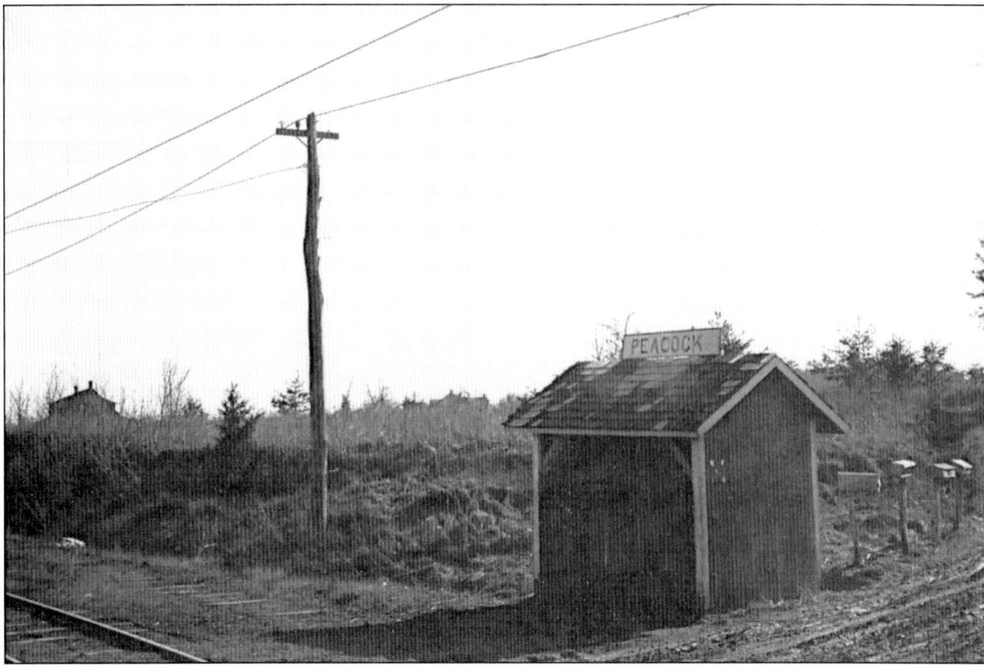

The W&OD Railway photographed the Peacock passenger shelter for its records. The shelter was on the east side of the tracks near present-day Peacock Station Road in the 8700 block of Old Dominion Drive, 12.2 miles west of Rosslyn. (Courtesy of NOVA Parks.)

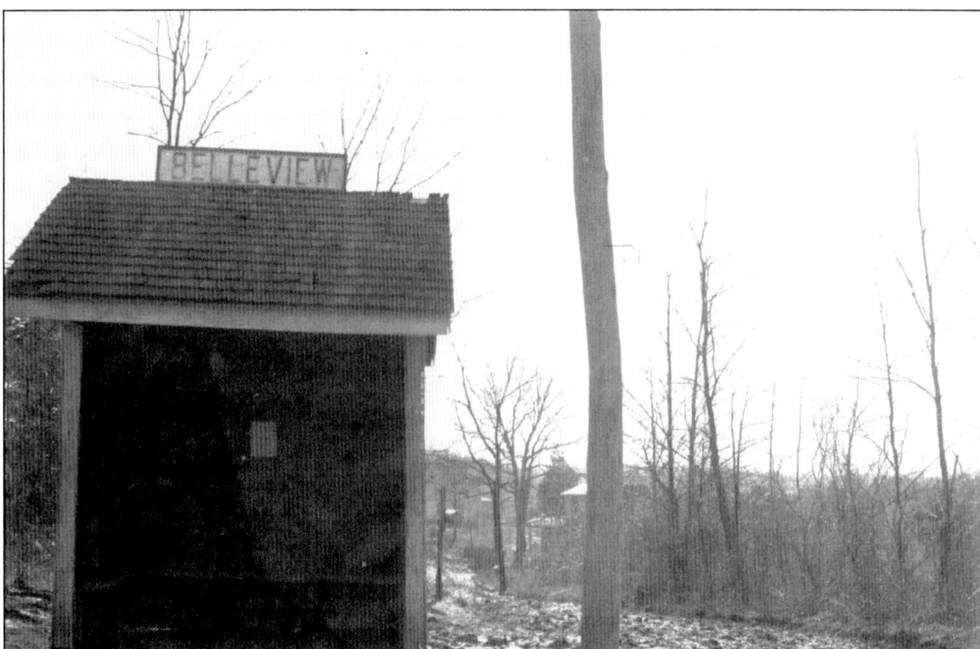

The Belleview passenger shelter was located near Bellview Road, 11.1 miles west of Rosslyn. It was typical of the three-sided shelters found along the GF&OD Railroad until the railroad was abandoned in 1934. (Courtesy of Herbert H. Harwood.)

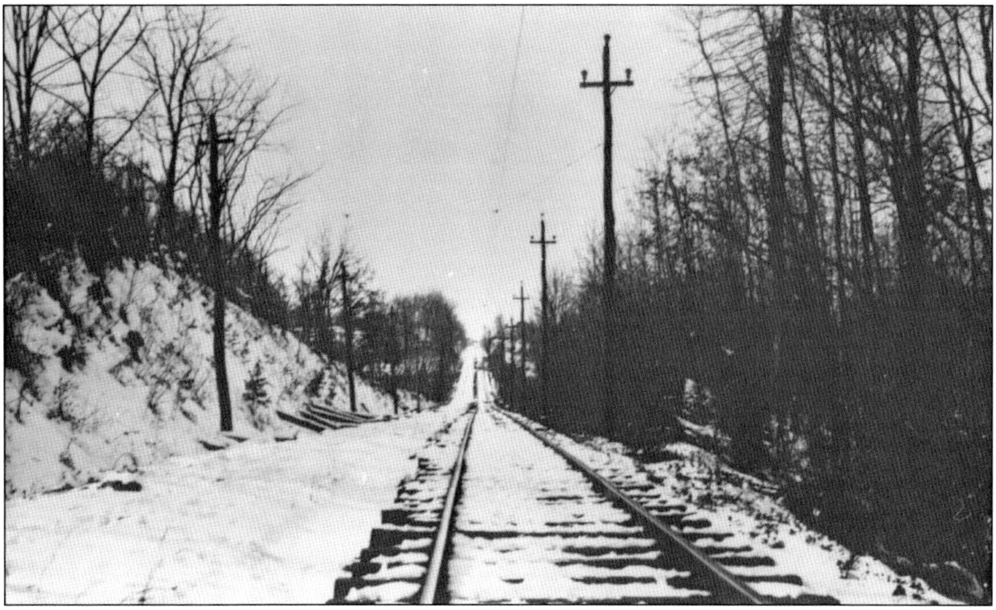

In this photograph, the W&OD Railway is about to finish removing the line to Great Falls. There are a few places where the line, present-day Old Dominion Drive, runs straight down a long slope and then back up: west of Spring Hill Road, near Rector Lane, and in the vicinity of Towlston Road. (Courtesy of Herbert H. Harwood.)

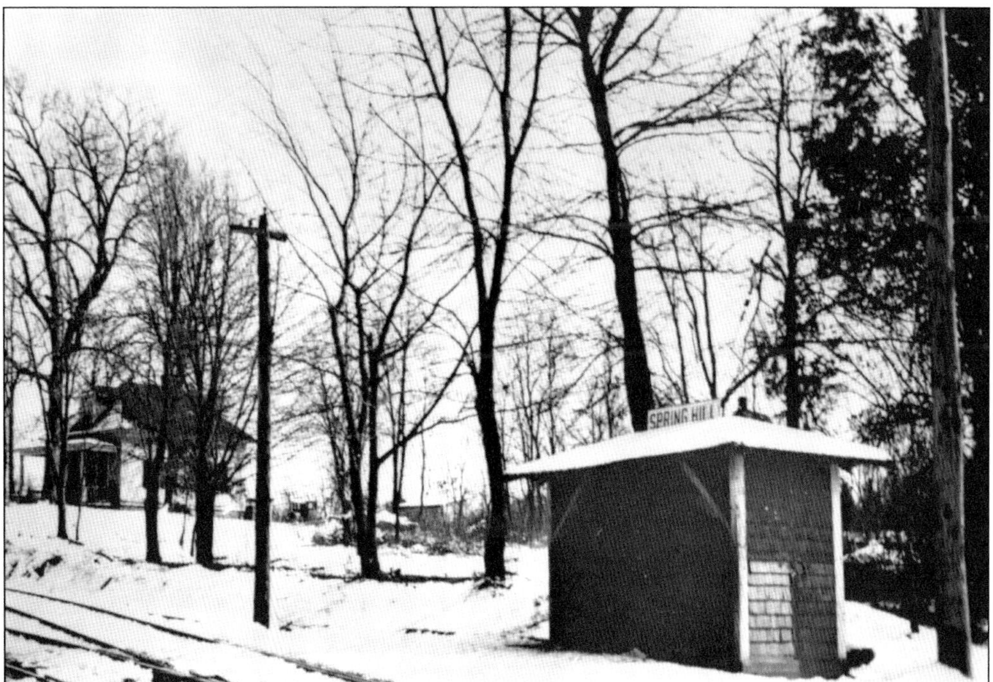

The Spring Hill passenger shelter was located 10.1 miles west of Rosslyn near present-day Spring Hill Road. Track facilities included this crossover that would allow westbound trains to change directions and head back toward Rosslyn. Spring Hill was the site of the only electrical substation on the Great Falls line. (Courtesy of Herbert H. Harwood.)

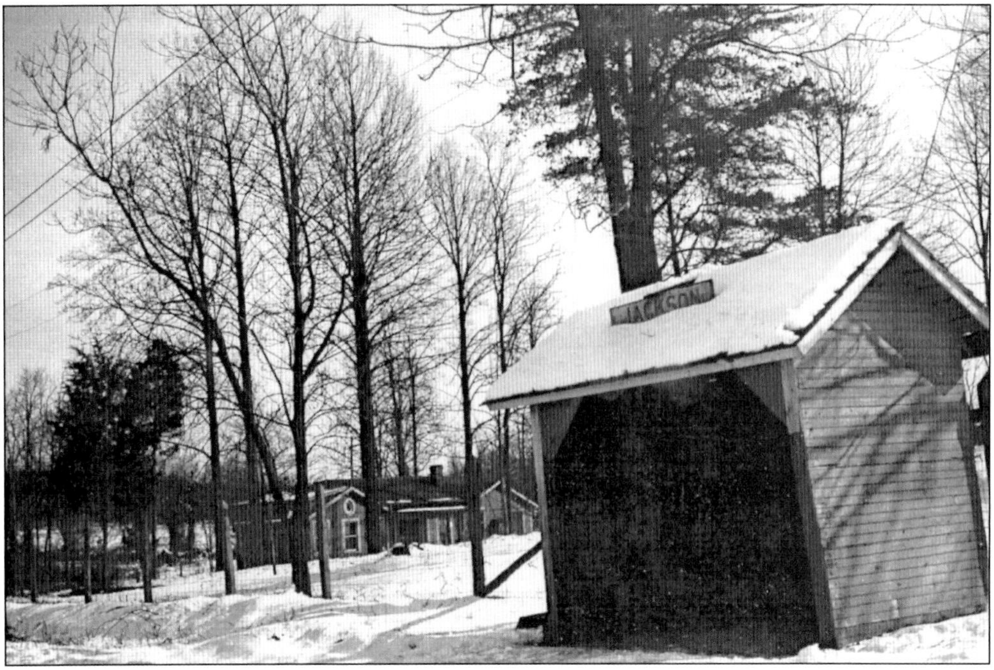

The Jackson passenger shelter was 900 feet west of Swinks Mill Road. This photograph was likely taken in the early 1930s, at the same time as the two pictures on the previous page, as the railroad was getting ready to abandon the Great Falls line. (Courtesy of NOVA Parks.)

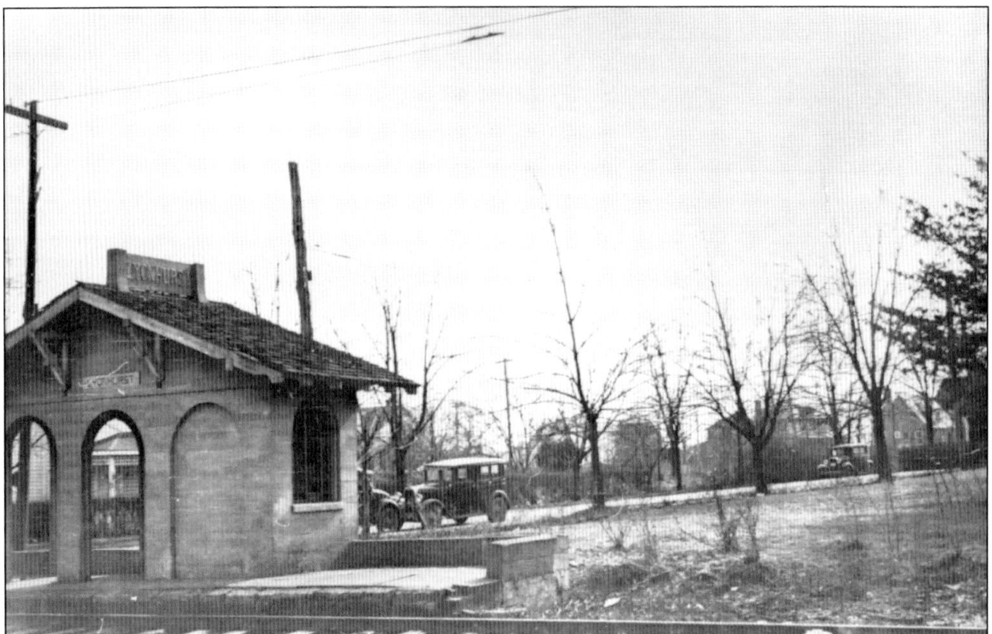

Lyonhurst was named after the home of Frank Lyon, a local lawyer and developer. The passenger shelter was unusual because it was constructed of concrete. Lyonhurst was near present-day Twenty-Fifth Street, 3.3 miles from Rosslyn, on the west side of the tracks. The photograph was taken by the W&OD Railway. (Courtesy of Herbert H. Harwood.)

Three

Leesburg

The town of Leesburg, the Loudoun County seat, sits at the intersection of two colonial roads: the Winchester-Alexandria Pike, now Virginia State Route 7/Market Street; and the Carolina Road, now US Route 15/King Street. The Carolina Road connected the northern colonies with the southern colonies.

With the arrival of the railroad in Leesburg on March 17, 1860, and its revival on June 1, 1867, following the Civil War, Leesburg became the commercial center of Loudoun County. Industries were laid out along the tracks from the Leesburg Lime Kiln on the east to J.T. Hirst Company on the west and north to the Wallace George Ice Plant on the south side of Loudoun Street SE.

Some interesting information for 1954 comes from the 1960 US Department of Agriculture Soil Survey for Loudoun County, Virginia. The main market was the livestock market in Leesburg. Most of the livestock and dairy products were sold in Baltimore and Washington, DC. The total number of farms was 1,438, decreasing at least since 1950. Total cropland harvested was 90,274 acres. About 311 dairy farms and 391 livestock farms were still running. Corn was the principal grain crop, but wheat, oats, and barley were important. Orchard grass was the most important grass; seed was harvested from 5,279 acres. Totals of 14,412 tons of commercial fertilizer and 25,199 tons of lime were used on the farms.

Dairy farming was primarily located east of the Catoctin Mountains, surrounding Leesburg. The reduction in dairy farming began with the purchase of 12 dairy farms for the construction of Dulles International Airport in 1955 and continued as airport influence led to the suburbanization of eastern Loudoun County.

In the late 1970s and early 1980s, commercial space in Leesburg was scarce. Beckham Dickerson, an architect with Kamstra-Dickerson Associates, and Bruce Brownell, owner of Bruce Brownell Inc., a construction firm, built the Market Station complex in association with the Town of Leesburg. Bob Lewis handled the financing. Market Station incorporates three structures from the railroad days: the W&OD freight station, the section foreman's house, and the C.C. Saffer & Brother feed and grain mill.

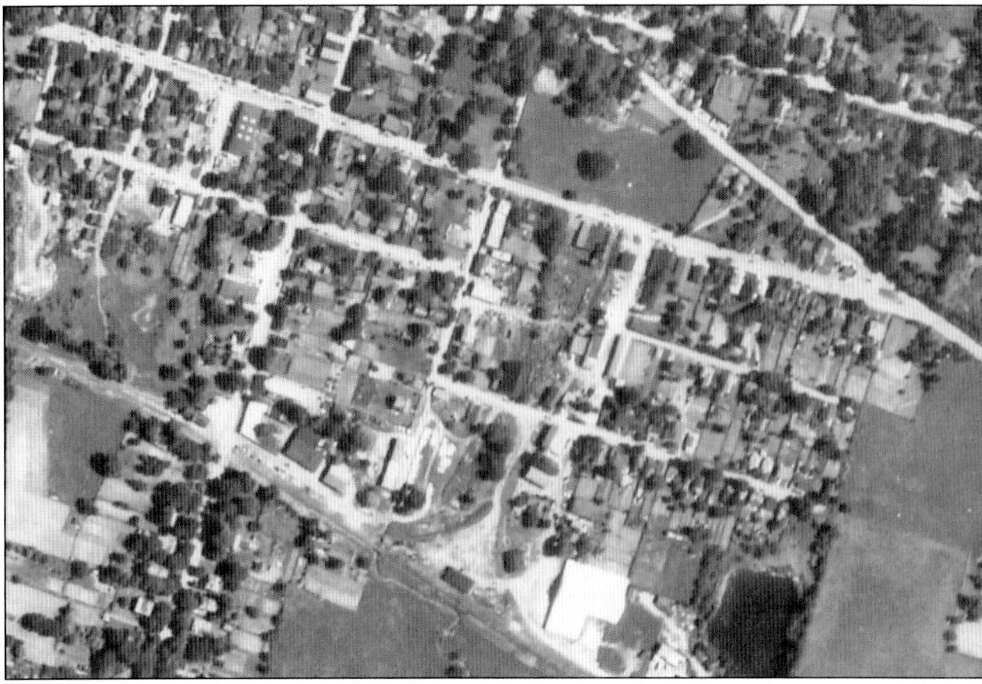

The map below shows the same area as the 1950 aerial photograph above. Some of the industrial buildings alongside the railroad are: (2) Loudoun County Stock Market. (3) C.C. Saffer Corn Mill, 1912. (4) Section foreman's house. (5) Norman & Harding fertilizer & feed, 1912. (6) C.C. Saffer mill, 1917–1968. (7) Saffer grain and hay storage building. (8) Store house. (9) Leesburg Feed and Grain. (10) Coal sales office. (11) Leesburg emergency power station and Wallace George Ice Plant. (12) Norman & Harding agricultural implements store. (13) Freight station. (14) Norris Brothers agricultural implements, 1894, and J.T. Hirst Company, 1930. (15) W&OD electric substation building. (16) Passenger station. (Above, courtesy of US Department of Agriculture, ASCS-APFO.)

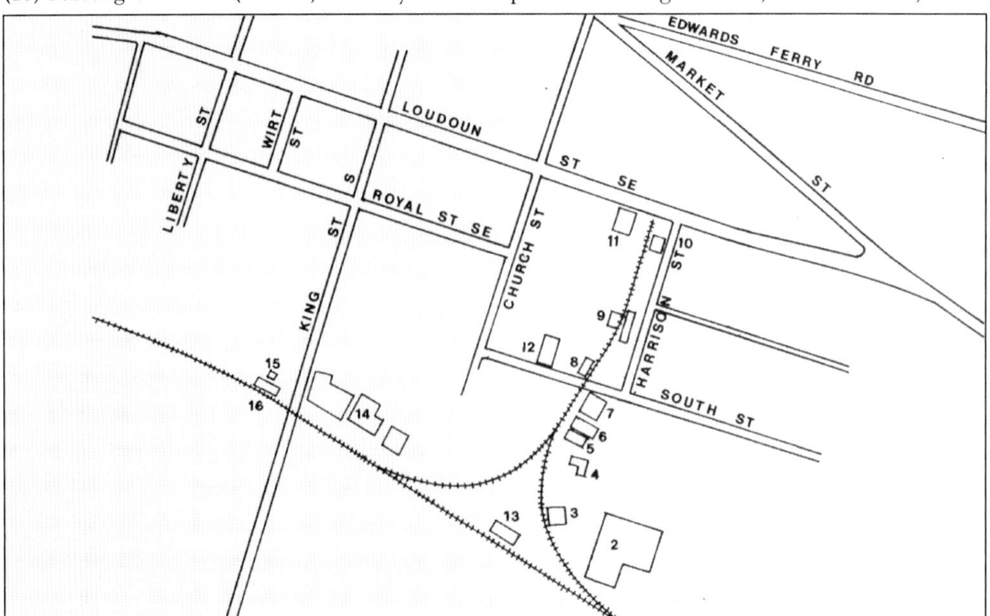

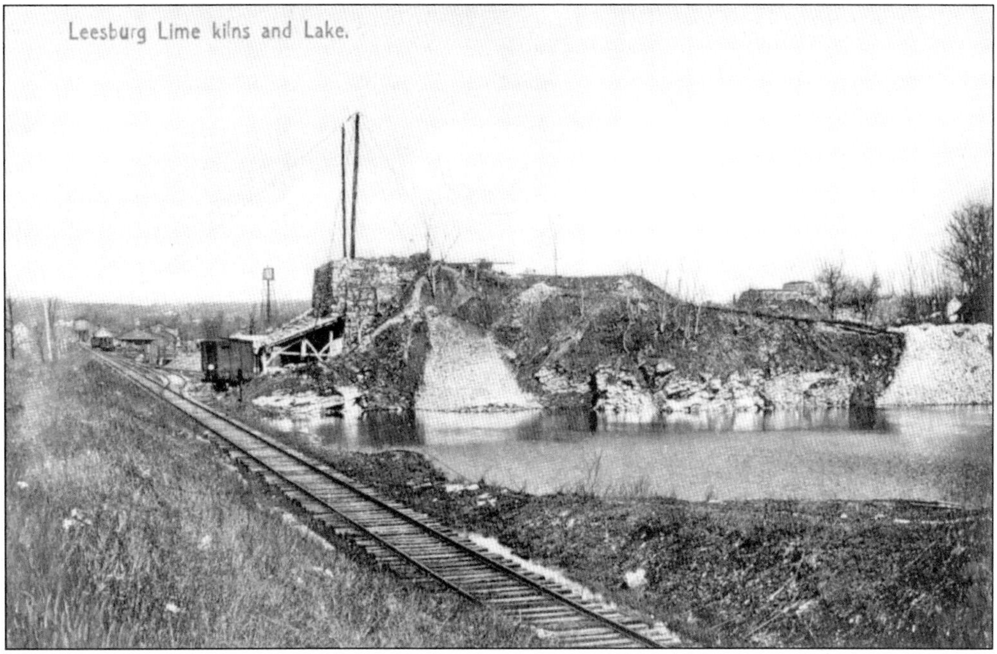

Based on the style of the boxcar's body, this photograph of the Leesburg Lime Kiln was probably taken in the early 1900s. Limestone from the quarry was used in the US Capitol building in Washington, DC. (Courtesy of NOVA Parks.)

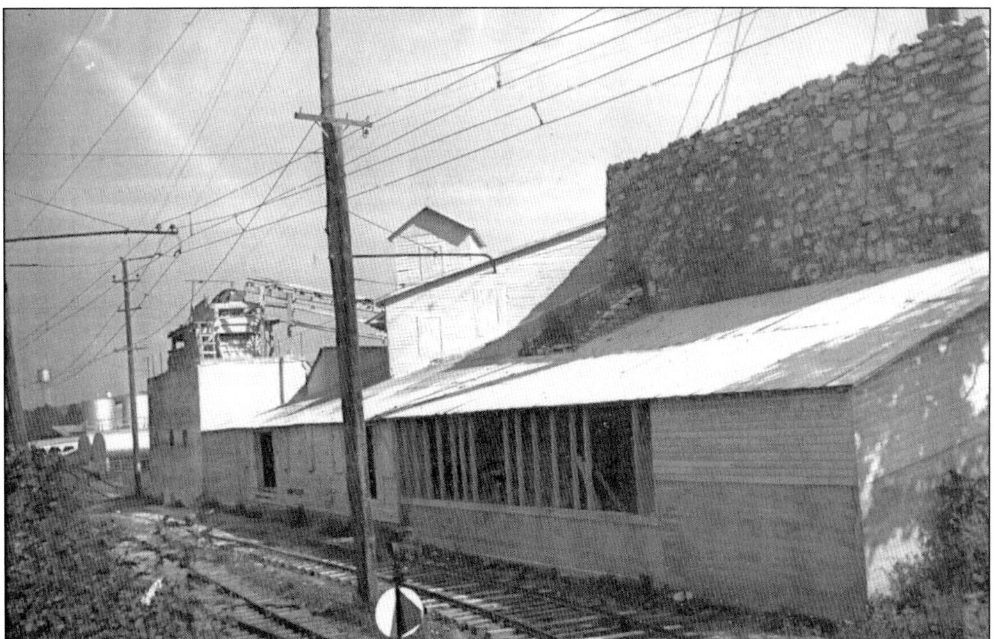

About 30 years later, the lime kiln operation is in full bore at the eastern end of Leesburg's industrial area. Lime was sold to farmers as a soil modifier, and lime rock was used on Loudoun County roads until the Trap Rock Quarry opened, offering a harder, more durable stone. (Courtesy of NOVA Parks.)

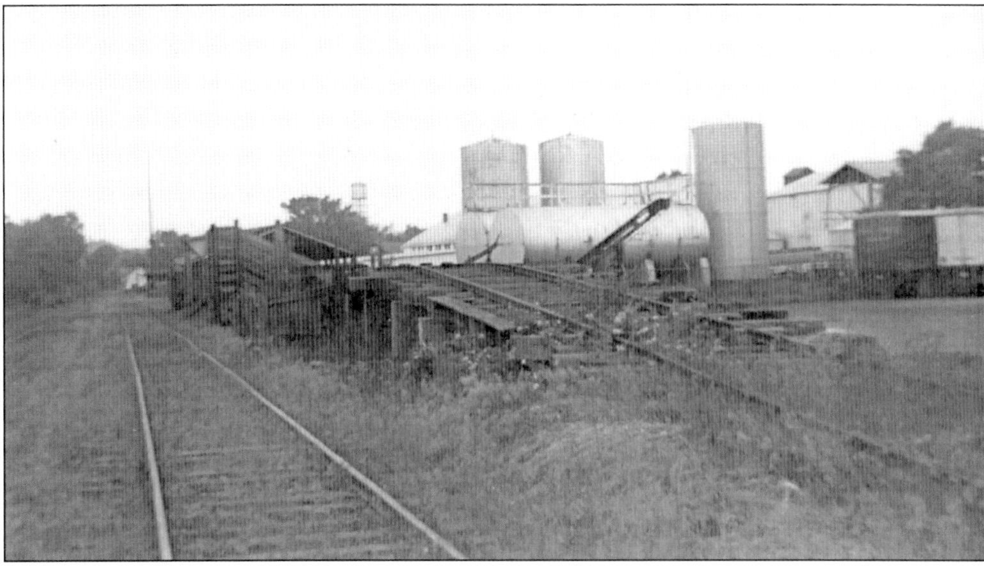

The short siding up the trestle provides a place to unload coal cars, as evidenced by the conveyor. Standard Oil Company tanks are in the center of this June 1957 picture taken by an unknown photographer. Behind them is the Loudoun County Livestock Market, and at left, just above the tracks, is the Leesburg passenger station. (Courtesy of NOVA Parks, Larry Crosen Collection.)

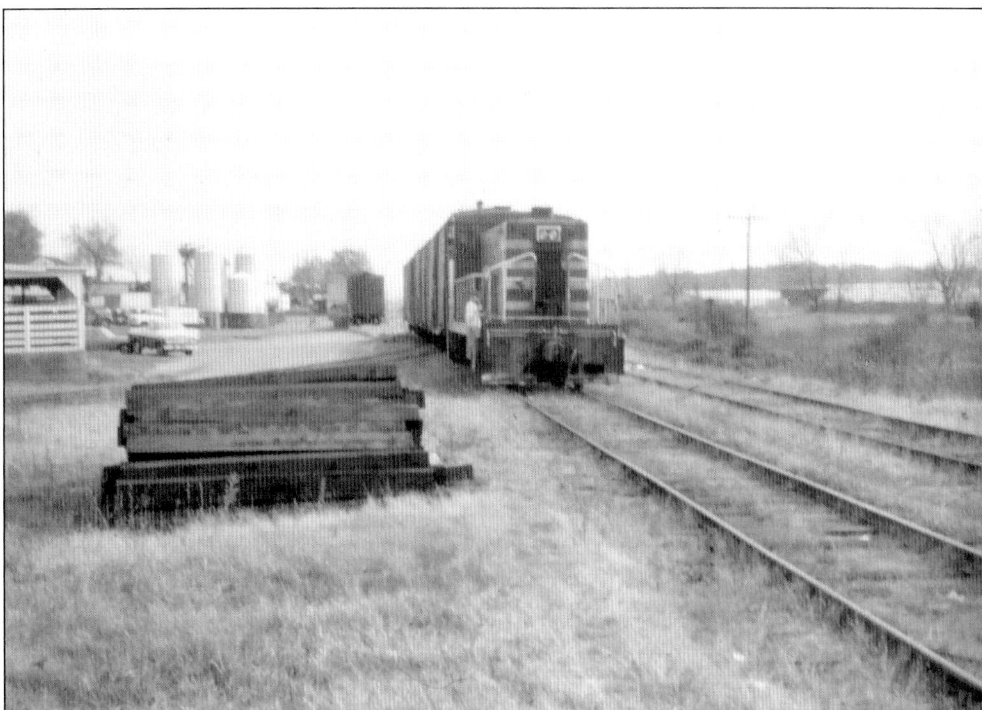

James E. Chapman visited Leesburg in November 1966 and took a series of photographs. Here, the daily freight is arriving behind General Electric 70-ton locomotive No. 57. The Loudoun County Livestock Market is just out of frame to the left.

James E. Chapman photographed the Loudoun County Livestock Market, located east of Harrison Street, in November 1966. Farmers and ranchers came here to auction horses, beef and dairy cattle, sheep, pigs, ducks, chickens, and turkeys. Dairymen would sell the cows they culled from their herds, as well as bulls and calves. The building, like so many along the line, succumbed to fire and was never rebuilt.

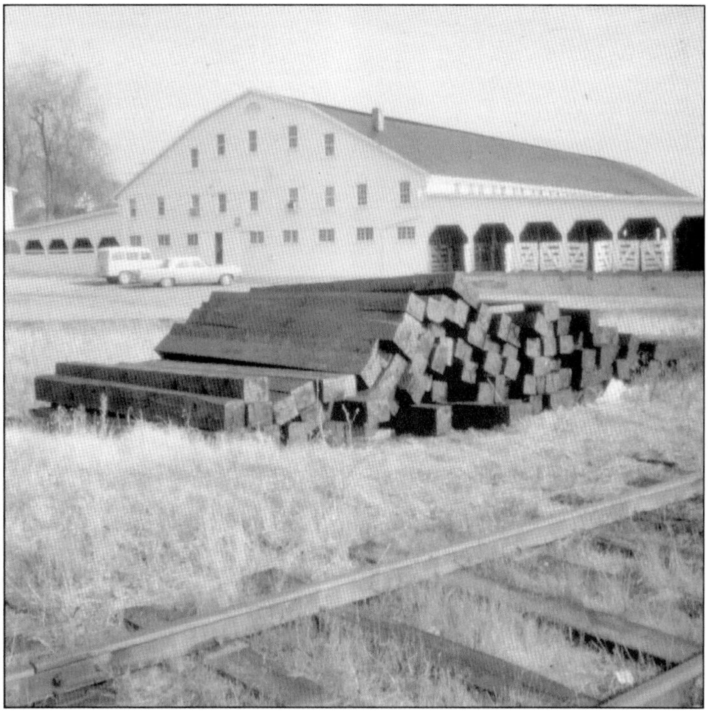

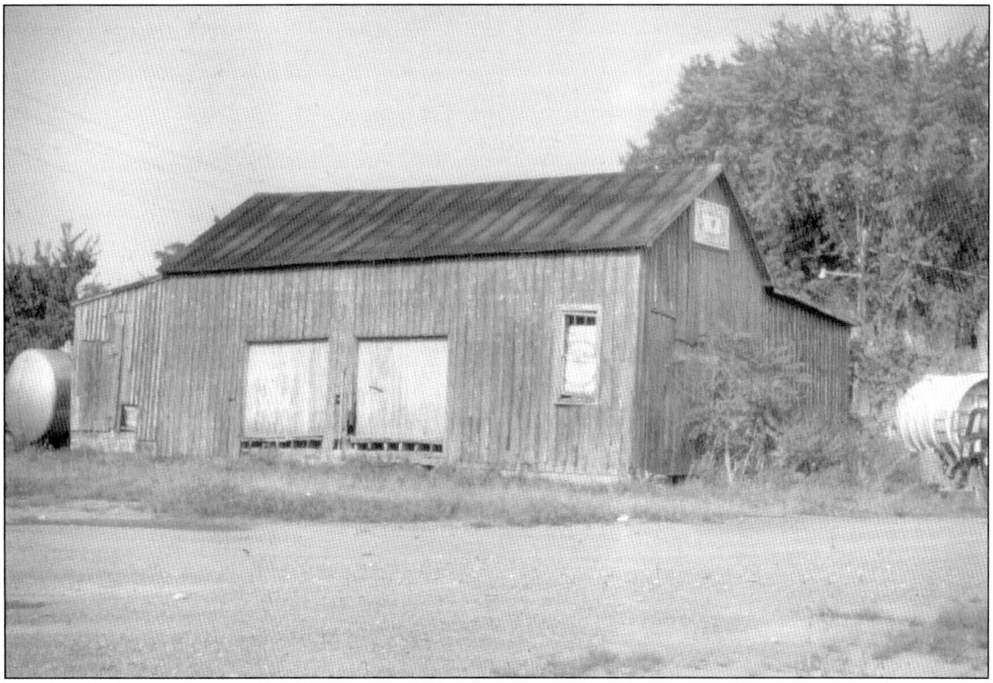

Early in the 20th century, C.C. Saffer used this building as a corn mill. Later, it was converted to store fertilizer and pesticides. The sign reads "Baugh's Animal Base Fertilizers," perhaps advertising Baugh and Sons Company of Philadelphia and Norfolk, Virginia, distributors of phosphate fertilizer and other agricultural chemicals. Seen here in August 1968, the trains are gone and the fertilizer storage building awaits its fate.

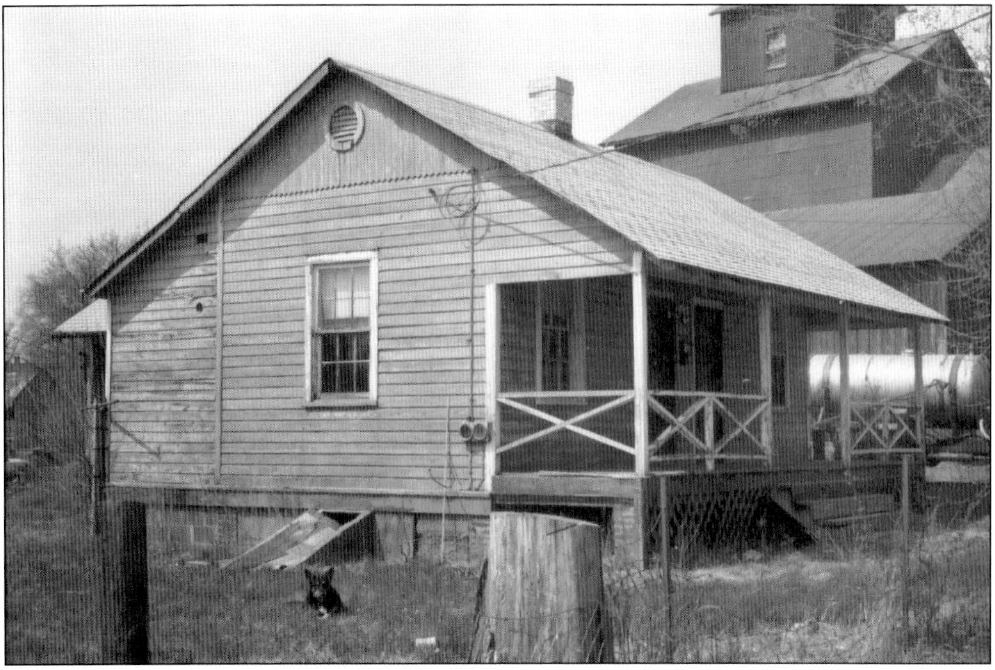

Roger Fox, one of the railroad's track gang supervisors, lived at this house from 1944 to 1965, when it was turned over to Wilbur Lee, another railroad employee. The house had an L-shaped floor plan with public rooms in the front and bedrooms in the rear. Residents had to use an outdoor toilet for many years. The structure was not in use when photographed in October 1968.

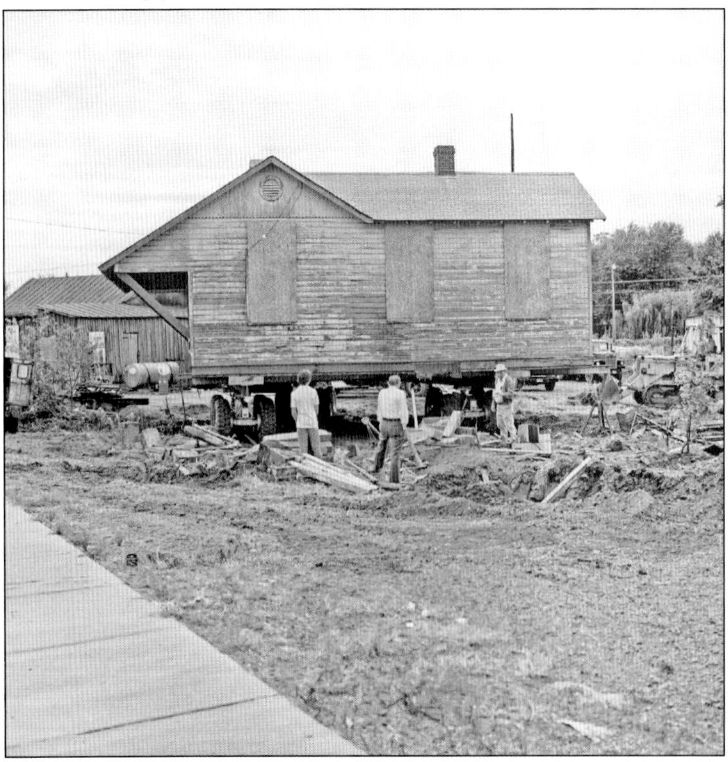

Neil Steinberg of Photoworks, in Leesburg, documented the conversion of the "wharf" area into the new Market Station commercial complex. Here, on October 5, 1984, the section foreman's house has been lowered onto rubber-tired dollies and is ready to be moved to its new home on Harrison Street. (Courtesy of Photoworks.)

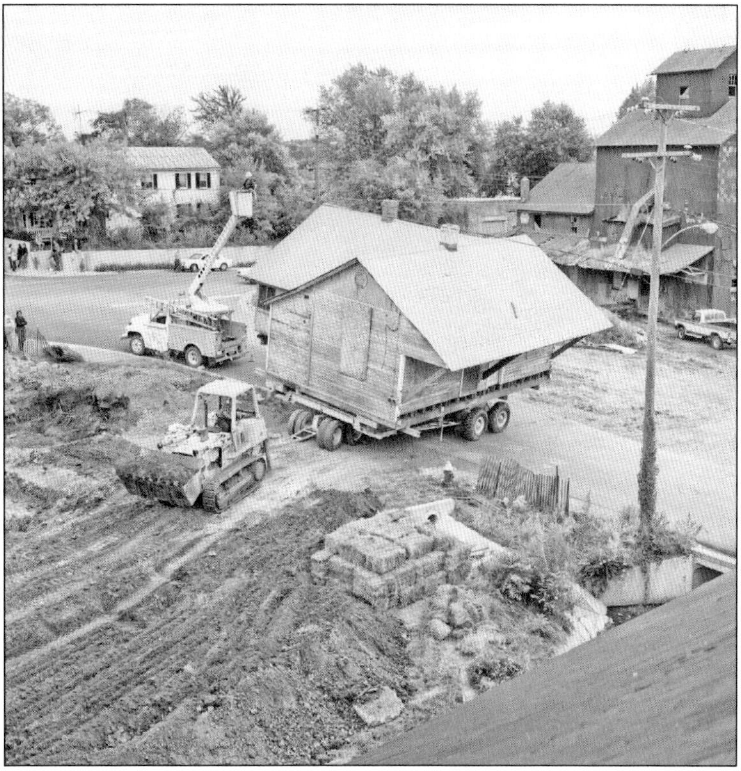

In what has to be the easiest method of moving a utility line out of the way, the C&P Telephone Company technician in the bucket truck is holding the cable up while the section foreman's house passes below. Neil Steinberg caught the house moving across South Street on October 5, 1984. (Courtesy of Photoworks.)

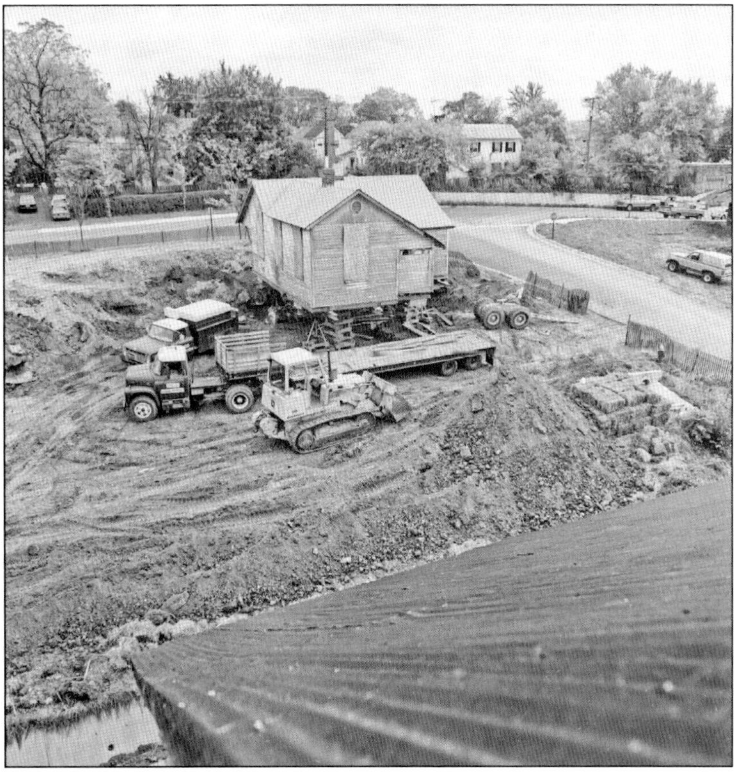

The section foreman's house is in its new location. Here, the house is resting on temporary timber cribbing that allowed the dollies to be retrieved. The next step will be to build up the foundation to support the house. The lead rubber-tired dolly sits at right. Today, the building is occupied by the Leesburg Cigar & Pipe store. (Courtesy of Photoworks.)

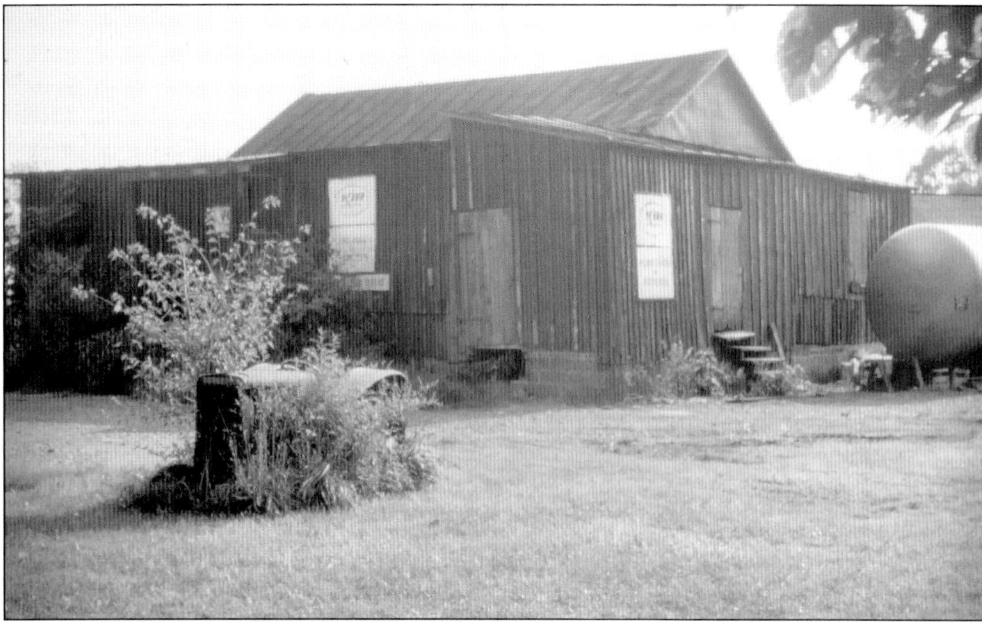

This August 1968 view from Harrison Street shows the rear of the fertilizer building seen on page 39. In 1912, it was C.C. Saffer's corn mill. Saffer sold salt blocks and also sold and installed milking machinery. The signs advertise plant foods and pesticides. The tractor would make an interesting detail item on a diorama or a model railroad.

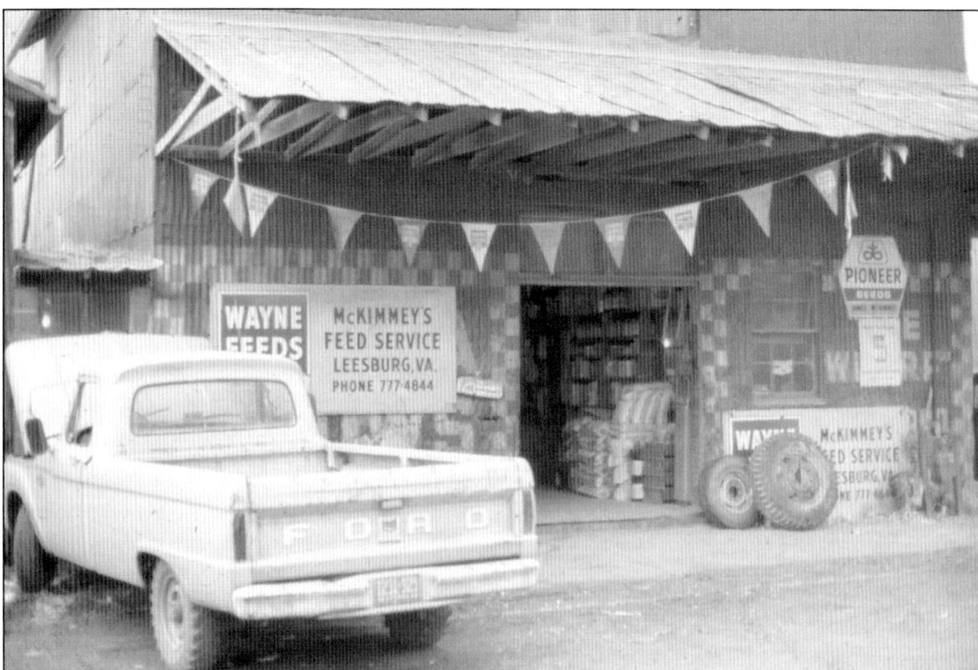

McKimmey's Feed Service rented C.C. Saffer's mill in November 1968. The author photographed the McKimmey storefront in December 1968. The store faced Harrison Street and was located under the shorter, eastern section of the C.C. Saffer mill. The triangular signs on the rope advertise Wayne Feeds.

This warehouse, pictured in December 1968, was located just south of the C.C. Saffer mill. Grains were unloaded from trucks, weighed, and elevated into the four storage bins located in the tall section of the mill. The mill bought wheat from the farmers, most of which was just cleaned and stored. C.C. Saffer would work until very late in the evening during the harvest season until all of the farmers' grain was unloaded.

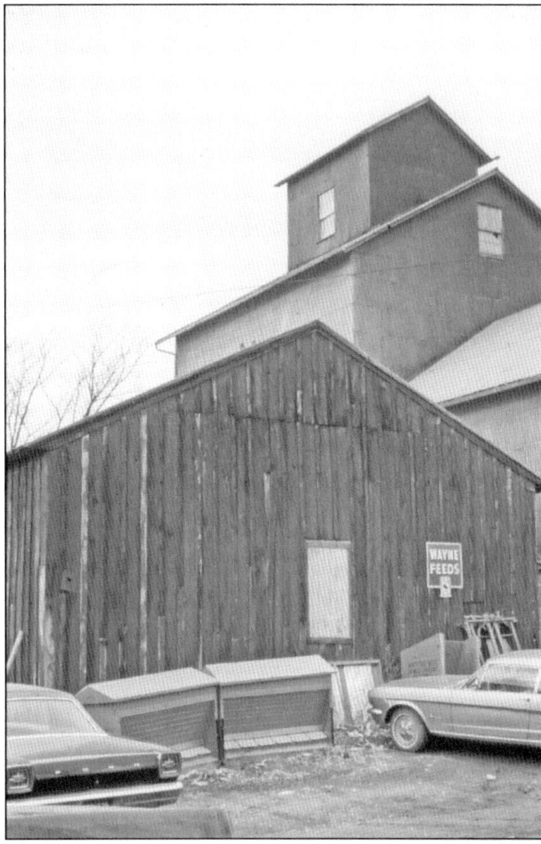

This view in August 1968 shows the south side of the storage building. The roof of the store section barely shows above the new cement block lean-to. The northwest corner of the section foreman's house is at right. The gray round object above the roof of the storage building might be the top of a small cyclone dust collector.

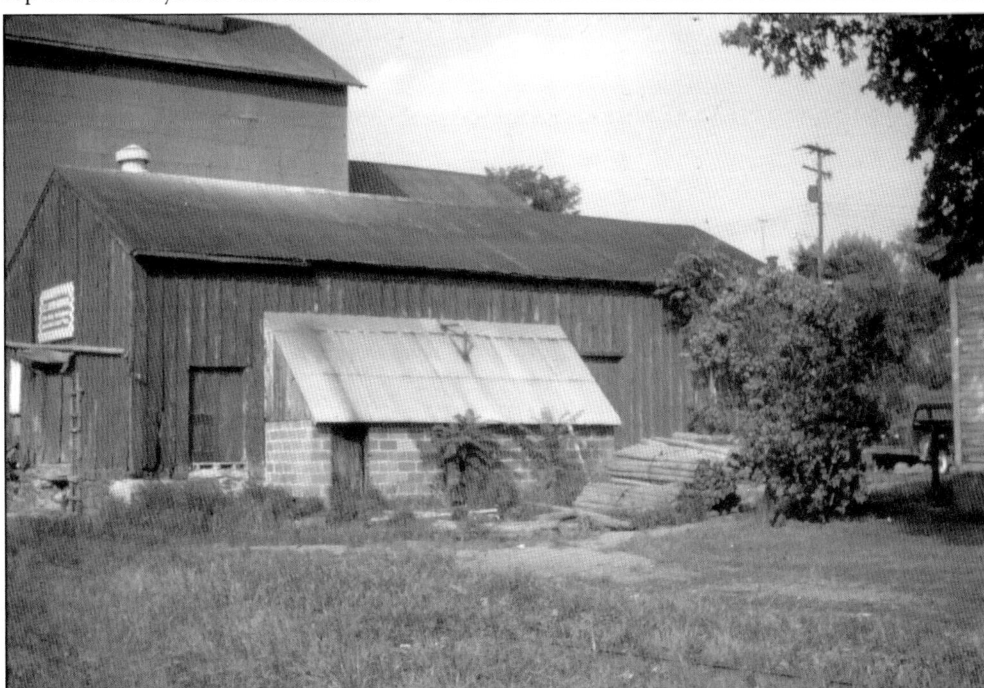

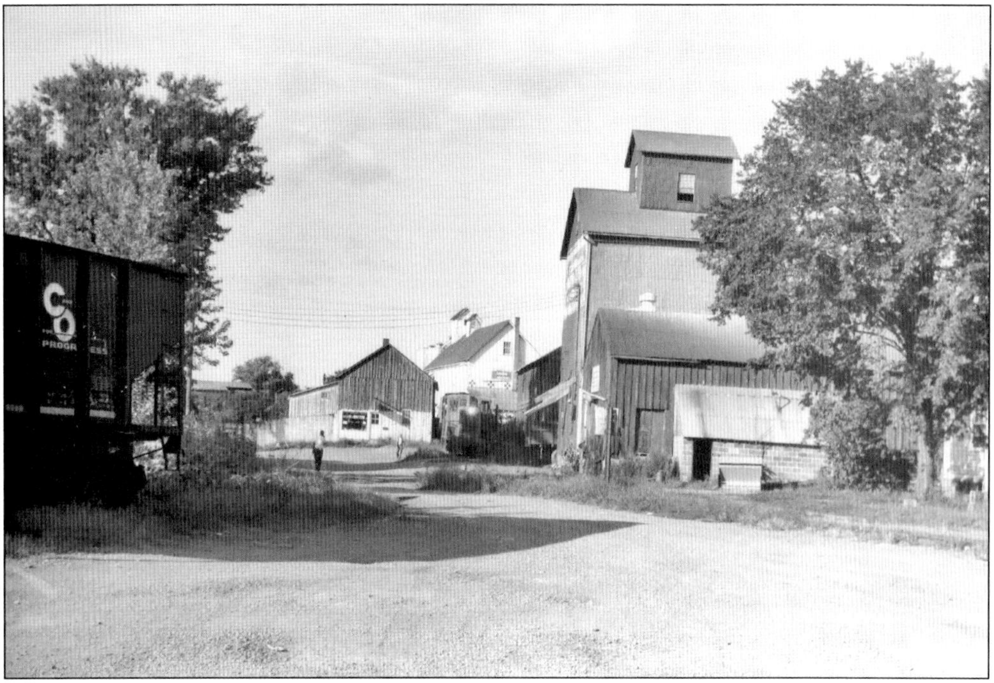

Thomas A. Coons traveled to Leesburg to catch some train action during the last year of operation in September 1967. General Electric locomotives No. 57 and No. 58 are switching cars on the blind end of the wye. The headlight of No. 58 is pointed toward Coons. (Courtesy of Thomas A. Coons.)

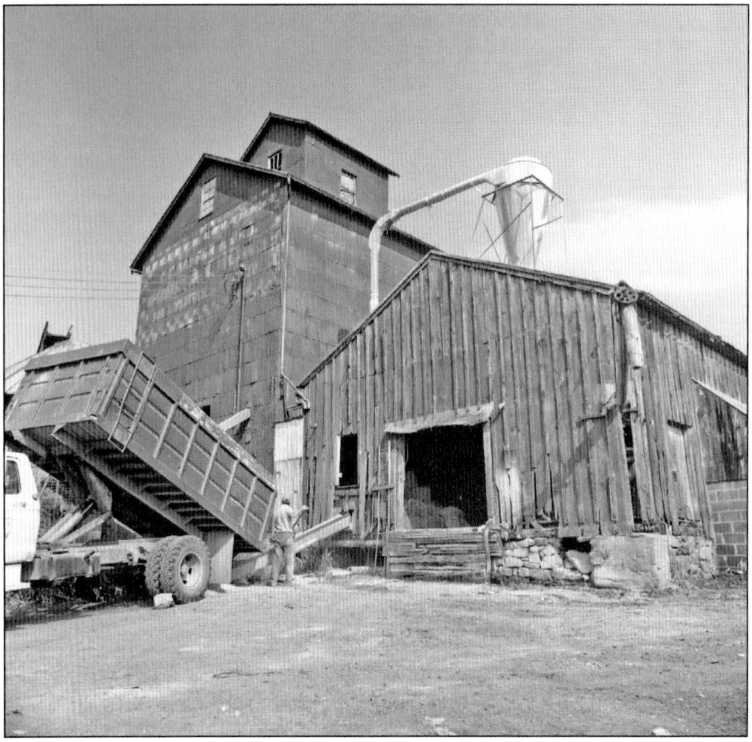

Neil Steinberg photographed what may have been the last delivery of grain to McKimmey's Feed Service in September 1984. After leaving the truck, the conveyor would take the grain to a scale to be weighed in. Then the grain would be elevated into the storage bins for holding until needed to make feed or for shipment out. (Courtesy of Photoworks.)

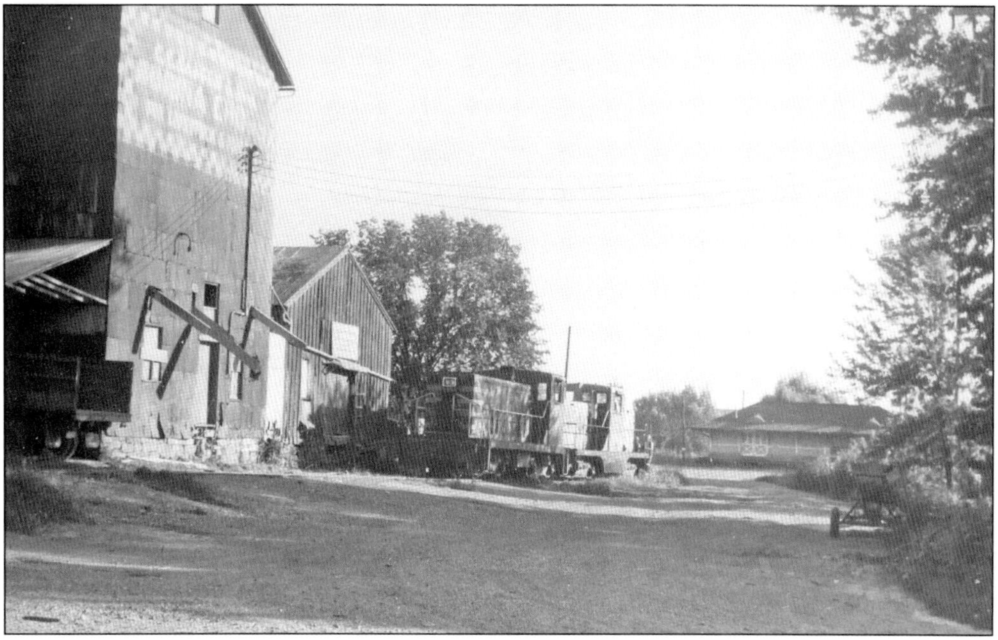

The three chutes sticking out of the elevator building provided a means of loading boxcars with grain. The sign at upper left reads "C.C. Saffer & Bro. Purina Chows for Livestock and Poultry." Looking south, Thomas A. Coons photographed No. 57 and No. 58 on the east leg of the wye in September 1967. (Courtesy of Thomas A. Coons.)

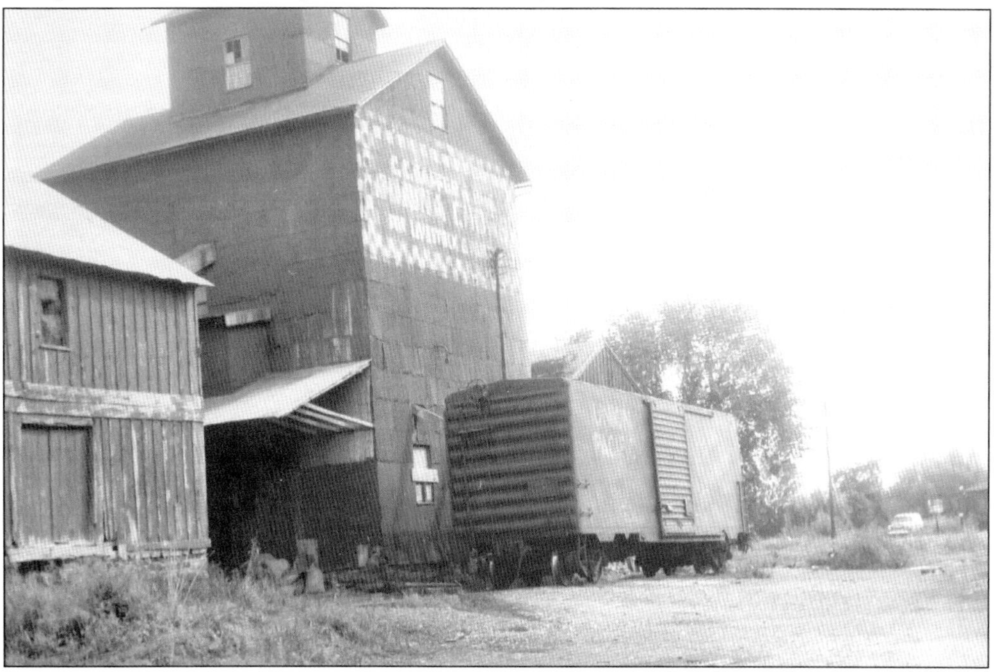

Chutes were used to load boxcars with grain, while augurs were used to unload them. Without seeing whether a chute or an augur is connected to this boxcar, it is not possible to determine whether it was being loaded or unloaded. Thomas A. Coons photographed the car in August 1967. (Courtesy of Thomas A. Coons.)

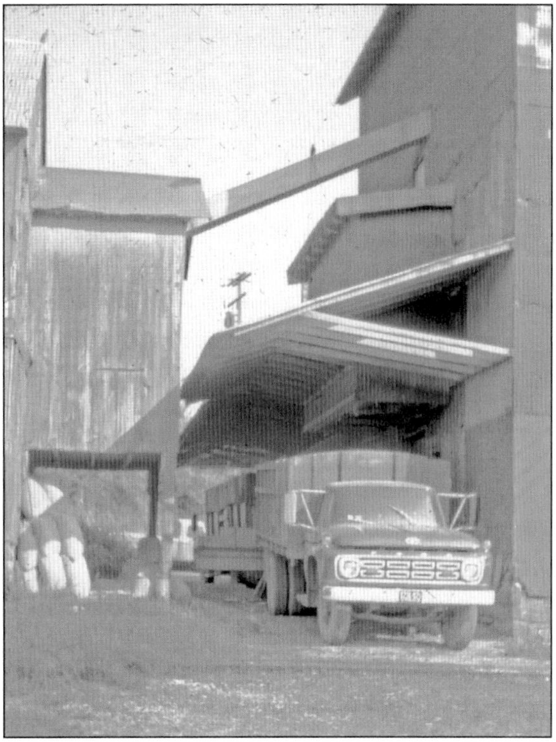

In August 1968, McKimmey's truck is ready for loading under the north-side awning of McKimmey's Feed Service. The square tube connecting the two buildings allows grain to be routed into the storage building at left. The photographer was looking east from the track side of the mill. The following photograph was taken on the same day.

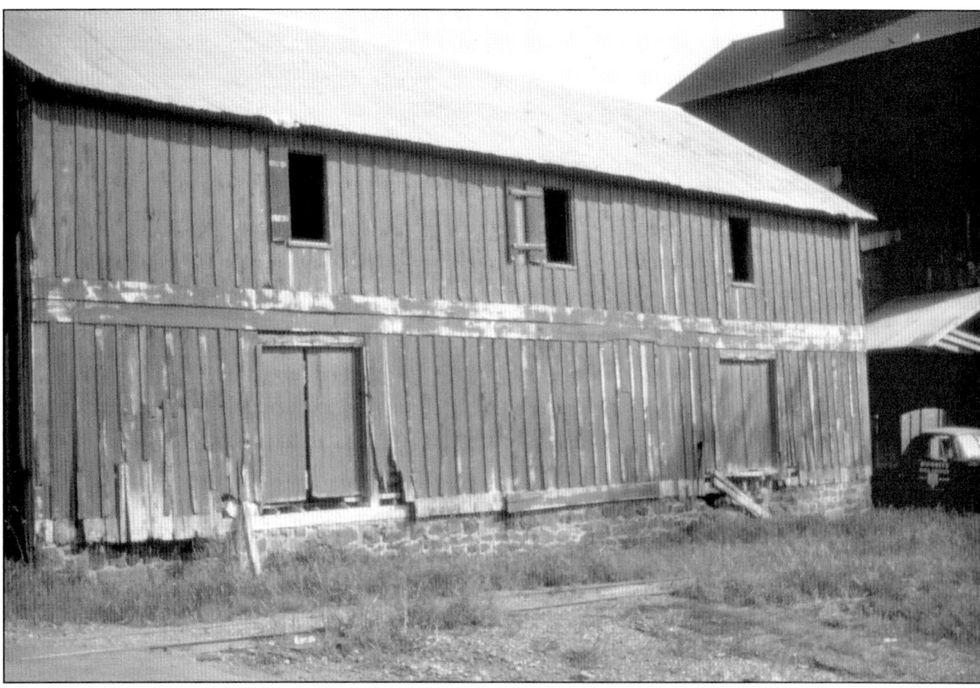

This building was used to store hay, which farmers would need in the late winter after their own supply of hay had been used up, and was probably also used to store grain. Wynne C. Saffer and William Sasher both remembered building forts out of hay bales and grain/feed bags in mill warehouses as children. Saffer's father told him not to play in the mill, as it was too dangerous.

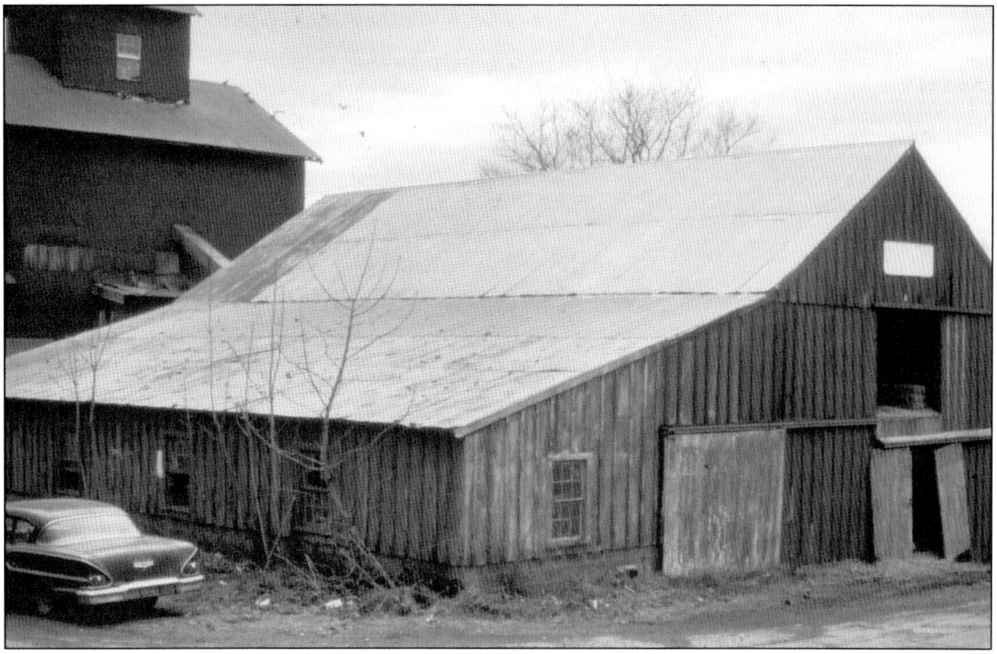

The photographer was standing on the north side of South Street facing southwest in December 1968 to take this picture of the McKimmey storage building. Built after 1898, the mill was purchased by the Saffer family in November 1917 and then sold to McKimmey in November 1968. The mill would receive feed, along with hay in winter, and ship wheat out.

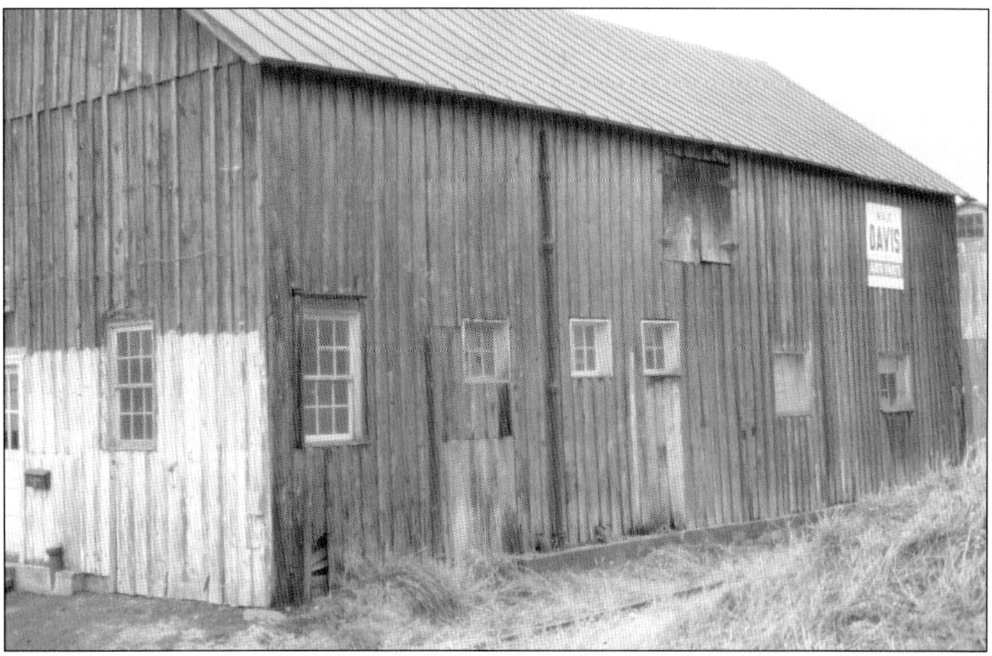

According to Wynne C. Saffer, there used to be a junkyard north of Saffer's mill surrounded by a stockade fence. The sign on this building reads "Max Davis & Co. Auto Parts." The end of the building at left faced south onto South Street. It was located almost opposite the Leesburg Feed and Grain Company. One rail is visible at the bottom of this December 1968 photograph.

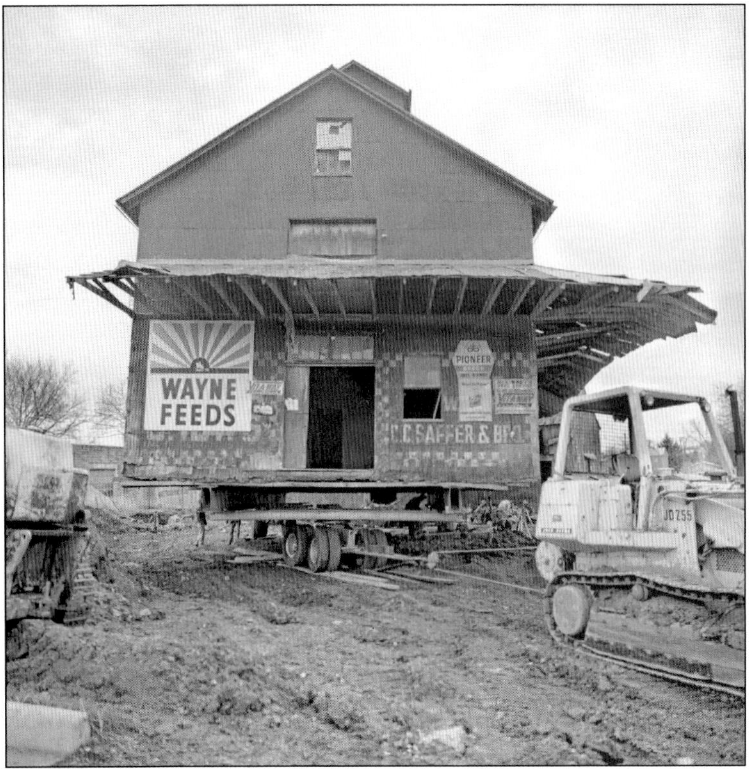

The front dolly under C.C. Saffer's mill has been hooked up to the winch on the back of the front loader. Three dollies are being used, connected by the steel cribbing. The double I-beams under the mill were located under the mill's internal columns to minimize structural stresses. Neil Steinberg captured the mill en route to its new home on December 18, 1984. (Courtesy of Photoworks.)

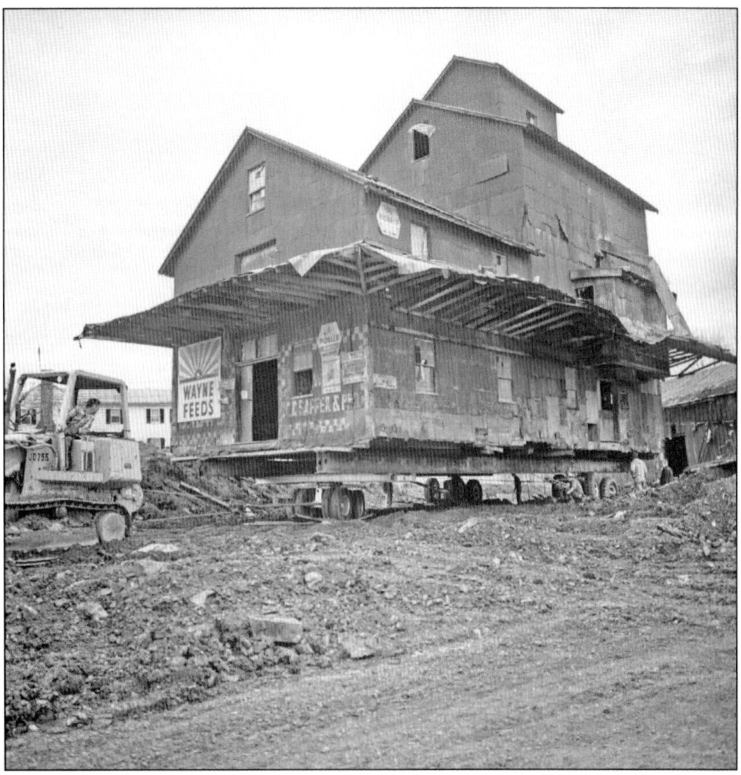

Crouse House Movers & Crane Service's crew is keeping a close eye on the dollies as the tractor pulls the building over a boardwalk. Many structures are moved on three supporting points to prevent wracking their frames. The sign at right reads "McKimmey's Feed Service. We Use and Recommend Vit-A-Way for Livestock, More than just a Mineral." Neil Steinberg photographed the action on December 18, 1984. (Courtesy of Photoworks.)

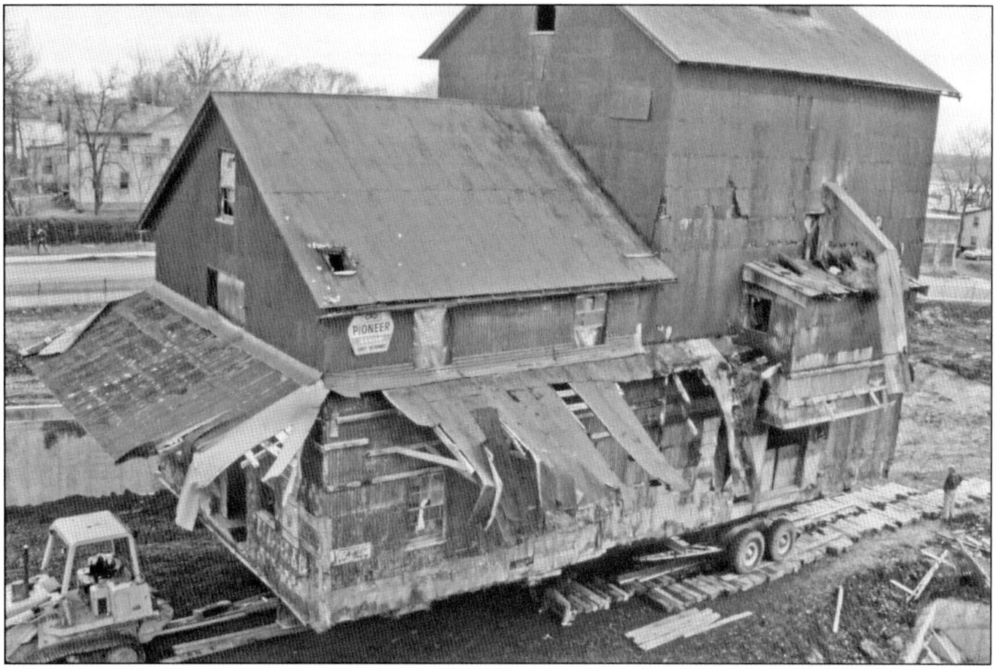

The building movers have placed a double corduroy road for the dollies. Mark Buckingham of Wolfe House & Building Movers estimated the weight of the mill to be 125 tons. Neil Steinberg photographed the mill a little farther along toward its final resting place on Harrison Street on December 20, 1984. The Tuscarora Mill Restaurant was the first tenant of Market Station. (Courtesy of Photoworks.)

The Saffer mill has been moved to its new resting place. The moving crews have set up cribbing, removed the dollies, and are leveling the mill in preparation for building its new foundation. Cribbing is typically made up of five-by-four-inch oak timbers. Neil Steinberg photographed this scene on January 28, 1985. (Courtesy of Photoworks.)

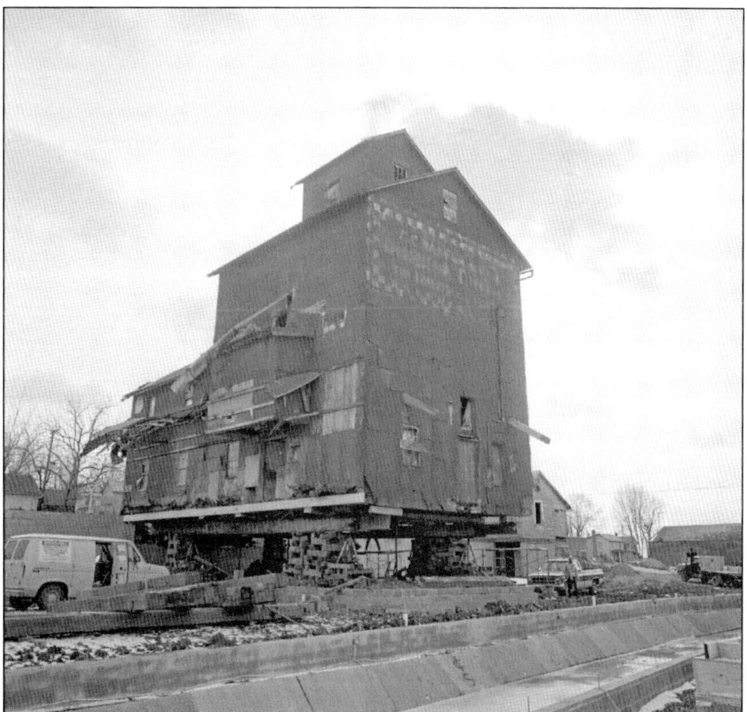

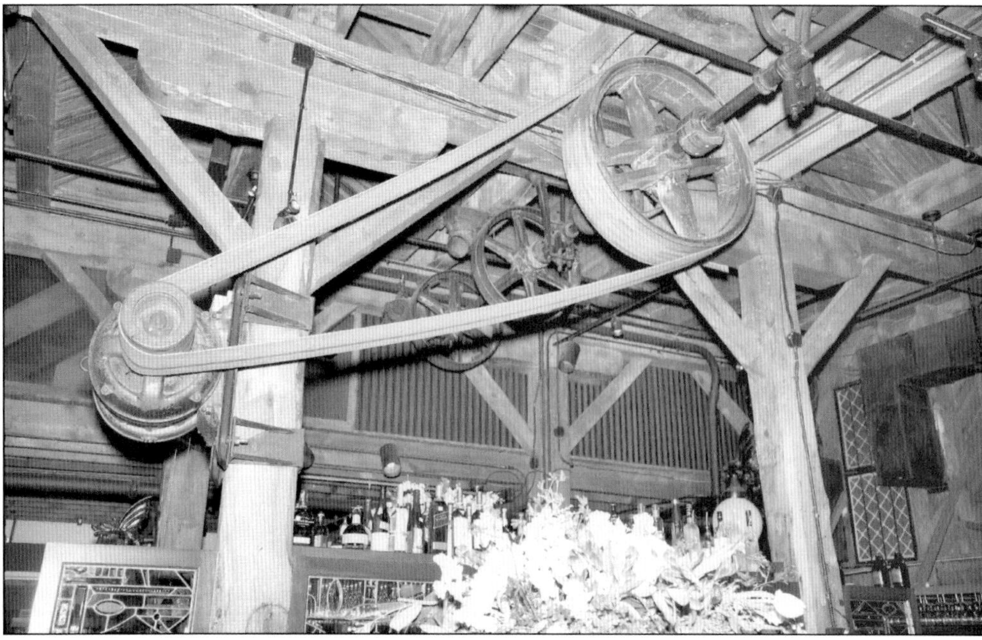

The mill's grain elevator powertrain of motor, belts, and wooden and steel belt wheels was kept as a part of the decor above the Tuscarora Mill Restaurant's bar and dining room, as seen on February 5, 2016. The motor ran on direct current when installed and was later converted to alternating current at no cost to the mill. (Access courtesy of the Tuscarora Mill Restaurant.)

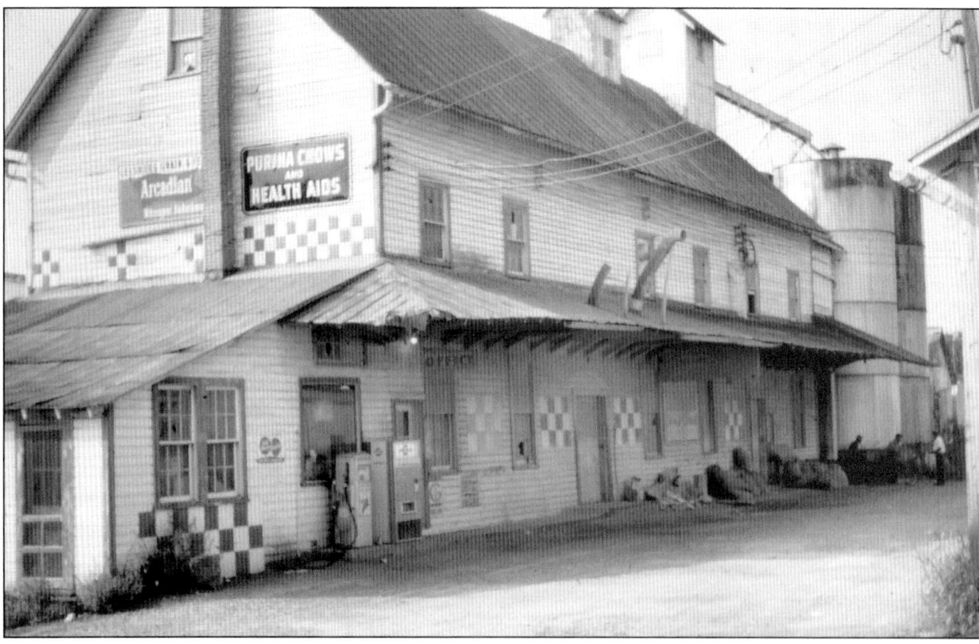

The Harrison Street side of the Leesburg Grain and Feed Company, owned by Herbert Bryant, is emblazoned with a Purina Chows and Health Aids sign and the red-and-white square Purina motif in August 1968. Equipment in the mill in 1912 included automatic scales, seven double milling rollers, purifiers, sifters, and dust collectors. Leesburg Feed and Grain could store 22,000 bushels of grain, the approximate output of 454 acres of corn.

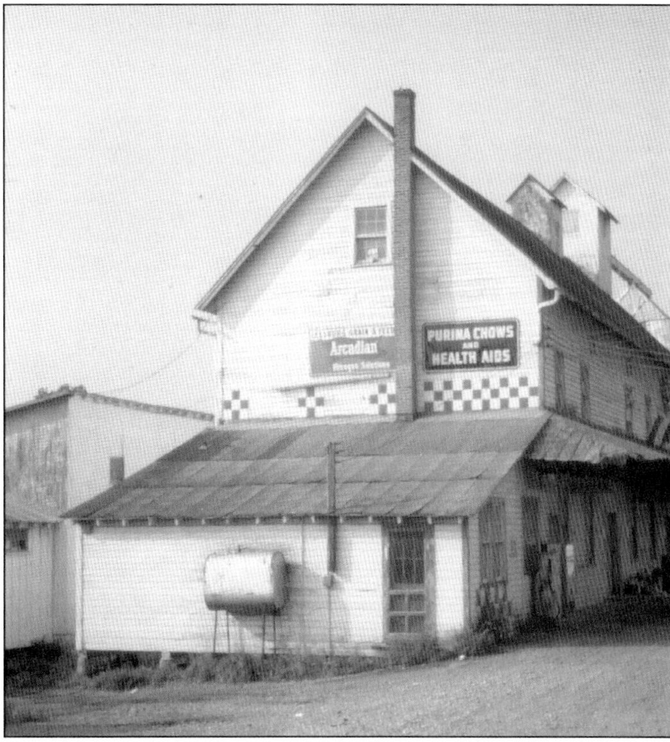

The lean-to with the fuel tank, seen here in August 1968, housed the plant's 40-horsepower engine. In double-roller milling, both rollers turn toward each other, but one roller runs faster than the other, grinding the grain. If the rollers ran at the same speed, the grain would be crushed. The rollers had serrations to aid the grinding.

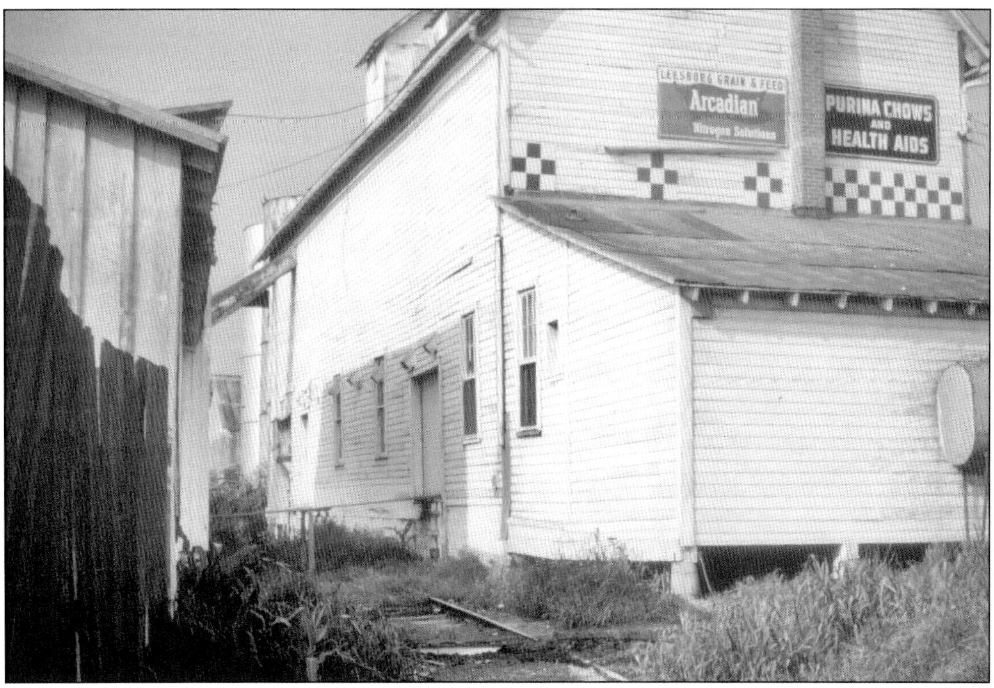

Leesburg Grain and Feed Company was just north of the C.C. Saffer mill on the same (east) side of the wye's extension toward Loudoun Street SE. This view from August 1968 shows what used to be the track side. Planks spread across the space allowed workers to easily pass from one building to the other.

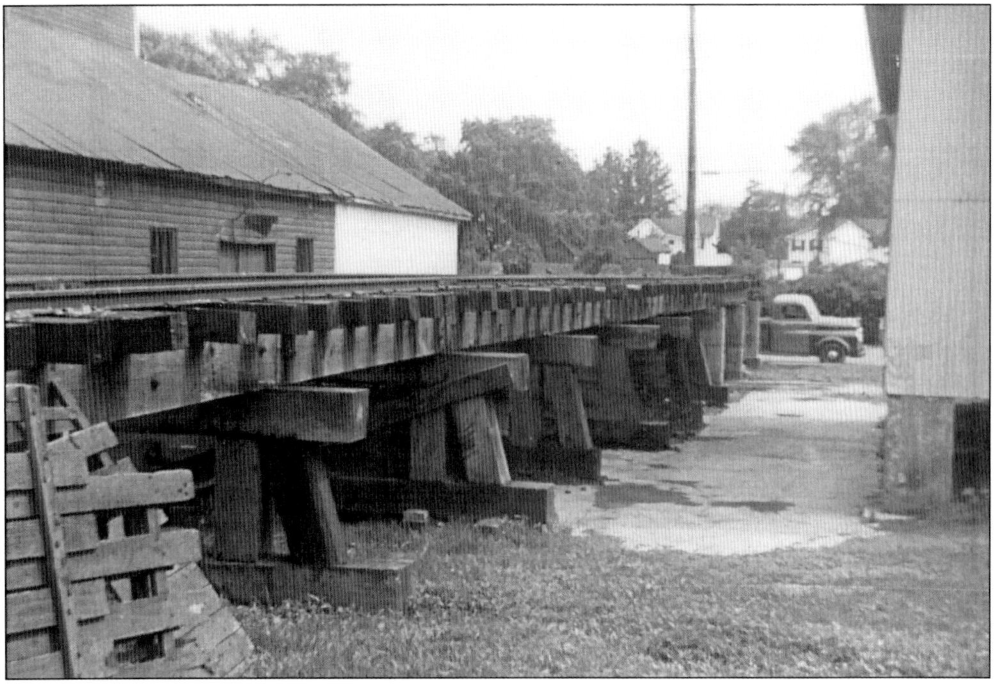

This trestle at the end of the wye supported hopper cars bringing in coal for the Leesburg emergency power plant. An ice plant was attached on its western side in 1912. This view from June 1958 looks north toward Loudoun Street. The Loudoun Packing Company, Food Division, was located in the building with the light-colored siding to the left of the trestle in 1968. (Courtesy of NOVA Parks.)

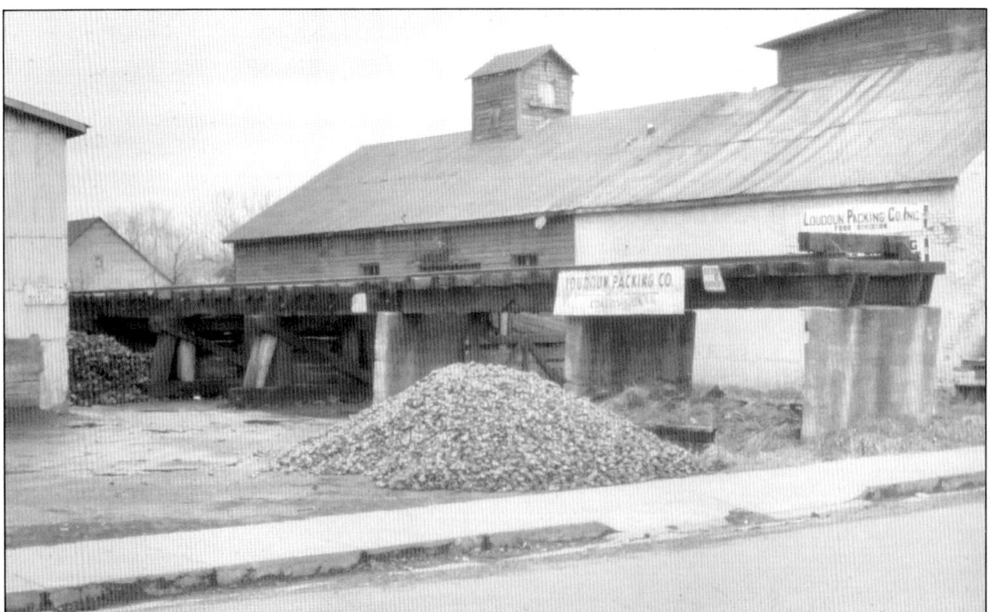

The sign on the trestle reads "Loudoun Packing Company, Coal Division." The author photographed the north end of the trestle in December 1968. The sign on the building reads "For Coal Apply Main Office, 37 East Loudoun St."

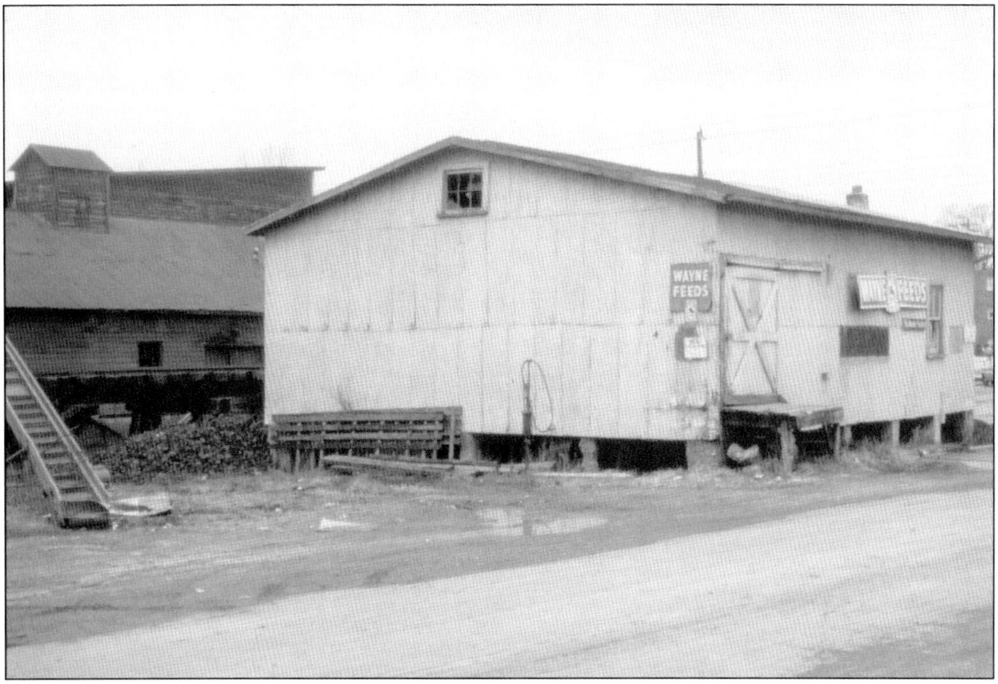

In late December 1968, the photographer was looking toward the center of town at the Wayne Feeds office, which probably doubled as the coal operation office. This building was on the corner of Harrison Street and Loudoun Street SE.

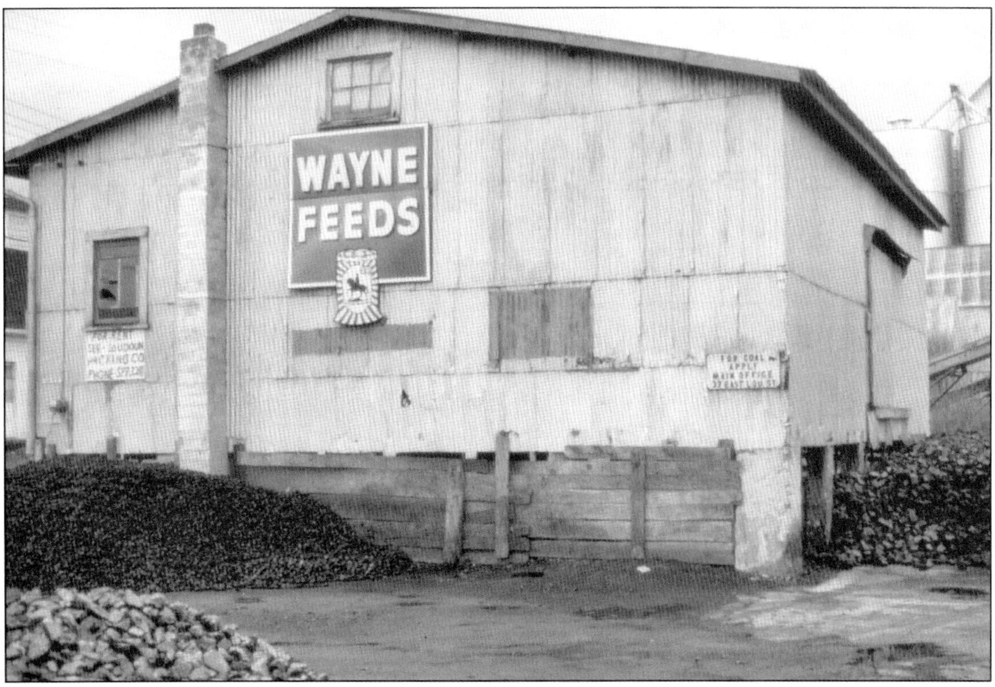

This is the north end and west side of the Wayne Feeds office as it appeared in December 1968. The grain silos of the Leesburg Feed and Grain Company are at upper right. Below them is a coal conveyor.

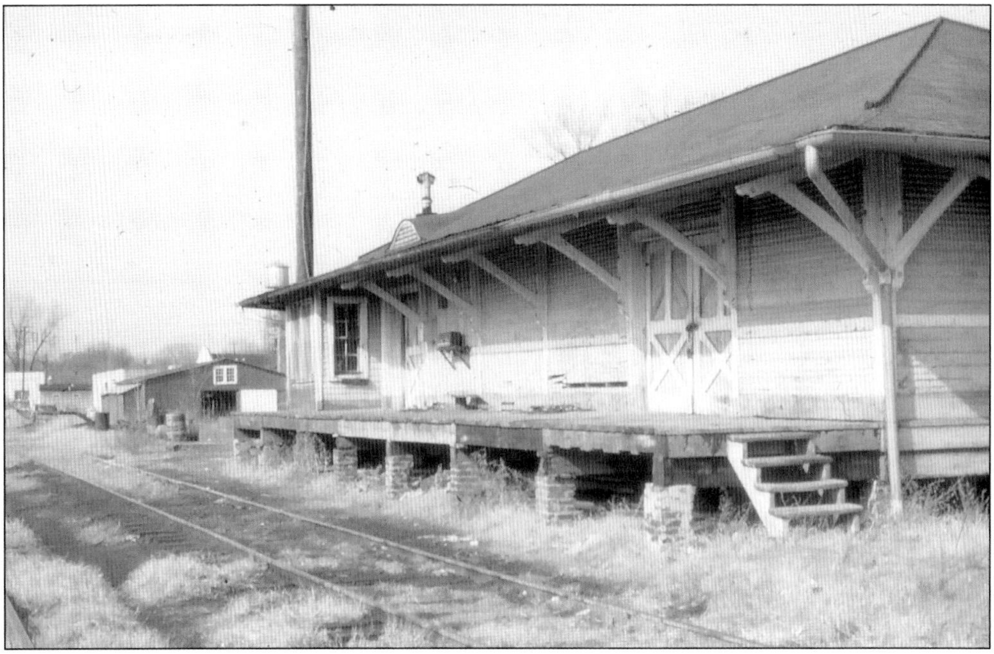

James E. Chapman photographed the freight station in November 1966. The November 2, 1898, freight station plans show two eyebrow dormers on the track side. When the railroad ceased passenger operations, it moved the Leesburg station agent's office to the freight station. The bay window was added so the station agent could look up and down the tracks.

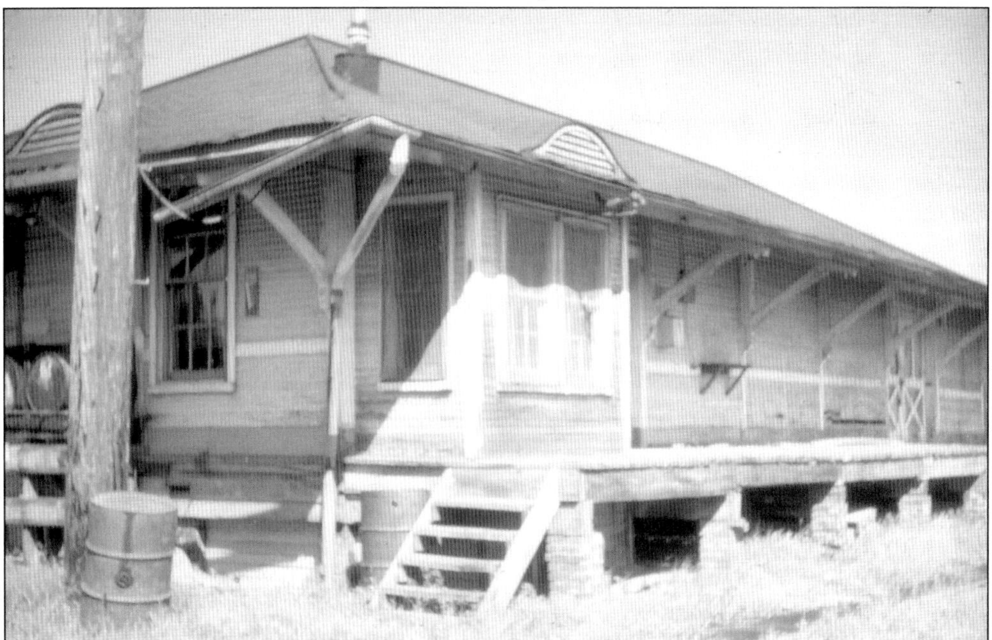

The agent's office on the southwest corner of the station can be seen in this view from August 1968. Just visible below the eyebrow dormer is a bracket that held a switch lantern. The lantern would have shown red down the tracks to indicate that the train crew needed to stop to pick up orders. The telephone pole was erected in 1956, when the railroad installed its radio system.

Neil Steinberg captured the freight station in its final resting place in September 1984. The move has just been completed, and one of the members of the moving crew is placing a timber under the wheels of the left-hand dolly to keep it in place until cribbing can be erected to support the station. Then the dollies can be removed and the foundation built. (Courtesy of Photoworks.)

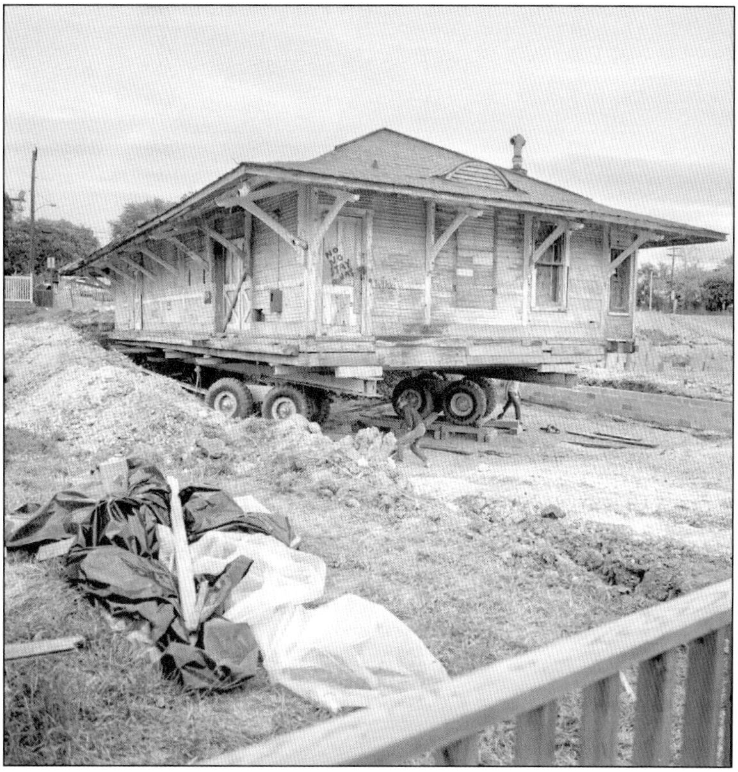

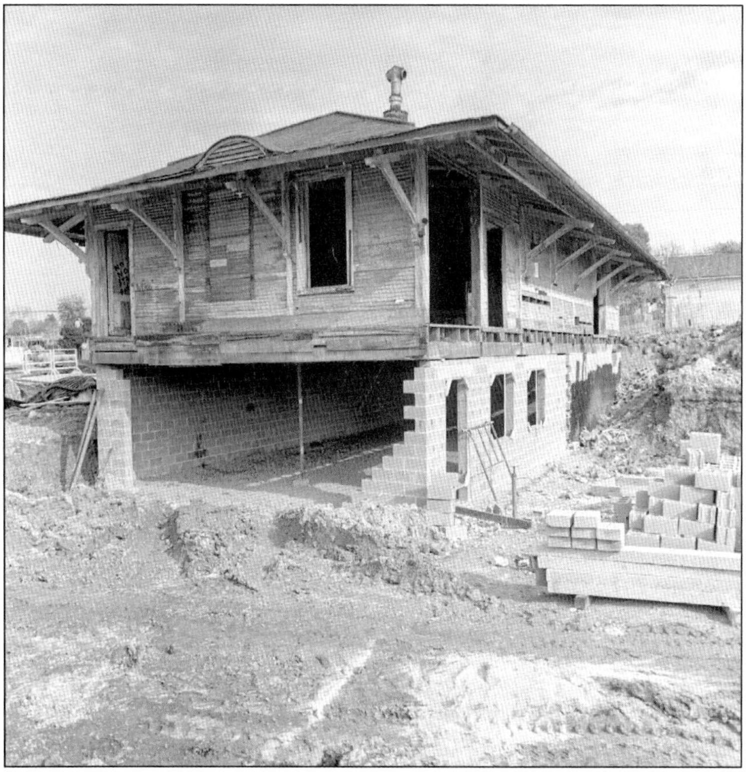

Beckham Dickerson planned to put the office bay (hole in the wall) on the northeast corner, not the southwest corner as seen in this photograph by Neil Steinberg taken on October 16, 1984. A custom milling cutter was needed to make new siding to cover the opening. Today, the freight station is occupied by Fire Works pizza. (Courtesy of Photoworks.)

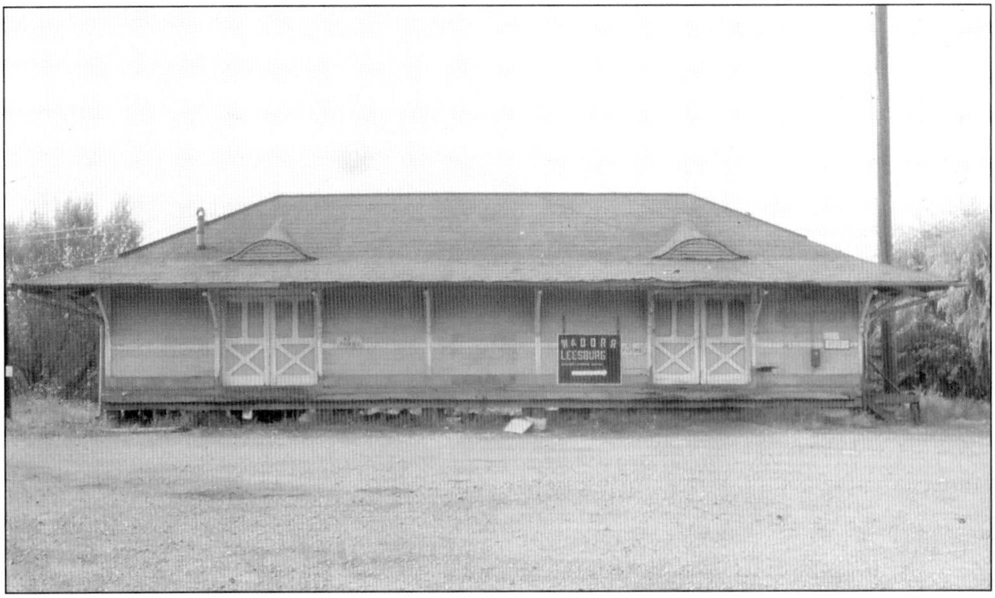

This view of the north side of the freight station in October 1968 shows the two eyebrow dormers and a sign labeled "W&OD RR Leesburg Freight & Express Agency." The station was painted in standard Southern Railway colors of green, yellow, and white. After the railroad ceased operations, the freight station was used to store storm windows and doors for a county energy efficiency program.

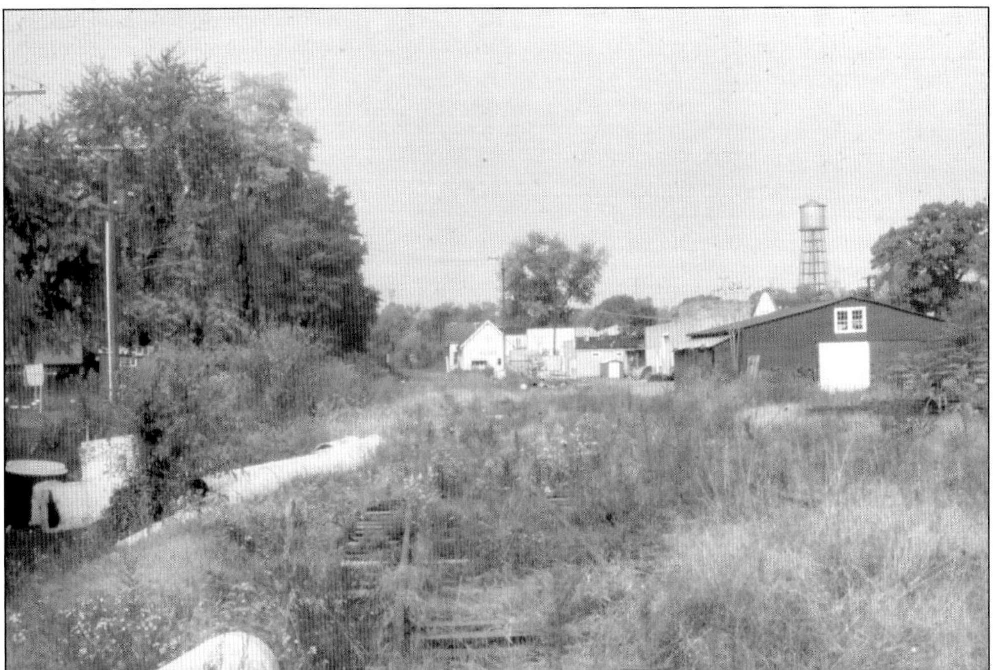

The railroad has been abandoned, as evidenced by the weeds growing over the rails in this October 1968 photograph. The Norris brothers, who built most of post–Civil War Leesburg, sold their business to J.T. Hirst in the 1920s. Hirst's lumber company buildings are on the right, where they sat on the east side of King Street. The passenger station is visible in the distance.

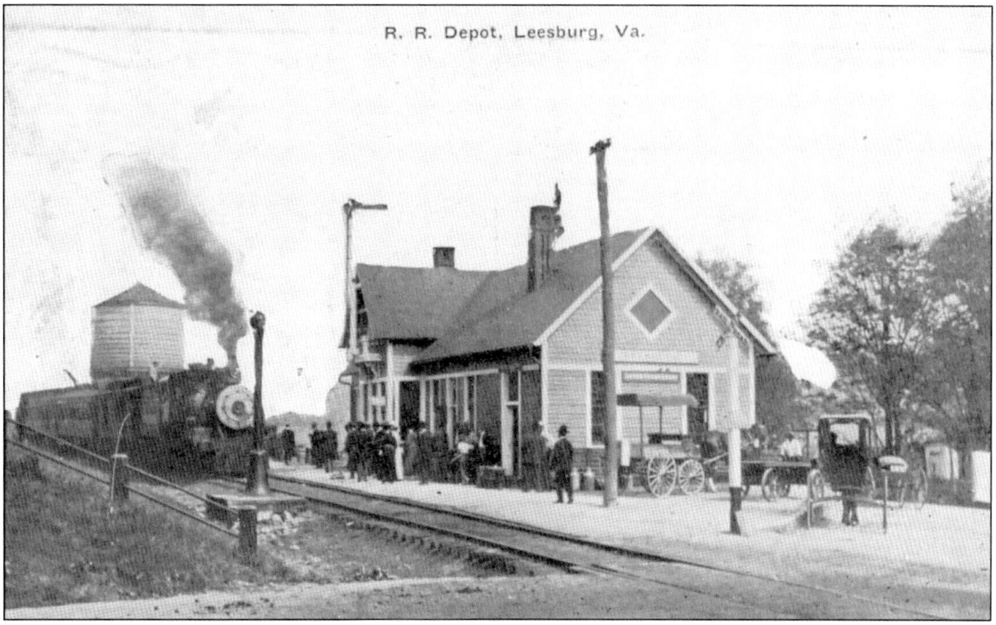

This pre-1918 postcard shows a steam train arriving at the passenger station from Bluemont. The post in front of the locomotive was a water spout to fill the locomotive's tender. The semaphore train order signal indicates that the next westbound train is to stop for orders. (Courtesy of C. Dennis Howard.)

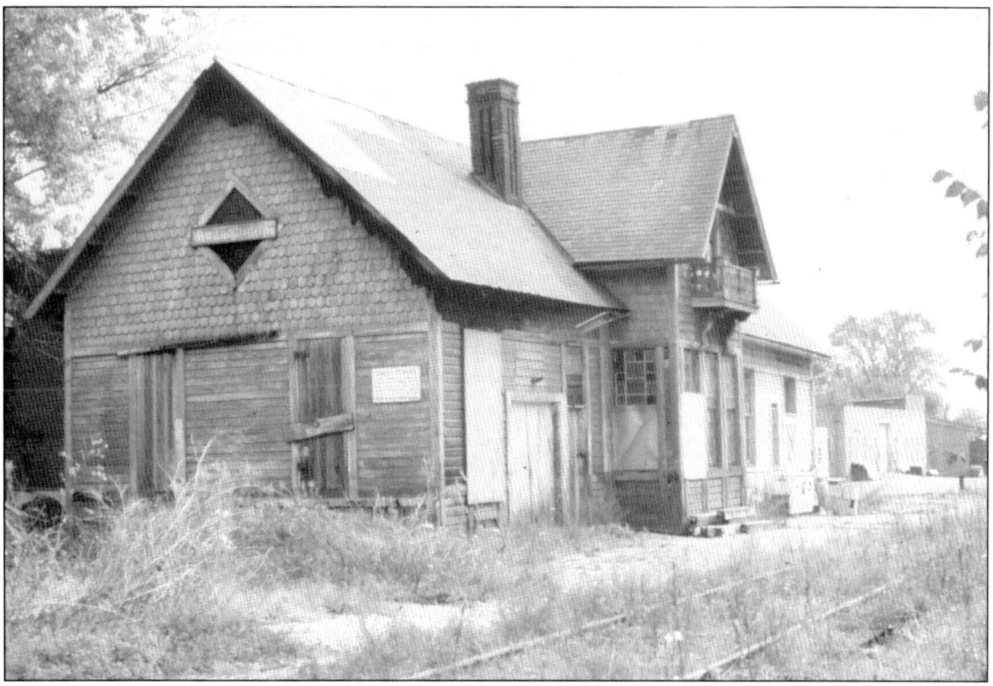

The Leesburg passenger station, like many other structures on the railroad, ended its days in a blaze. The station, as seen here in October 1968, had suffered the first of three fires. The last occurred in 1969. Fire was a constant threat to wooden railroad structures, and many of the stations burned before they could live out their useful lives.

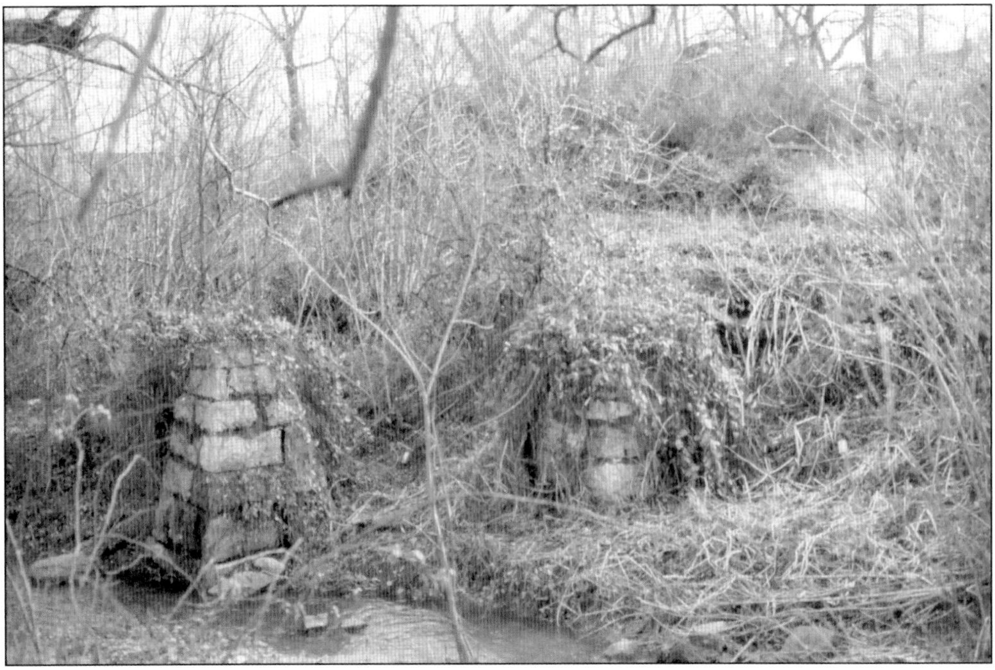

According to Interstate Commerce Commission Valuation Report notes and the Southern Railway Standards of the Department of Maintenance of Way and Structures, the piers shown in this December 1968 photograph supported a 48,000-gallon water tank. Water was pumped from the creek below (a tributary of Town Branch). Perhaps one of the station ticket agents was assigned water pump duty.

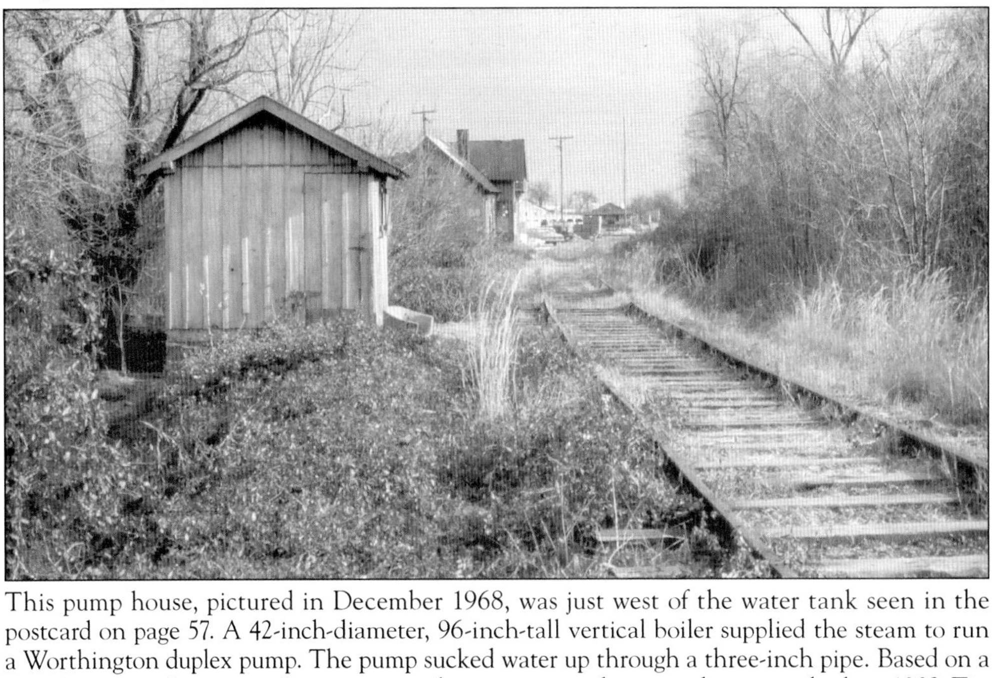

This pump house, pictured in December 1968, was just west of the water tank seen in the postcard on page 57. A 42-inch-diameter, 96-inch-tall vertical boiler supplied the steam to run a Worthington duplex pump. The pump sucked water up through a three-inch pipe. Based on a 1918 Interstate Commerce Commission valuation report, this pump house was built in 1903. Tin shingles undoubtedly contributed to its long survival.

Four

PURCELLVILLE

The arrival of the first train into Purcellville on April 1, 1874, was serenaded by bands from Leesburg, Hamilton, and Philomont. Purcellville then became the commercial center of western Loudoun County. Now farmers had a place where they could bring their cattle and grain to sell and a convenient place to pick up farm supplies, fertilizer, feed, kerosene, and other household items. Mills turned some of their wheat into flour and corn into cornmeal for household use. Businesses along the tracks included a cooper shop; a lime and cement storage building; a guano warehouse; a milling, feed, and meal company; a lumber and milling company; a fuel depot; a farm implements warehouse; a cattle yard; and an apple packinghouse.

The railroad provided a cheap means to transport grain to markets in Washington, DC, Alexandria, and Baltimore. The railroad made it possible for farmers to raise cows and produce milk, since the railroad could transport the milk to Washington dairies quickly enough to prevent spoilage. The railroad gave rise to the dairy industry of Loudoun County. According to Doug Lee, cattle always seemed to show up on weekends after coming in from the west. Because the cattle had to be fed and watered every so many hours, train crews would have to be called to take the cars to their destinations. A lot of cattle were shipped to Baltimore in the fall. In later years (1950s–1960s), there was a cinder block manufacturing plant on the north side of the tracks at the east end of town. This plant received one car of cinders every couple of weeks. On the west side of town, a concrete company set up where the cattle yard had been. The concrete company received hoppers of cement.

Bruce Brownell remodeled several buildings in Purcellville as well as those of Market Station. The Contee Adams Seed Company now houses the Trail's End Cycling Company. The Loudoun Valley Milling Company has become Magnolia's at the Mill restaurant. The Purcellville railroad station was rescued and restored by the Purcellville Preservation Association.

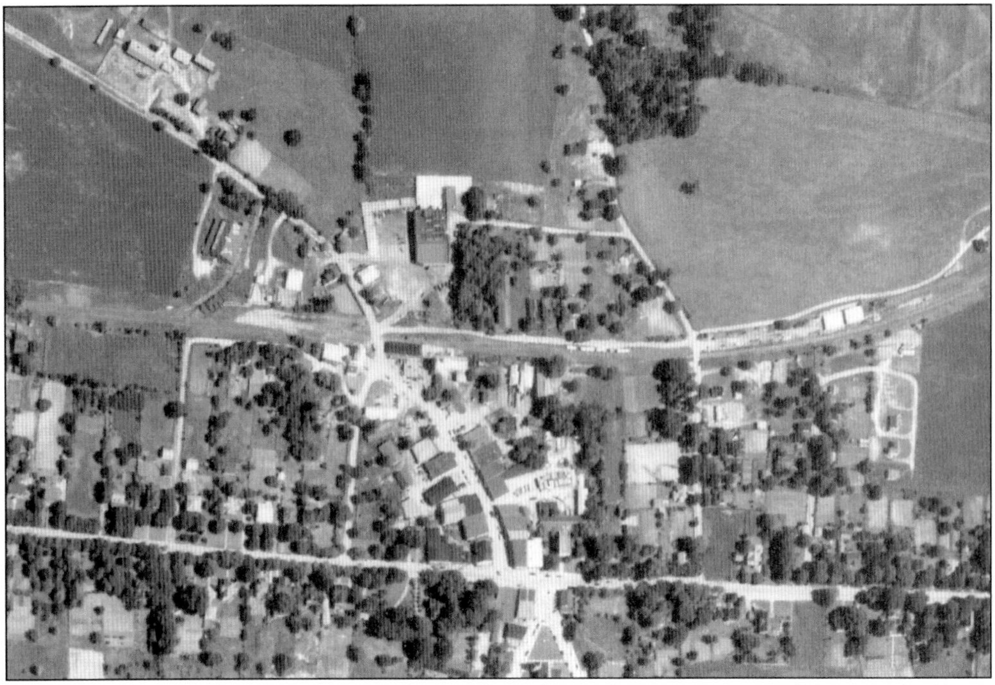

By August 17, 1956, when this photograph was taken, the tracks running west to Bluemont had been gone for 17 years. The end of the track is just long enough for crews to switch cars in and out of the apple packing plant at far left between Hillsboro Road and the railroad. Standard Oil Company had its depot just east of the packing plant. (Courtesy of US Department of Agriculture.)

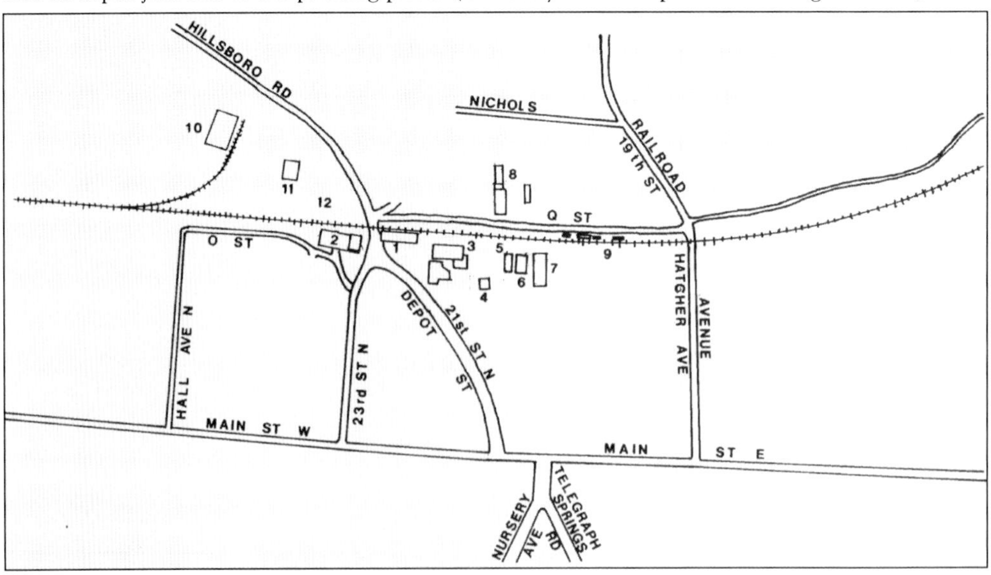

The roads and railroad on this map were traced from the aerial photo above. Numbered locations are: (1) Combination passenger-and-freight railroad station. (2) Brown & Welsh Mill, later Contee Adams Seed Company. (3) Loudoun Valley Milling Company. (4) Barrel factory. (5) Guano warehouse. (6) Lime and cement warehouse. (7) Cooper's shop. (8) Case Brothers Lumber and Planing Mill. (9) Texas Oil Company tank farm. (10) Apple packing plant. (11) Bulk oil depot. (12) Cattle pen.

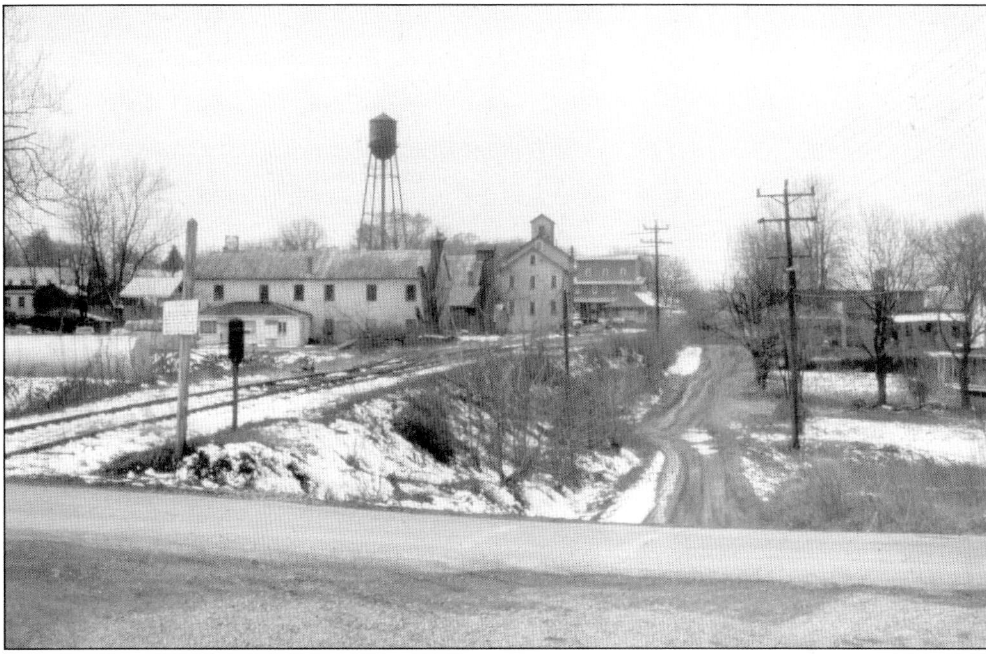

This view looks west from Railroad Avenue, now Nineteenth Street, toward the industrial center in April 1969. The rails would be taken up in just a few months. The large building under the water tower is the old cooper shop, where barrels for packing apples and flour were assembled. The grain elevator head of the Loudoun Valley Milling Company is prominent on the horizon.

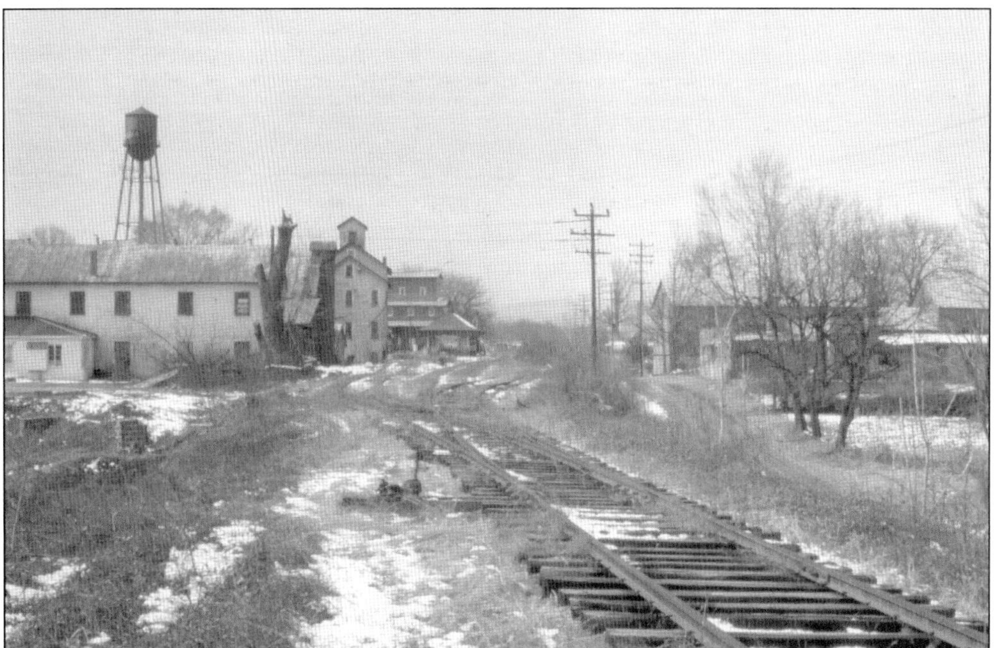

Moving to the left 20 yards, the photographer is looking down the roadbed toward the station. Contee Adams Seed Company is visible above and to the left of the station in this April 1969 photograph.

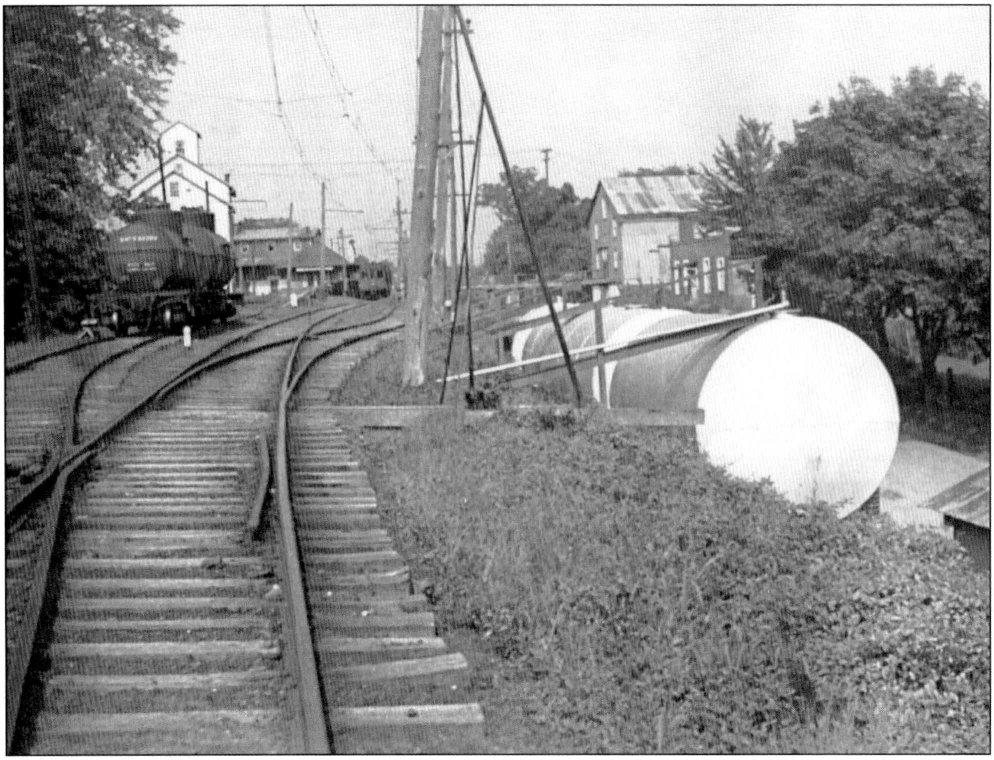

This photograph from the 1930s shows tank cars on the siding at left. Liquids likely included No. 2 fuel oil and kerosene. They were emptied into the silver oil tanks at right via an underground pipe. These tanks are visible in the aerial photograph on page 60. The Case Brothers Lumber and Planing Mill facilities can be seen above the tanks. (Courtesy of NOVA Parks.)

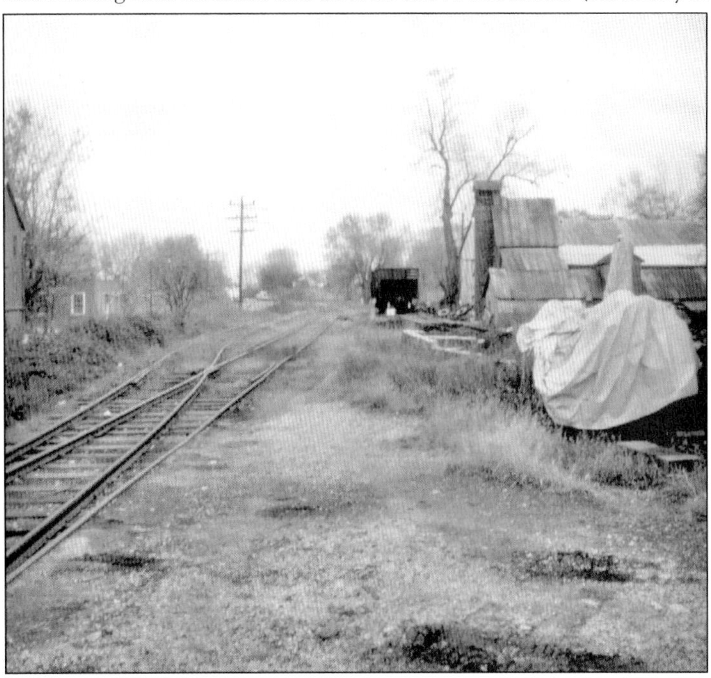

James E. Chapman photographed the east end of Purcellville looking west from just east of the Loudoun Valley Milling Company in February 1967. The edge of a Case Brothers building can be seen at far left.

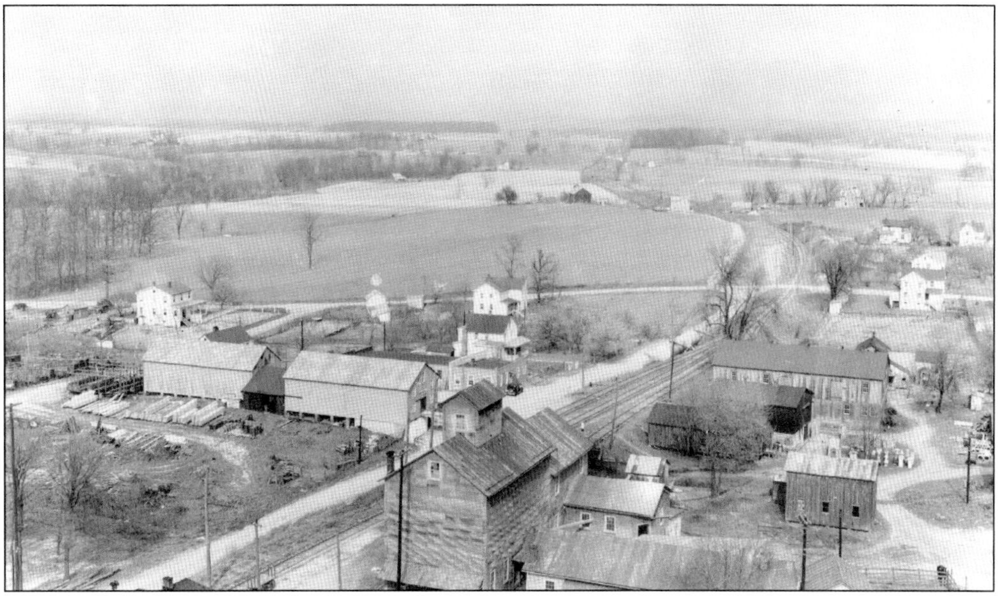

Looking east from the water tower in 1934, the Case Brothers Lumber and Planing Mill facilities are at center stage left. The near Case Brothers building at right housed building supplies. The building to its left was the lumber warehouse. The actual planing mill building is above the building supplies warehouse and Loudoun Valley Milling Company. (Photograph by Russell Gregg, courtesy of Edward Nichols, NOVA Parks collection.)

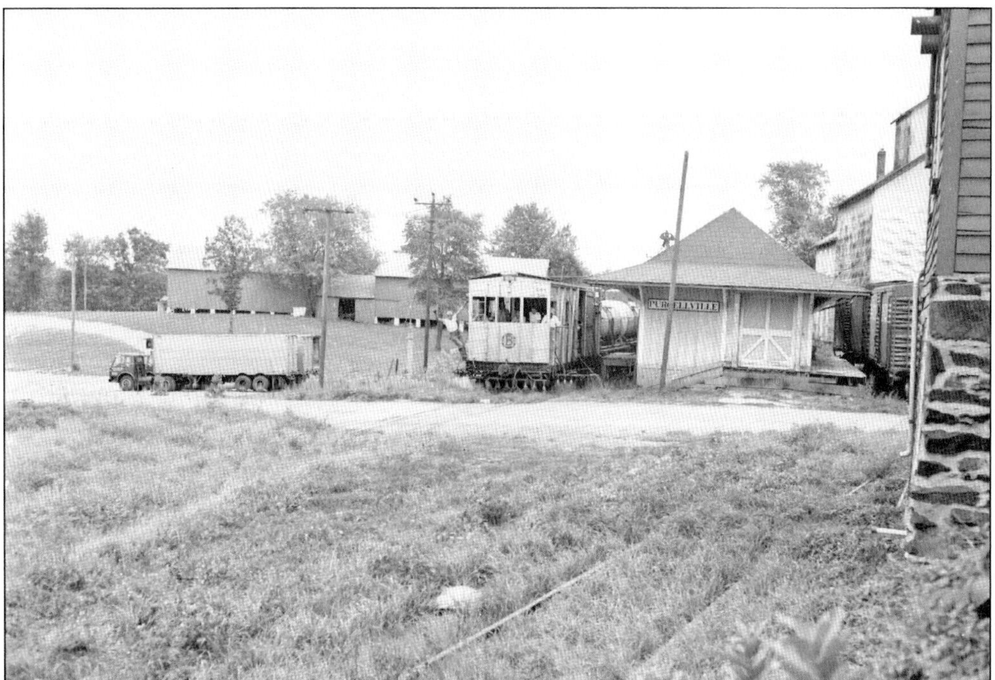

David Marcham photographed the weed train completing its annual run in August 1956. The buildings in the rear belong to the Case Brothers Lumber and Milling Company. Boxcars are on the team track beside the station. Hillsboro Road crosses the tracks. (Courtesy of NOVA Parks.)

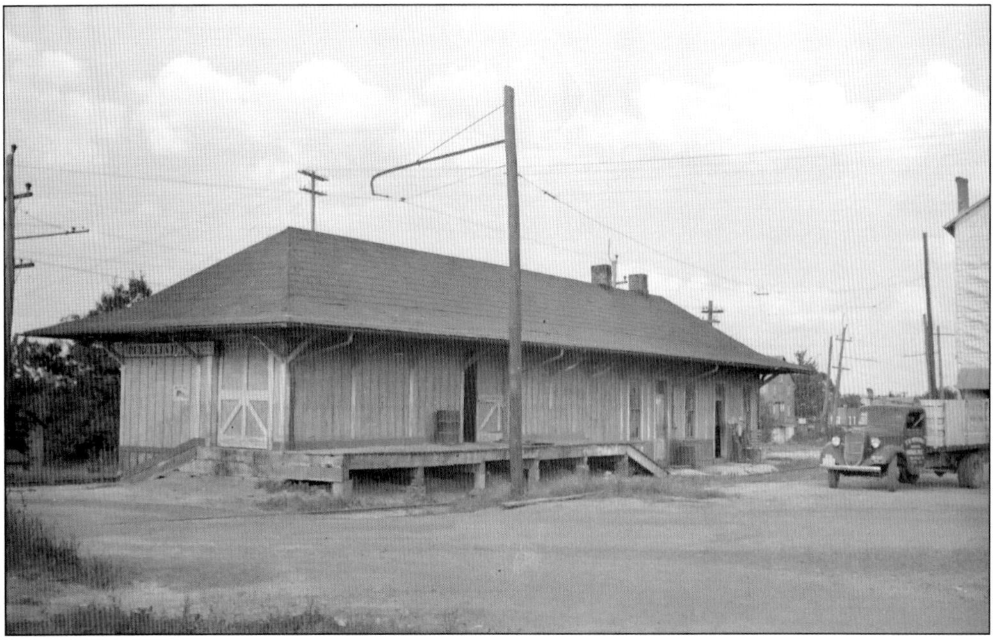

John F. Burns took an end-of-the-era trip to Purcellville on September 14, 1940. This view shows the south side of the station with the overhead wires still in place. Asa Janney recalled that Edward Nichols Jr. unloaded farm supplies for the hardware store from boxcars set out on the track on this side of the station.

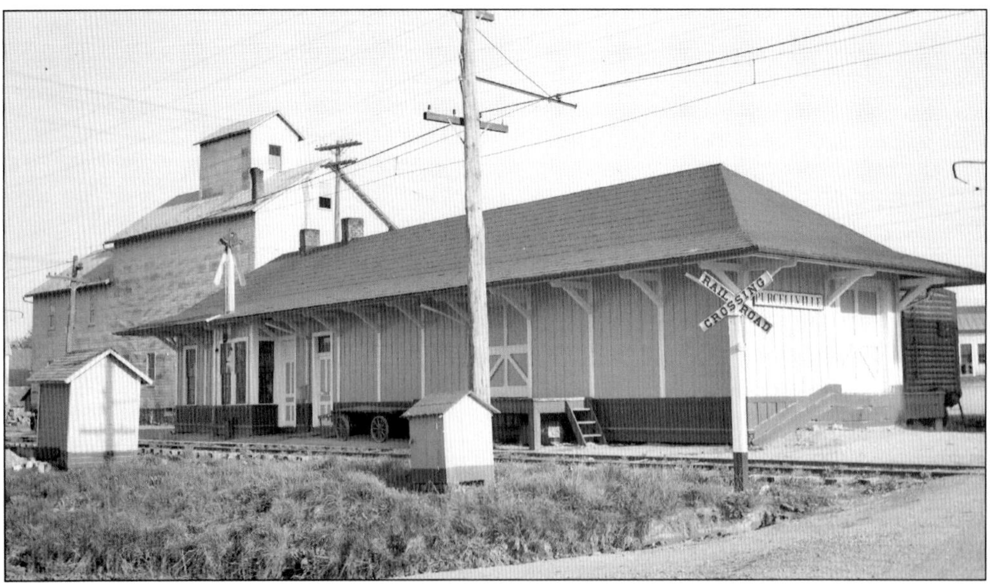

At left is an oil house in this 1930s photograph by Joseph Weyraugh. The J.R. Smith & Company mill, which became Loudoun Valley Milling Company in 1907 upon purchase by Samuel E. Rogers, produced three grades of flour known as Imperial Patent, Loudoun Family, and Ketoctin using the improved double roller process. (Courtesy of NOVA Parks.)

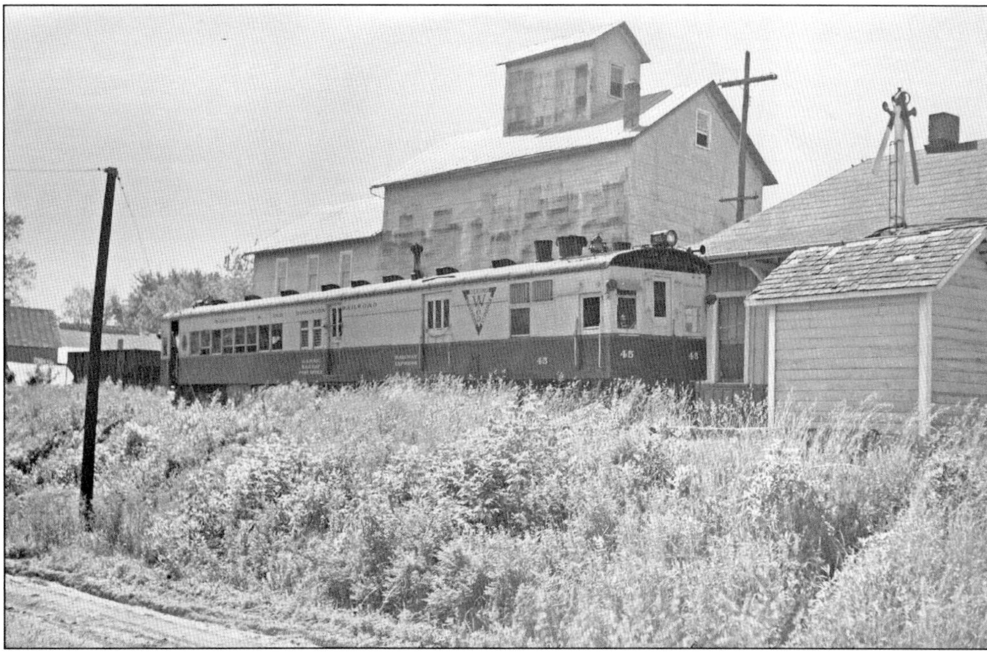

John F. Burns photographed diesel-electric car No. 45 on May 30, 1951. John R. Smith and John T. Hirst built a mill at this site in 1874. The mill burned in 1882, was rebuilt the following year, and burned again in 1904 after sparks from a steam locomotive switching cars set it on fire. The sides of the mill were then covered in tin sheeting to prevent further fires.

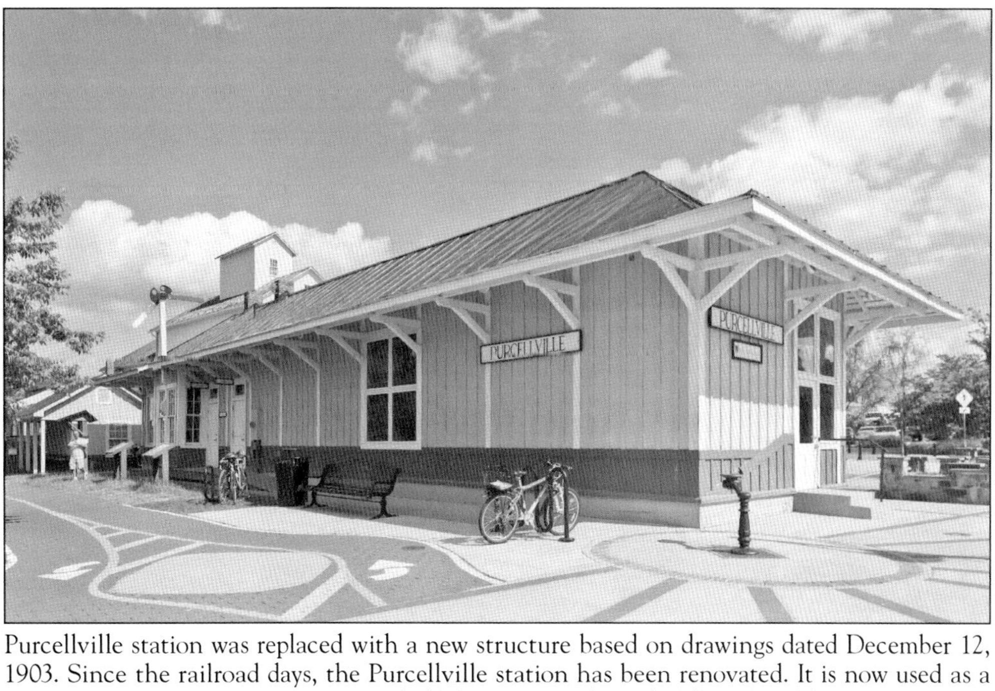

Purcellville station was replaced with a new structure based on drawings dated December 12, 1903. Since the railroad days, the Purcellville station has been renovated. It is now used as a community center. Wine tastings are held from spring through fall in the old east-end waiting room. Meetings are held in the west end's renovated freight room. The W&OD Regional Trail ends where the photographer stood on February 24, 2015.

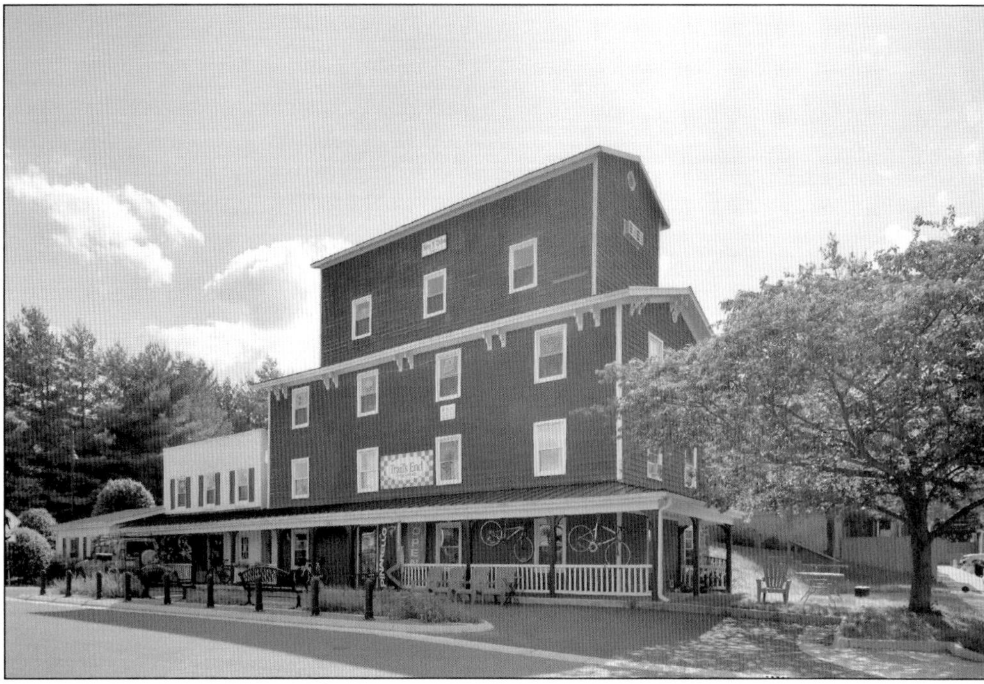

The former Contee Adams Seed Company was renovated by Bruce Brownell Inc. Today, it houses the Trail's End Cycling Company, as seen in this February 24, 2015, photograph. Known as "Mr. Orchard Grass," Contee Adams bought orchard grass seed from local farmers during World War II. He sold the seed to the government to use as packing for ammunition, artillery shells, small arms, and rifles.

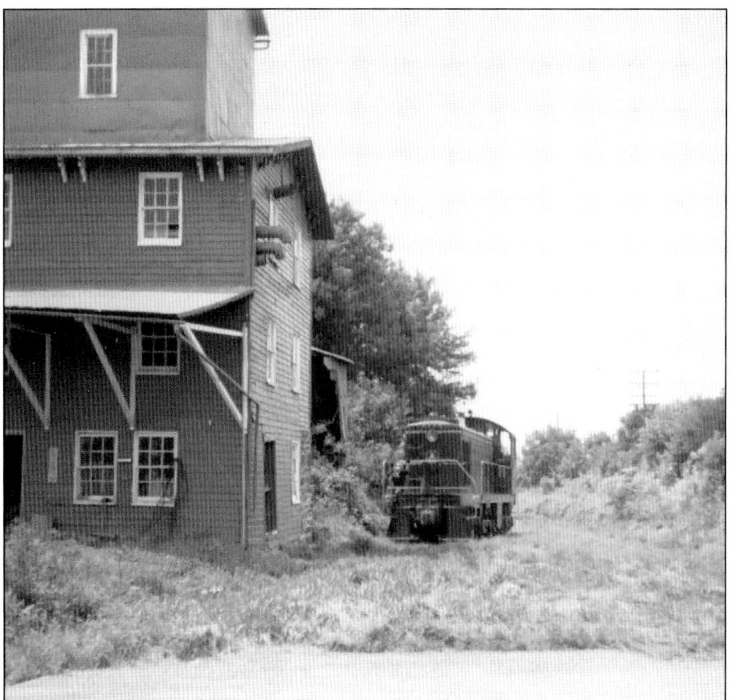

Thomas A. Coons captured the last days of railroad operations in August 1968. Here, a rented Chesapeake & Ohio ALCO type S-1 switching locomotive is working the siding in Purcellville in what may have been the last train in Purcellville. The annual weed spraying train had not been seen for years. (Courtesy of Thomas A. Coons.)

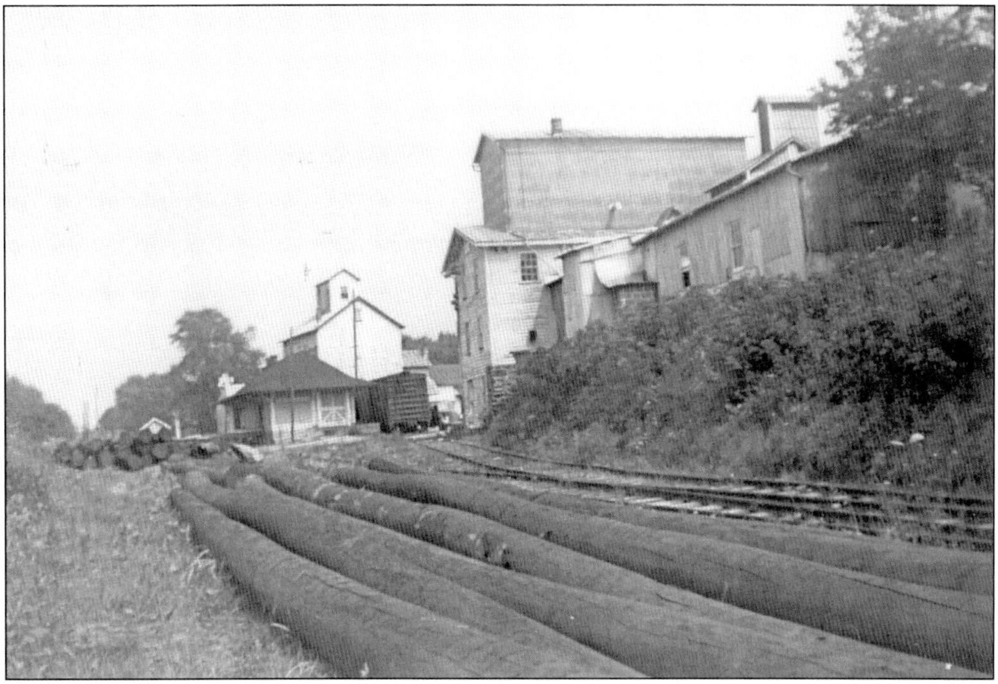

The Chesapeake & Potomac Telephone Company is the likely customer of these telephone poles on the ground. The farm implements warehouse is visible on the west (near) side of the Contee Adams Seed Company building. (Courtesy of NOVA Parks.)

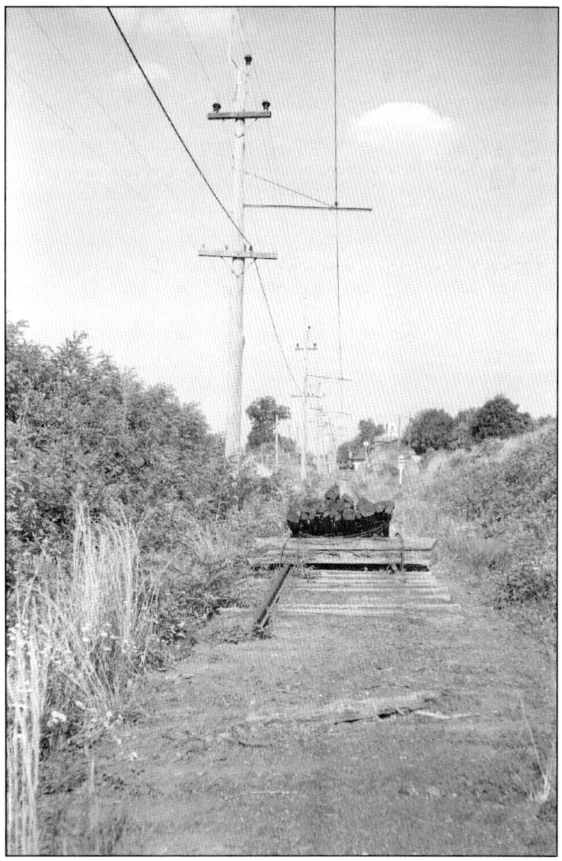

John F. Burns photographed the end of the line on September 14, 1940. The whistle sign at right tells the engineer to blow two long blasts followed by two short blasts to let the station agent and any passengers know that a train is approaching. Purcellville was the end of the railroad from February 14, 1939, when the railroad abandoned the tracks west to Bluemont, until the end.

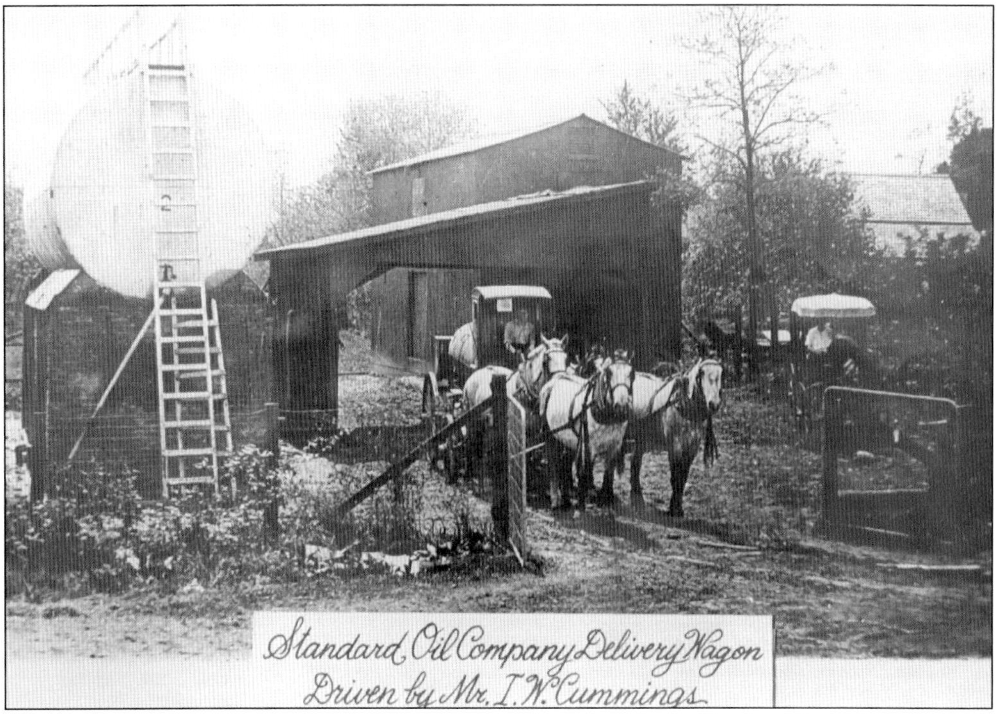

Before trucks became common in the 1940s, Loudouners received oil via horse-drawn tank wagons. Four horses were needed to handle the weight. The product might have been kerosene for lamps or heating oil. (Courtesy of NOVA Parks.)

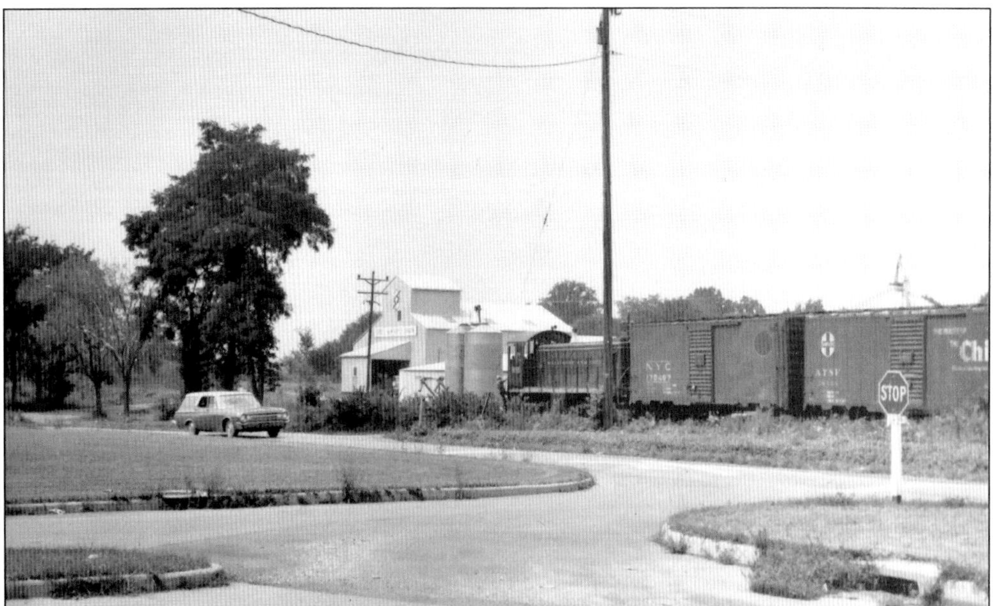

Thomas A. Coons photographed the train leaving Purcellville in August 1968 as it passed the Southern States facility east of town. The sign reads "Seed & Farm Supply Division." Loudoun Valley High School is to the back of the photographer. (Courtesy of Thomas A. Coons.)

Five

MILLS

Early American mills had to be located along streams for water power. With the development of the steam engine, mills could be located in more central locations or, in the case of the W&OD, along the railroad with its efficient transportation.

This chapter focuses on feed and grain mills that served Loudoun County's agricultural interests. Flour mills were located in Leesburg, Purcellville, and Round Hill. Feed mills, which mixed various grains and other materials to create food for beef and dairy cattle, horses, and other livestock, were located in Herndon, Sterling, Ashburn, Leesburg, Paeonian Springs, Hamilton, Purcellville, and Bluemont. Each mill had a means of receiving and storing grain from farmers or from boxcar shipments, an area for processing the grain (milling corn or wheat or just cleaning and/or drying the grain), and silos and warehouse areas to store the cleaned, finished grains or bagged meal or flour. Feed mills had additional areas for mixing and storing bagged feed.

The mill business is one of quantity, price, and competition. In order for a miller to make money, he had to process a large quantity of grain on slim margins. He was in competition with fellow millers to buy grain from farmers at the highest price, but then he needed to sell the grain at an even higher price to the markets in Baltimore and Washington in order to make any money. One part of this equation was the ability to hold a large quantity of grain until market prices went up. The Rogers family increased its buying and selling power by purchasing several mills along the rail line west of Leesburg. William S. Jenkins also owned several milling operations. C.C. Saffer left the milling business when the volume of grain decreased with the loss of farms to suburbanization.

Mills are known for the dust they generate. This dust can be flammable and even explosive under the right conditions of density and moisture. With or without the aid of combustible grain and flour dust, a number of mills along the railroad burned over the years, including three in Bluemont, one in Paeonian Springs, and one in Leesburg.

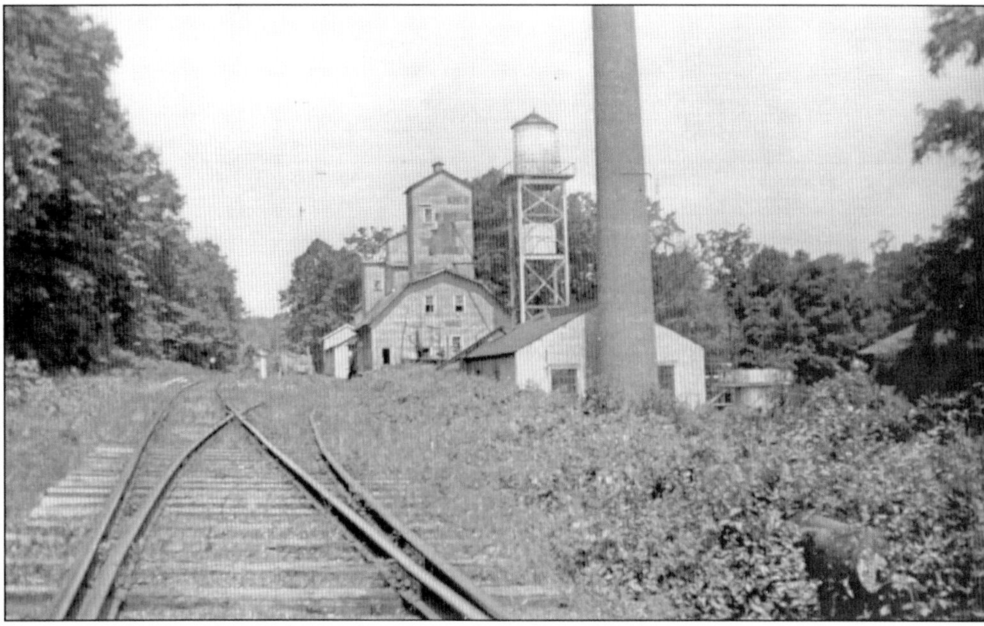

Looking west toward Herndon and present-day Reston, the A. Smith Bowman Distillery boiler house is the near structure with the smokestack. Coal from hopper cars was carried on the conveyor leaning on the roof to the left of the water tower. Smith Bowman and his sons applied for a distillery permit in March 1934. The first bottled bourbon was sold in 1938. (Courtesy of NOVA Parks.)

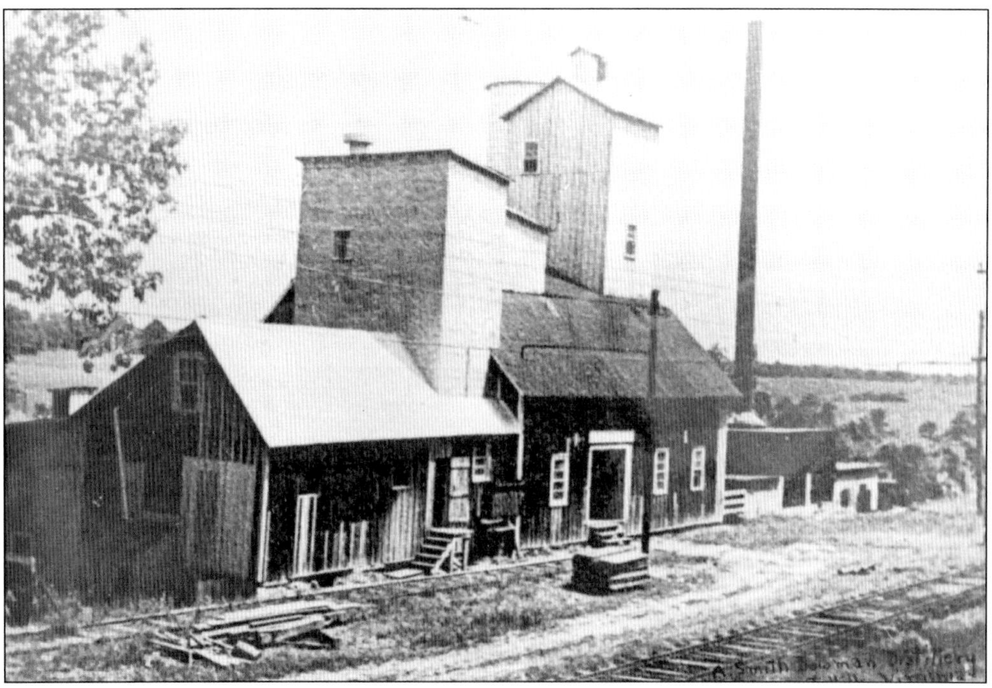

The building at center is the still house, where bourbon was created. It included cookers and fermenters. To its left is the bottling house. A. Smith Bowman Distillery is known for its Virginia straight bourbon whiskey. (Courtesy of Fairfax County Public Library Photographic Archive.)

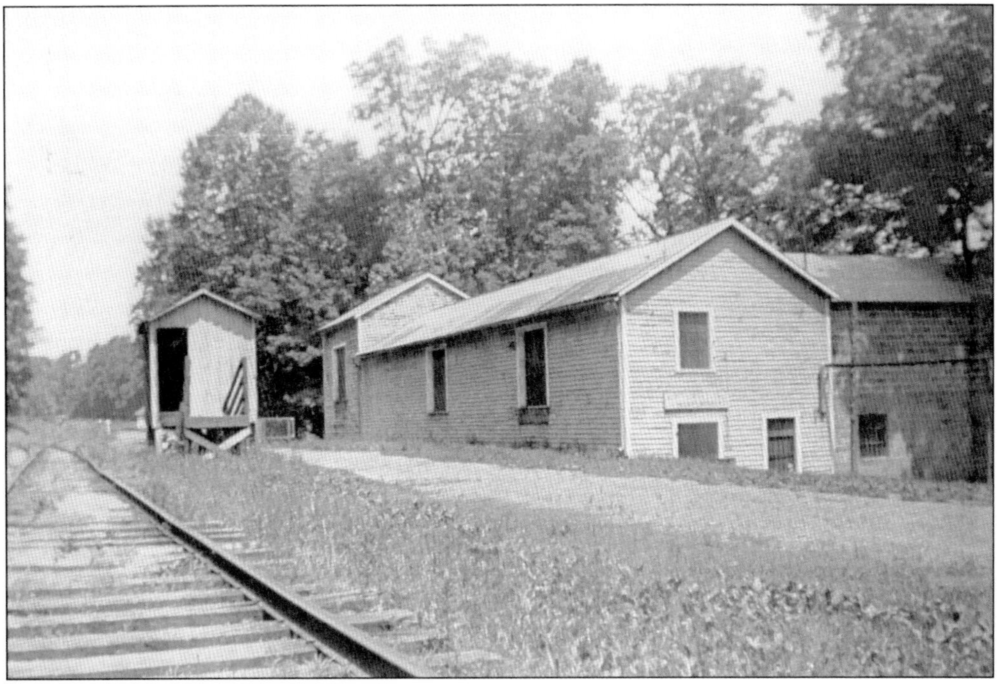

At center is the distillery's warehouse, where the bourbon was kept while it aged. The railroad hauled coal, barrels, corn, and bottles to the distillery. (Courtesy of NOVA Parks.)

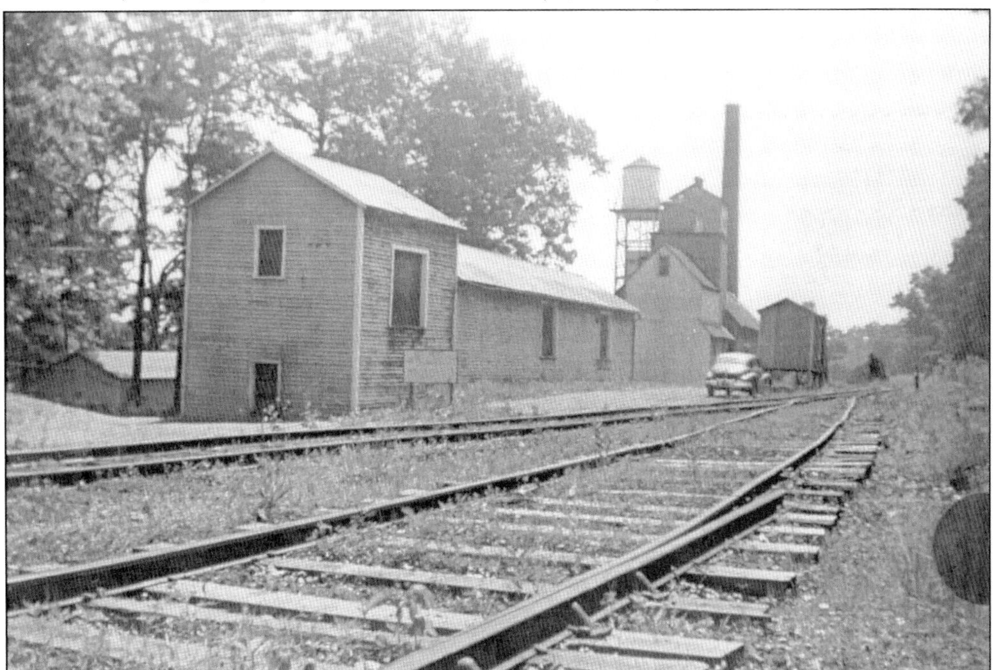

This view shows the west end of the warehouse. The distillery office was out of sight to the left. At lower right, the single rail with a pointed rail beside it is a derail. The switch stand would move the pointed rail away from the straight rail so that a runaway car would roll onto the ground instead of onto the main line. (Courtesy of NOVA Parks.)

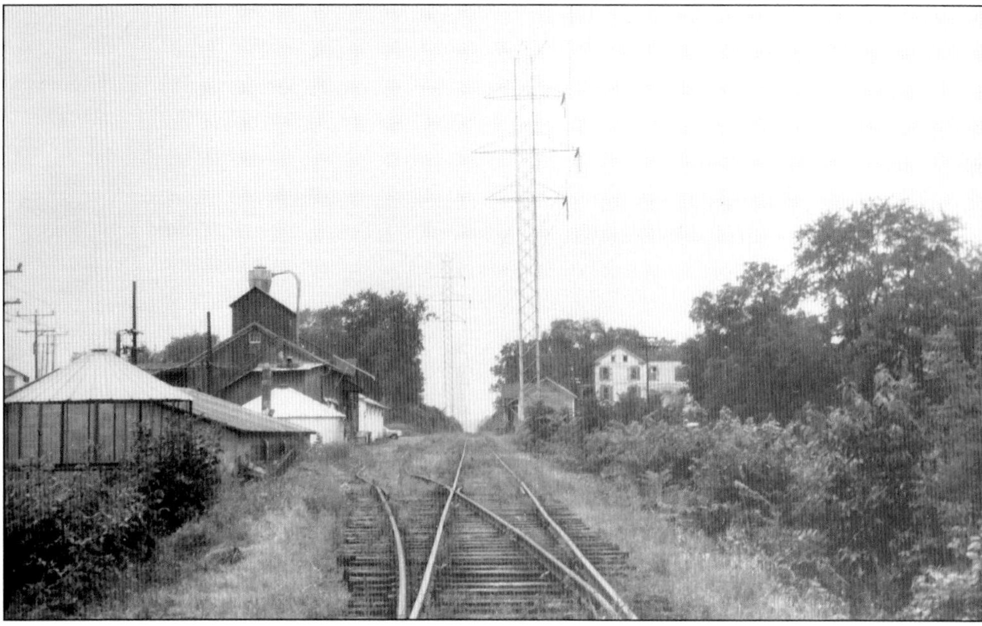

Thomas A. Coons photographed the Ashburn Milling Company in August 1967. M.L. Kendrick constructed the first mill building in the 1870s. His son passed the operation to Webb Hutchinson. W.S. Jenkins Co. purchased the mill in the late 1910s and sold it to Ernest T. Harding in 1930. William E. Fletcher renamed the mill Ashburn Milling Company after he bought it in 1944. (Courtesy of Thomas A. Coons.)

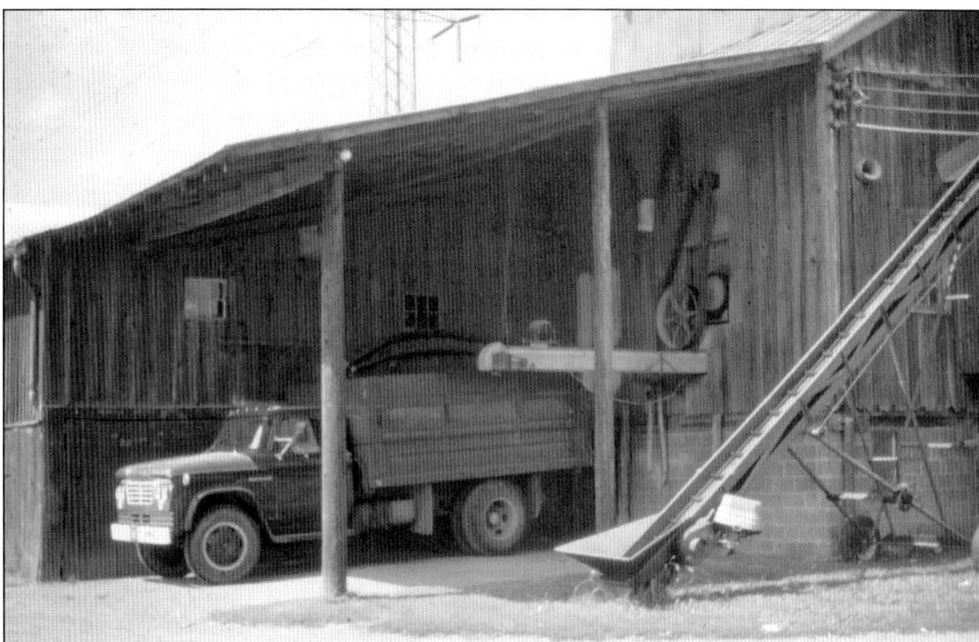

This truck appears to be receiving a load of grain from the spout sticking out of the building in August 1968. The railroad carried loaded boxcars of wheat outbound during the winter and brought in an occasional load of feed. The mill operation was closed on December 30, 1973, because it could not pay high enough wages. The company continued to sell feed for another decade.

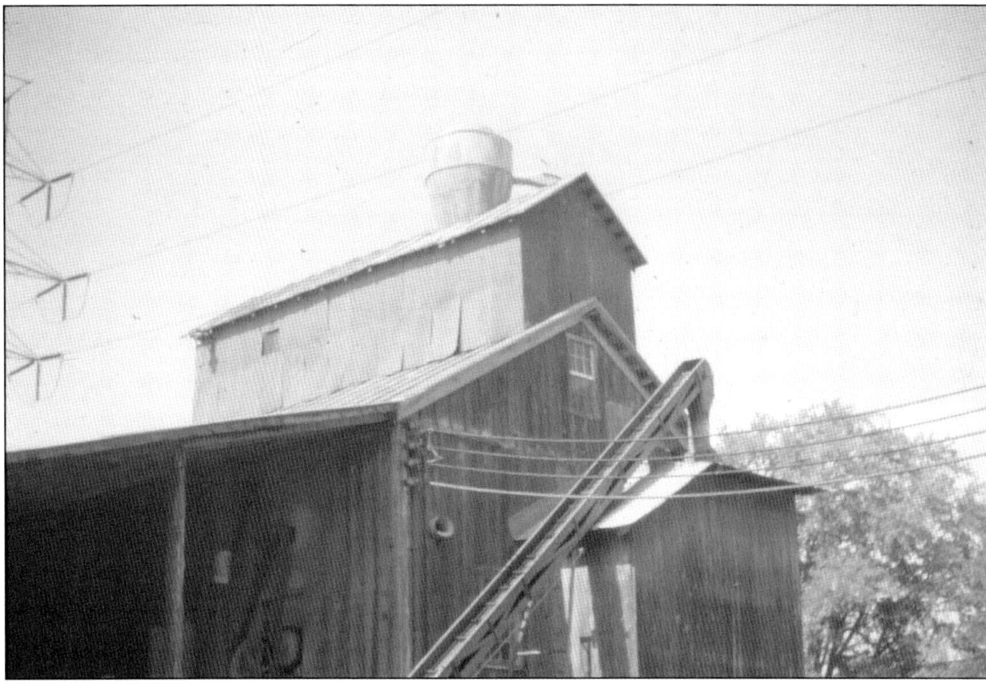

The conveyor dumped its grain into the shed at the east end of the mill. Once weighed, the grain was moved to the elevators, where it ran into storage bins in the building behind the shed. The mill's product was known as Red Rose Flour. Newspaper accounts of the mill's history do not mention any fires, so perhaps the elevator building dates to the 1870s.

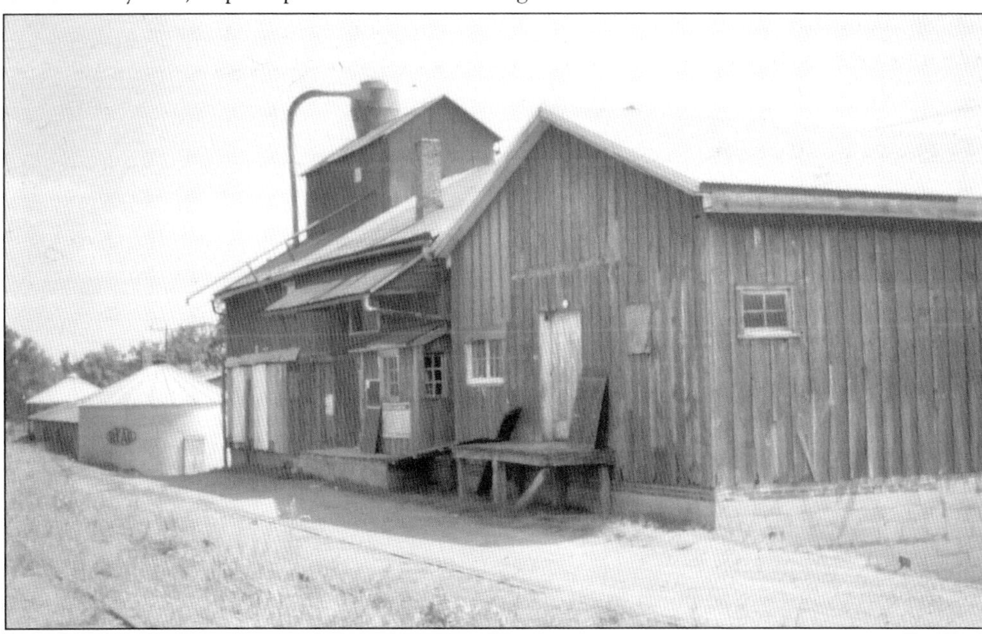

William S. Jenkins bought the steam-powered mill with capitalist Wallace George and later enlarged it. The author suggests that the section of the complex on the west end, seen here in August 1968, is that enlargement, which probably served as a warehouse. The Ashburn Milling Company complex is now the Olde Mill Furniture & Design showroom.

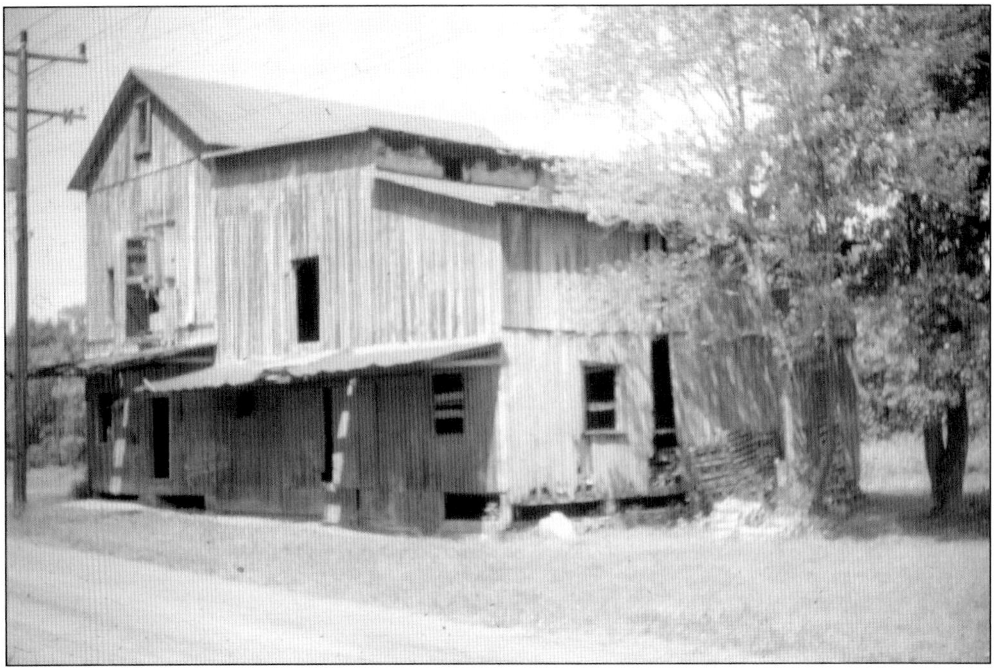

The Sterling mill was still standing in August 1968 alongside Ruritan Circle. The railroad siding swung away from the main line to run along the north side of the mill. The grist and flour mill was first powered by a steam engine under Ernest T. Harding's ownership. Under Edward Chick, it was powered by gasoline, followed in 1929 by electricity.

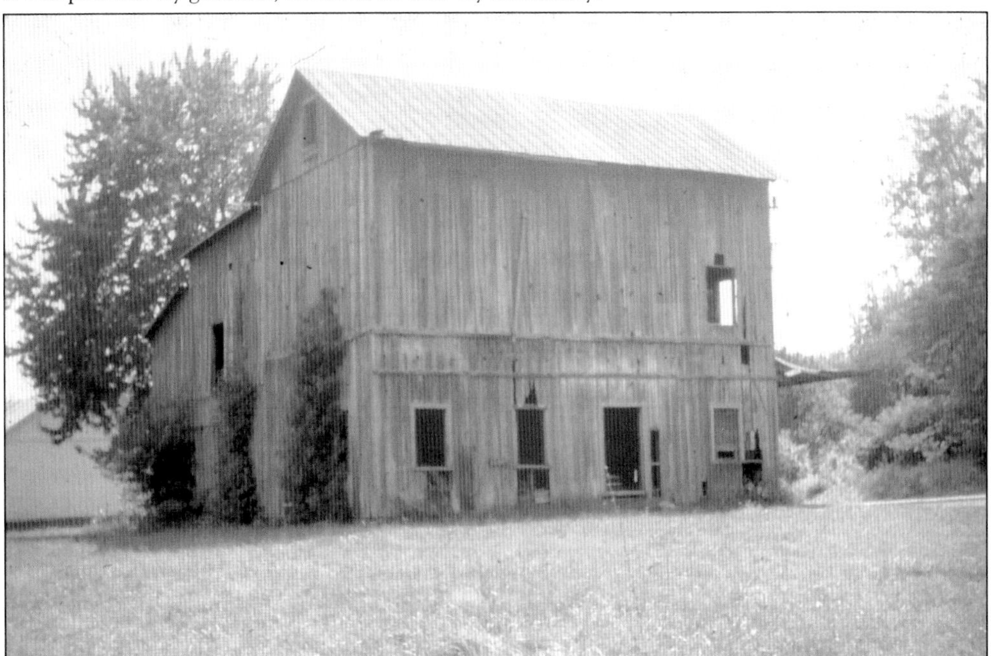

Richard "Dick" Tavenner performed the miller duties for many years. The mill was operated until 1934 and finally burned down in 1970. The north and west sides of the mill show years of wear in August 1968.

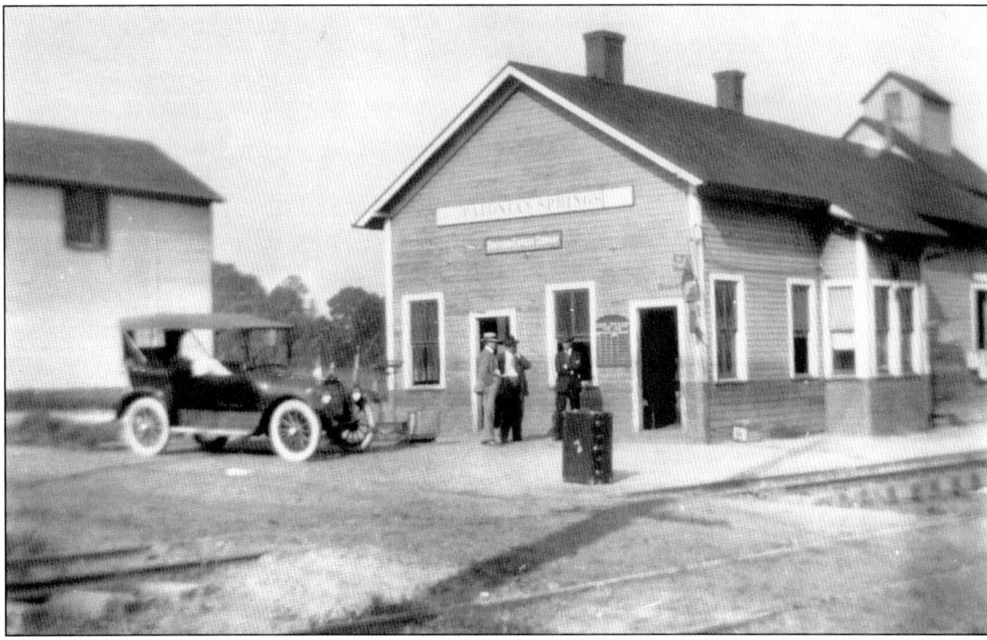

The elevator head house is just visible above the Paeonian Springs station at right in this 1920s photograph. This mill, built by John R. Smith and John T. Hirst in the 1890s, was almost a twin of the Loudoun Valley Milling Company plant in Purcellville. The Purcellville mill mechanic was frequently called here to fix the mill's gasoline engine. The mill burned about 1925. (Courtesy of NOVA Parks.)

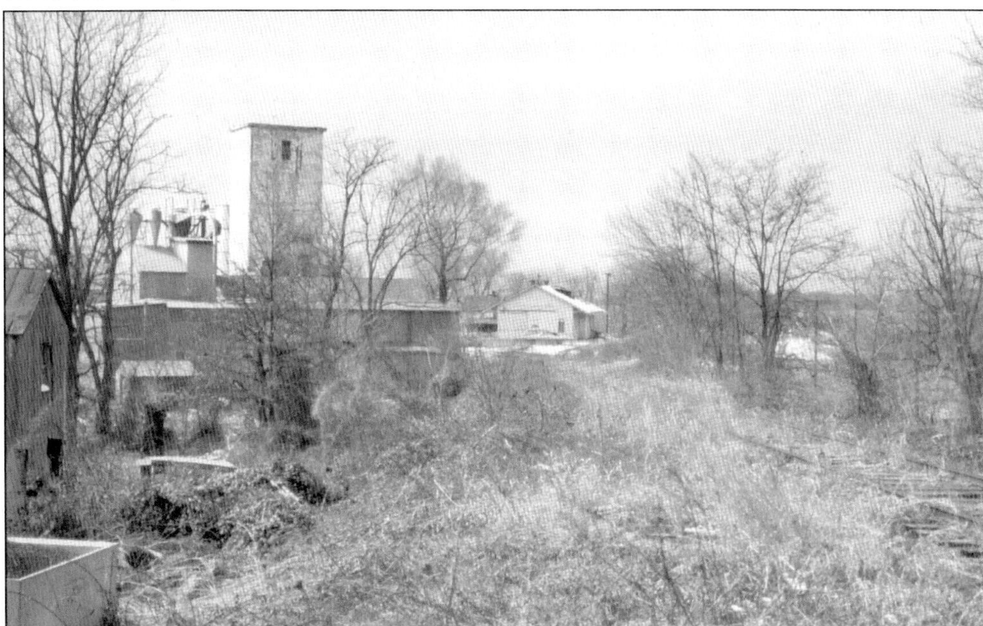

In this west-facing April 1969 photograph, the Loudoun County Milling Company is at left center. Hamilton station is at center rear. The small building below the cyclone separators housed the boiler for the feed pellet steam press. The Loudoun Valley County Company is the sole surviving mill along the W&OD.

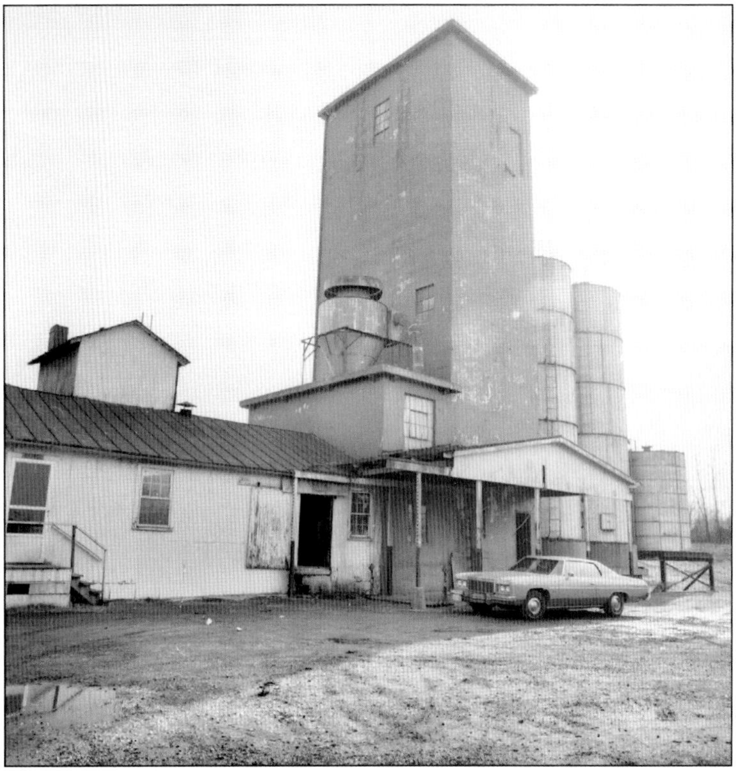

This mill's original structure is at left, where the office is today. Whole-grain corn is received through a small trap door in the concrete pavement under the awning. At one time, a cable would be hooked to the front of a truck, and a winch would lift the front of the truck, tilting it so that the grain would flow out the back.

Corn, barley, and oats are stored in the elevator and silos at left. The warehouse above the box truck was added to the original structure, followed by the 60-foot-high corn elevator about 1922. Later, the feed mixing room was built under the cyclone dust collectors. This is where grains are mixed with other ingredients to make Loudoun Supreme Feed. Grown-Big Hog Feed was another specialty feed.

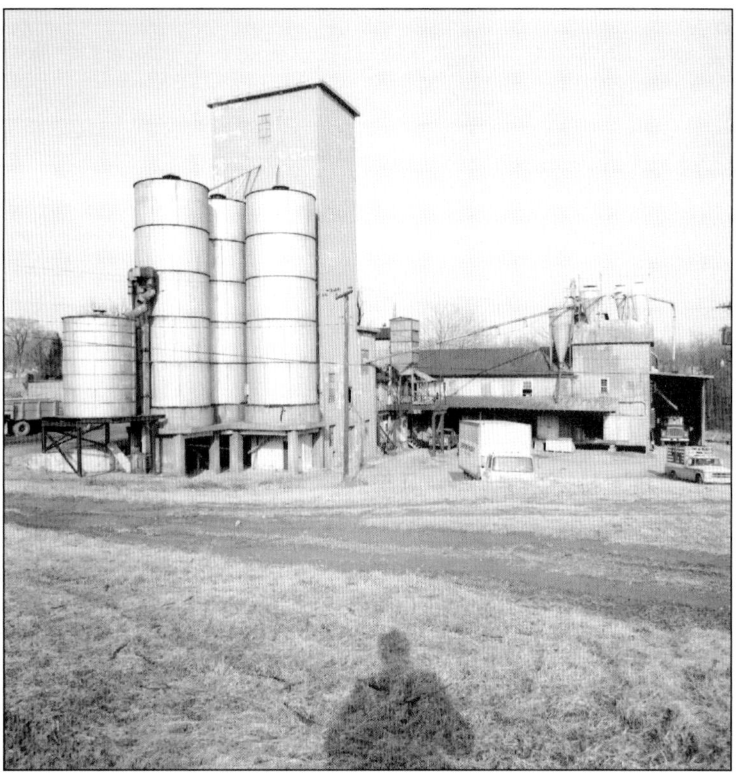

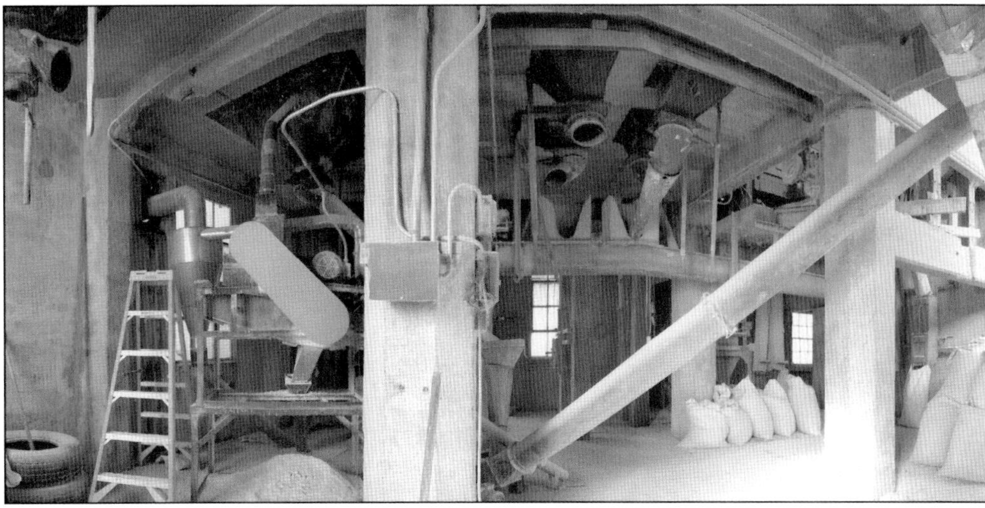

This view is a composite of three photographs taken on November 12, 2014, accounting for the distorted structural posts. This room is under the concrete towers at the west end of the mill complex. The small machine at left by the step ladder cracks corn.

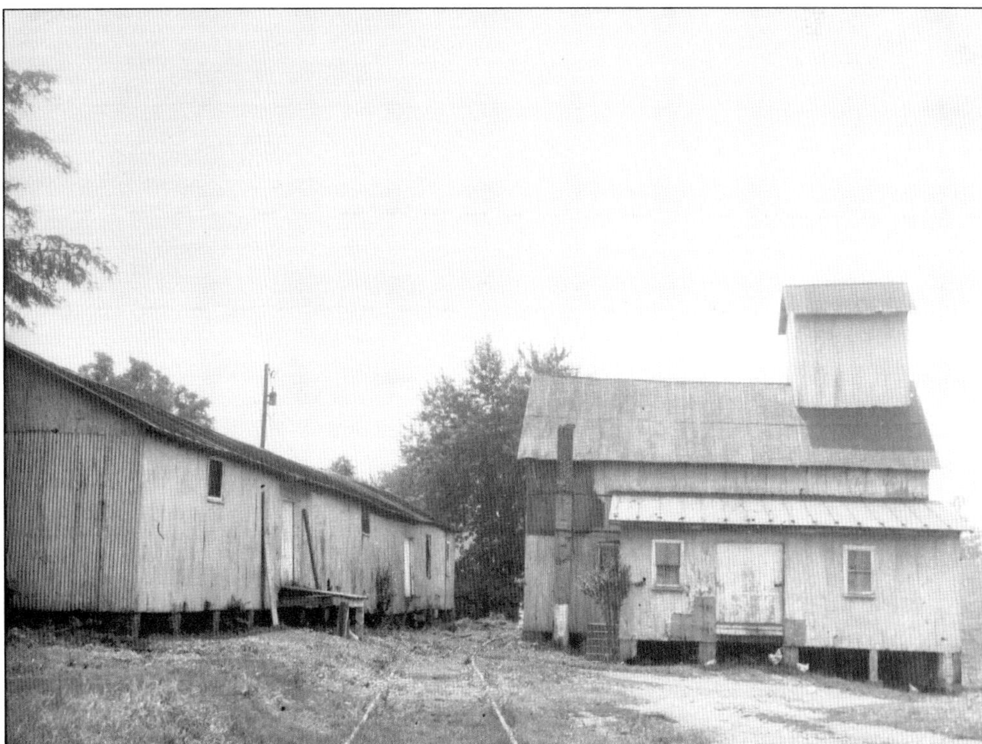

This view shows the old mill across the street from the Loudoun County Milling Company's Hamilton plant in August 1968. It was originally built by W.S. Jenkins in 1888 as a feed mill. The building with the cupola was the warehouse of Herbert Bryant's son in June 1919. Now owned by Loudoun County Milling, it is referred to as the old mixing room. (Courtesy of Thomas A. Coons.)

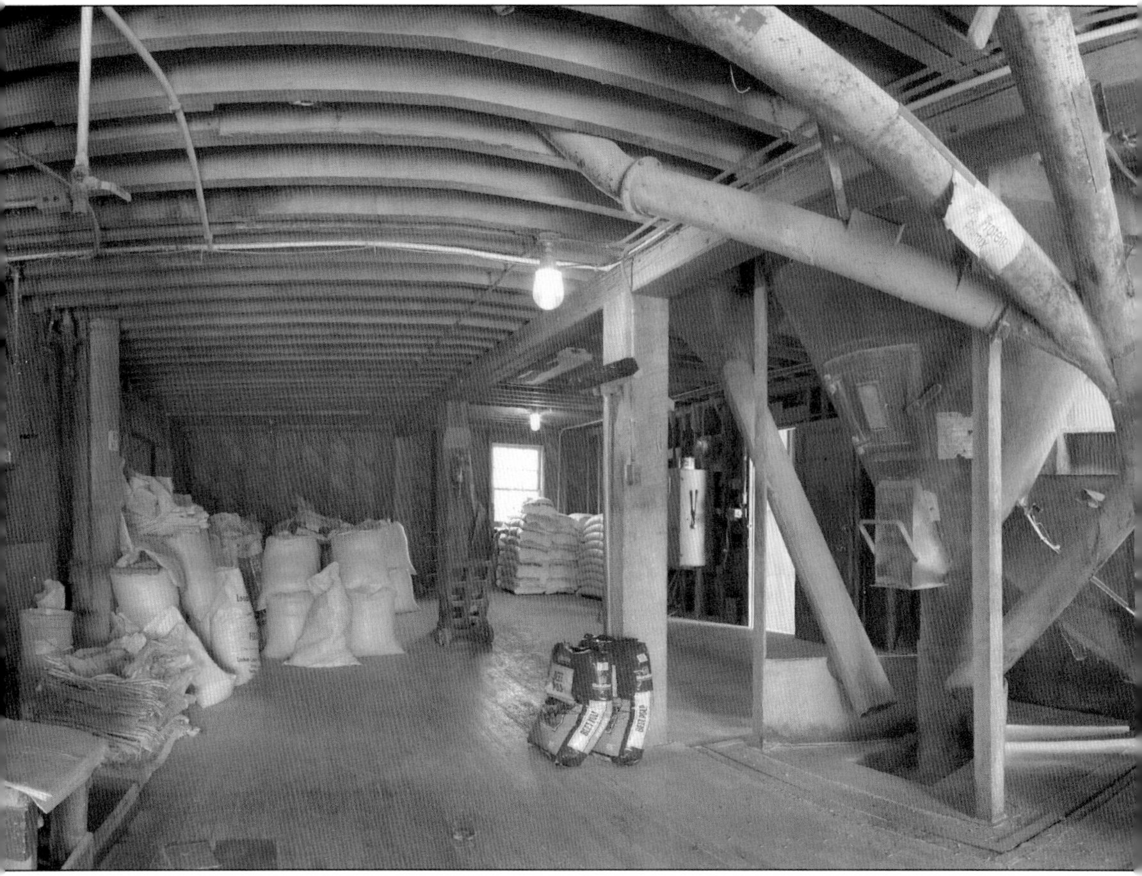

Above, this room (photographed on November 12, 2014) features two vertical feed mixers made by the still-in-business Kelly Duplex Mill and Manufacturing Company of Springfield, Ohio. The mixing process is a bit like the game Chutes and Ladders. Round pipes drop corn, barley, and/or oats, protein premix, and minerals into a receiving pit below the funnel-shaped hopper. An augur inside a tube inside the mixer picks up the grain and minerals and lifts them to the top of the mixing chamber, where they fall outside the augur. The contents of the

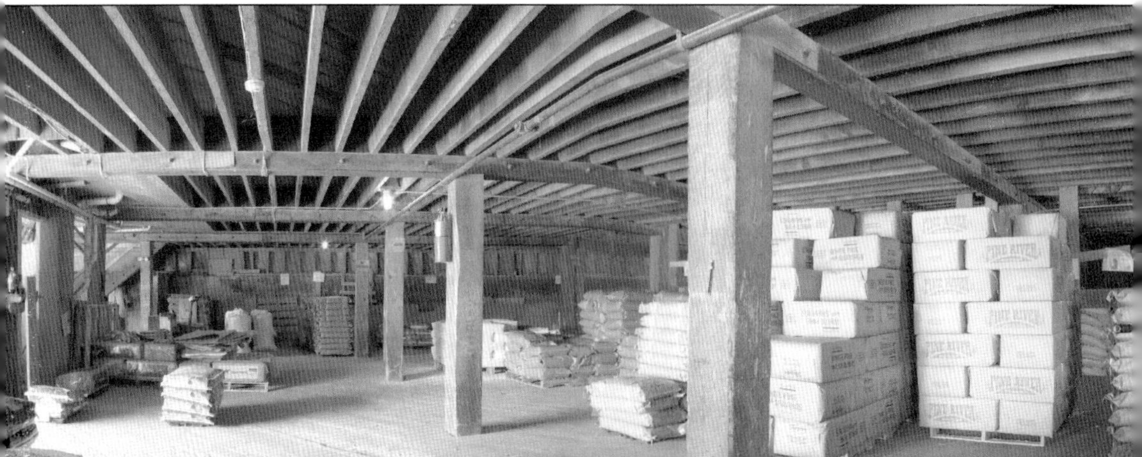

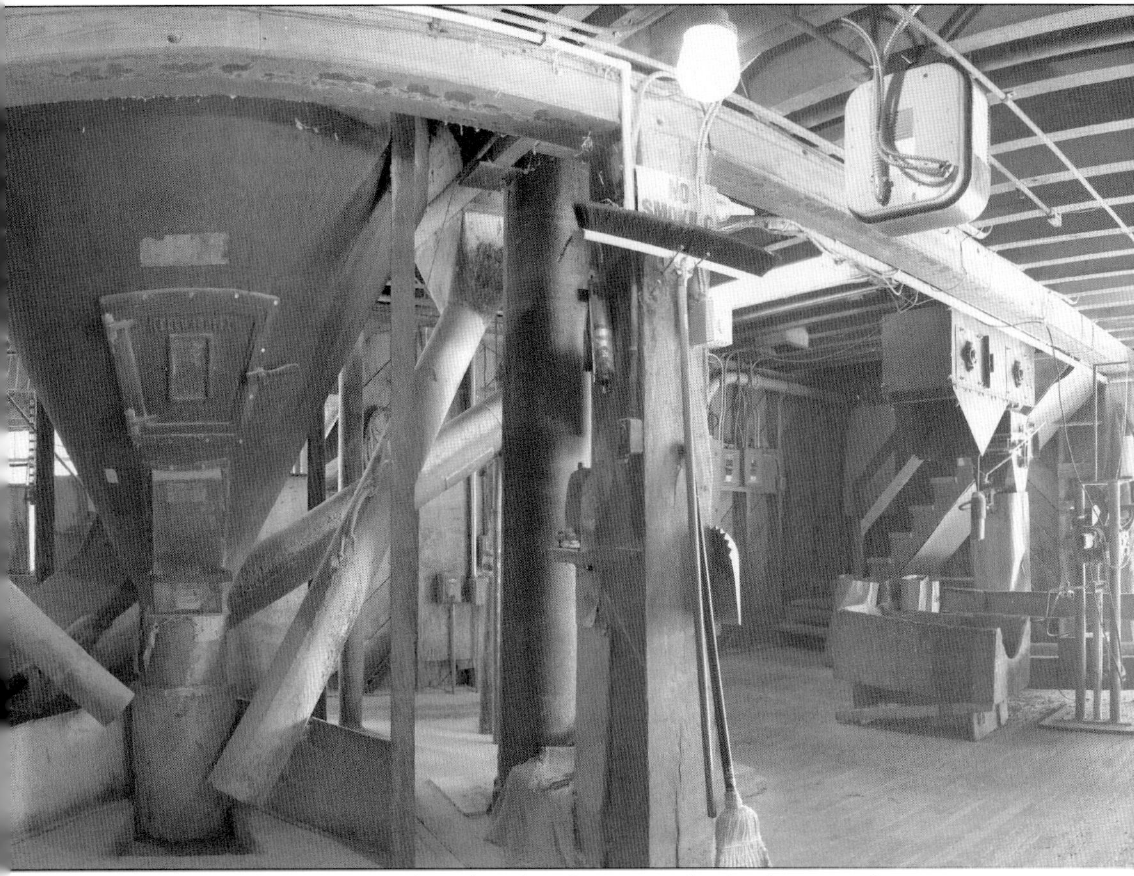

funnel are emptied into rectangular tubes that drop into a bucket between the two mixers at the rear, from which the mixed feed is augured up again and over to the bagging machine at right. Each vertical feed mixer is on a weighing scale. Below, manufactured bags of feed are kept on the first floor of the warehouse along with other products purchased wholesale for the mill's retail operations.

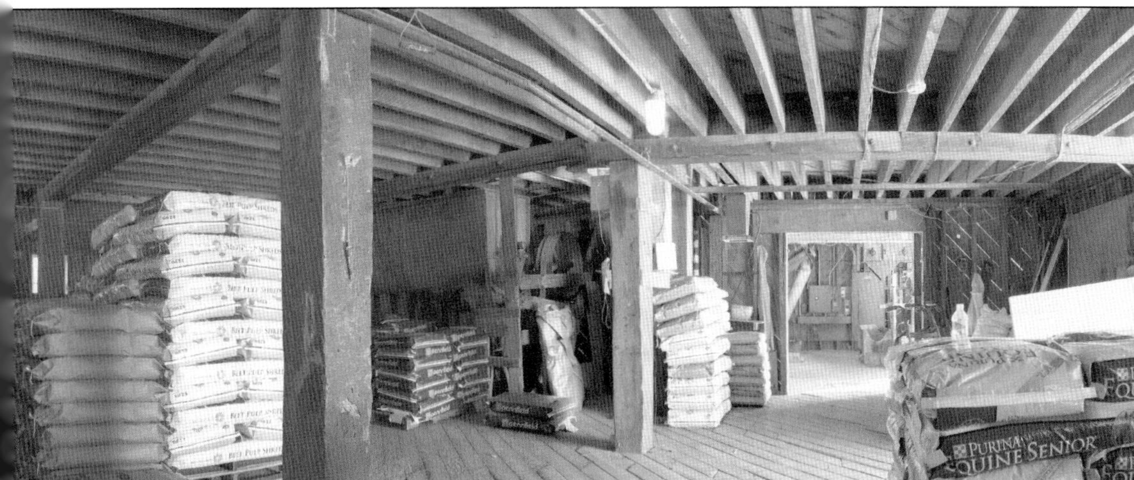

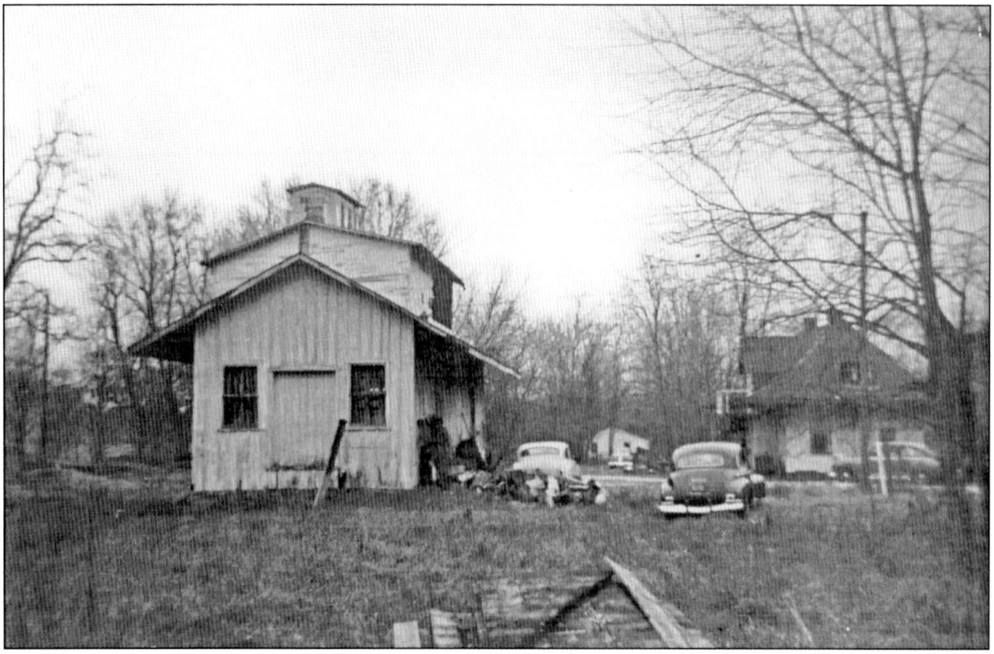

This November 1957 photograph shows the west end of the freight station and Round Hill Milling Company. The flour mill was one of Round Hill's largest firms. Its flour was sold under the Southern Pride label. Flour and wheat were shipped primarily to customers in southern Virginia. (Courtesy of NOVA Parks, Larry Crosen Collection.)

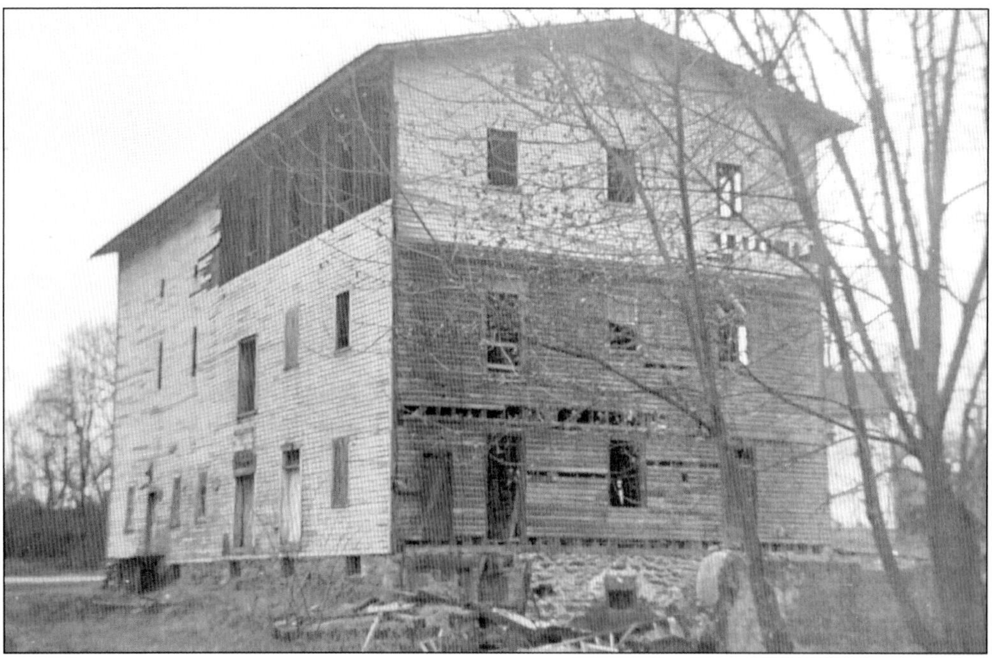

This November 1957 photograph shows the east end of the Round Hill mill. Originally built by John R. Smith and John T. Hirst in 1878, the coal-fired, steam-powered mill was sold to Samuel E. Rogers in 1907. Josephus "Joe" Carr Rogers managed the The mill was torn down in 1959. (Courtesy of NOVA Parks, Larry Crosen Collection.)

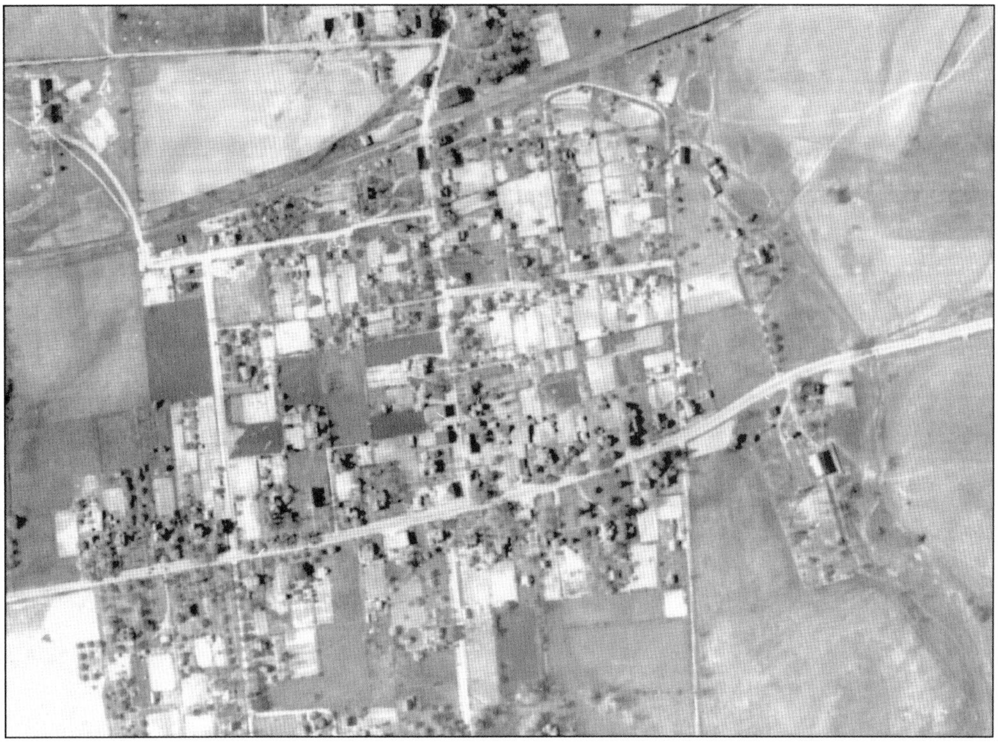

The railroad line to Bluemont runs across the top of this March 31, 1937, photograph of Round Hill. Main Street, running north to south, connects the station to Loudoun Street (Route 7). The Round Hill Mill and its shadow are above the tracks and to the right of Main Street; the passenger station is below. (Courtesy of National Archives.)

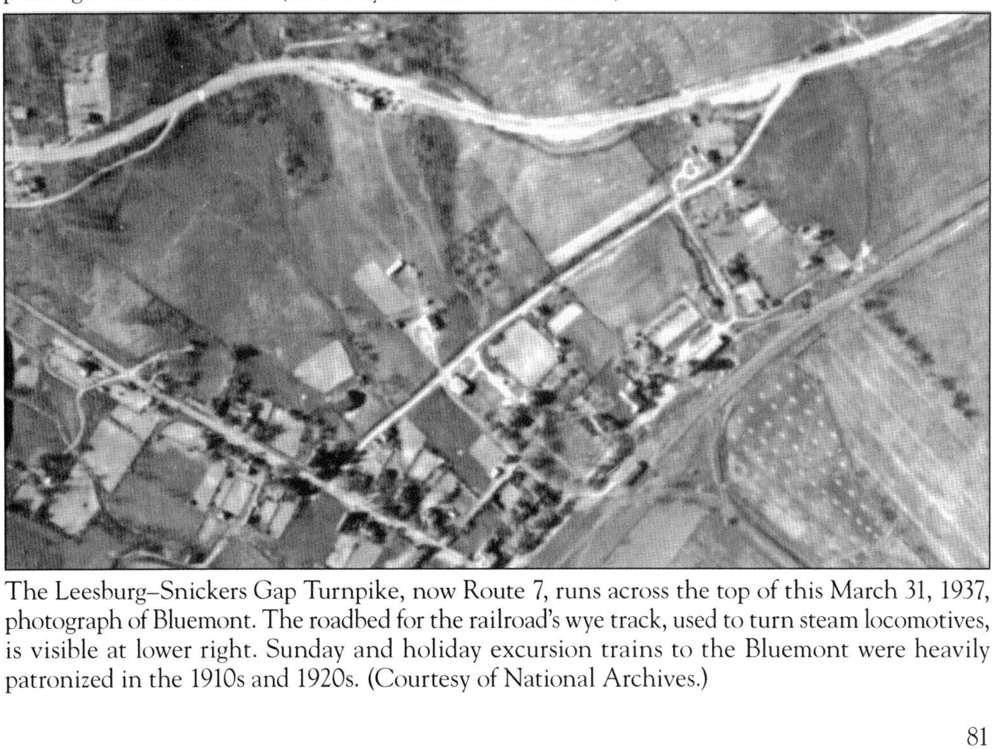

The Leesburg–Snickers Gap Turnpike, now Route 7, runs across the top of this March 31, 1937, photograph of Bluemont. The roadbed for the railroad's wye track, used to turn steam locomotives, is visible at lower right. Sunday and holiday excursion trains to the Bluemont were heavily patronized in the 1910s and 1920s. (Courtesy of National Archives.)

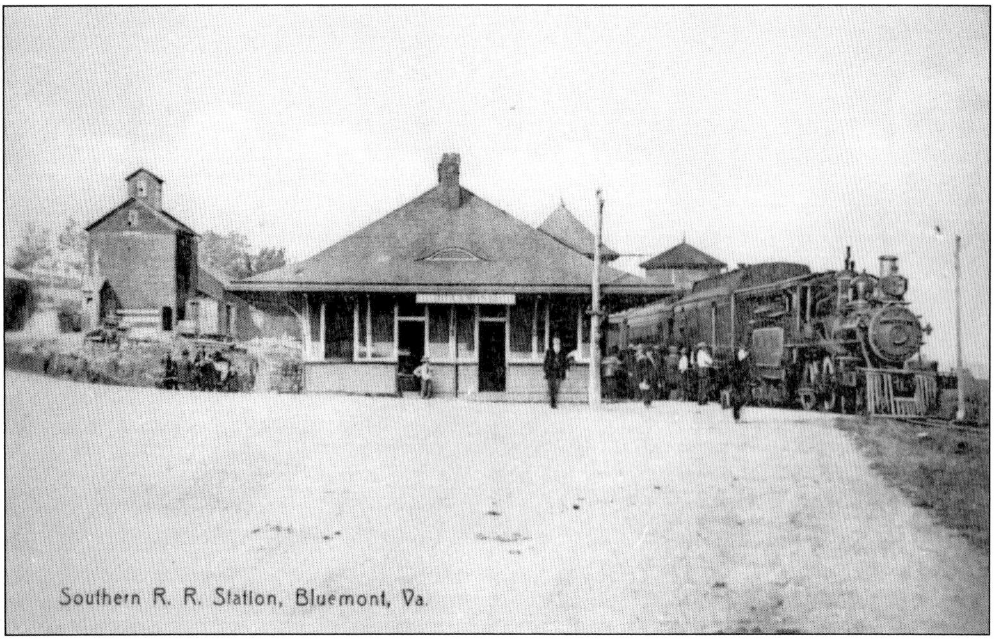

Smith and Hirst raised the first grain elevator in 1900, the year the Southern Railway came to Bluemont. It dealt in wheat, corn, fertilizers, flour, meal, feed, grass seeds, and so on. This c. 1900–1912 postcard shows one of the first three wooden grain elevators. The first two elevators burned in 1909, while the third burned in 1918. The station also burned down about 1920. (Courtesy of C. Dennis Howard.)

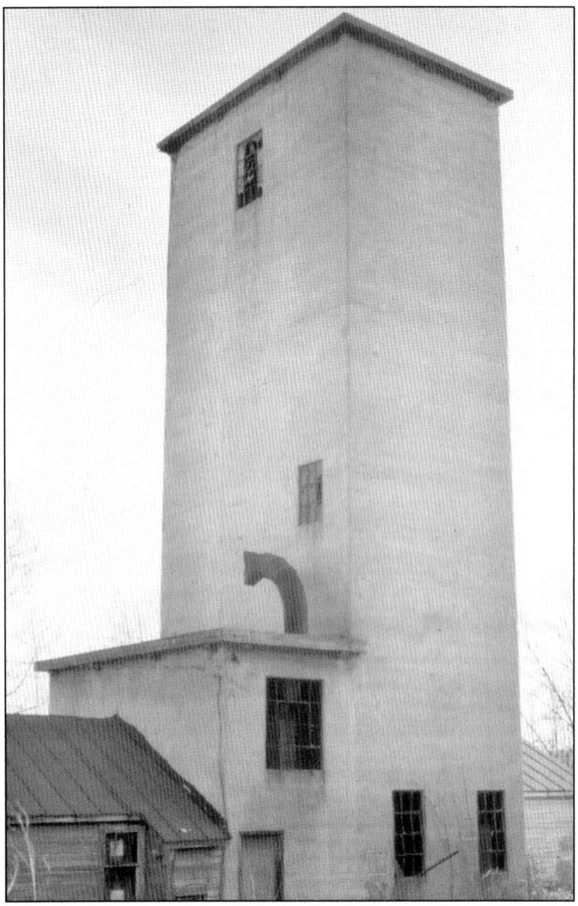

The author captured this view of the north side of the mill's 90-foot concrete elevator in December 1968. This fourth elevator was built for Wilkins-Rogers in 1920. Its long shadow can be seen just above the wye track in the photograph on page 81.

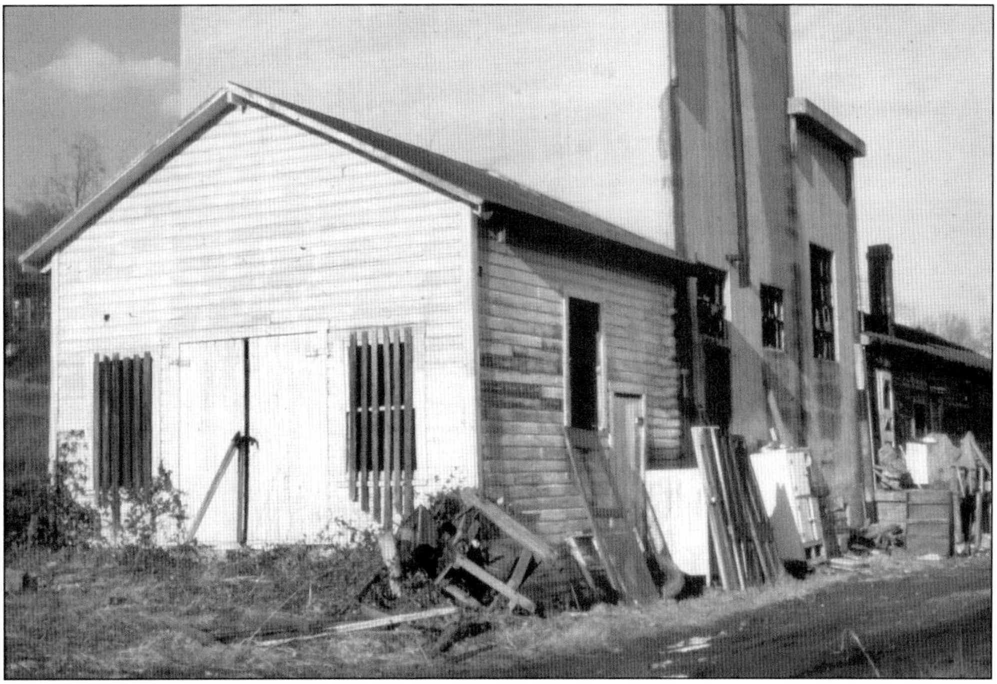

The mill was a sore spot aesthetically when photographed in December 1968. The wooden shed in the foreground eventually burned. This location is occupied today by Rosemary's Hair Design. The author missed an opportunity when he forgot to take the measurements of the steps at the loading platform. The steps are likely from one of the railroad's interurban cars.

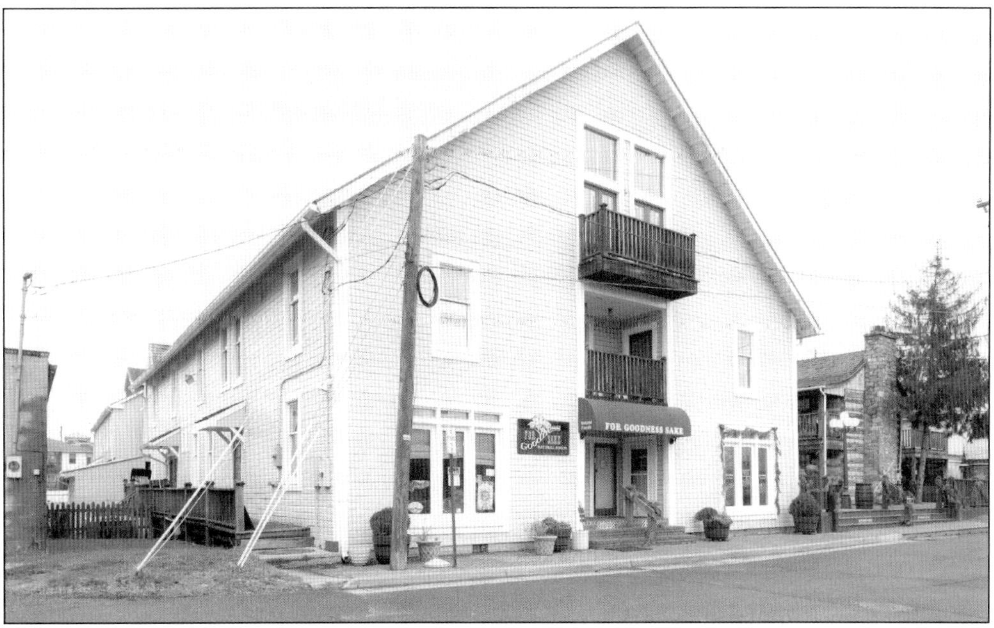

The Norman & Harding warehouse was renovated where it stood to become a part of Market Station, as seen on December 30, 2015. Salted herring was sold by the barrel from the warehouse, the salt odor giving rise to the "wharf" designation of the area. Asa Moore Janney recalled his father buying a barrel of a thousand herring for $20 and then eating a herring a day for breakfast.

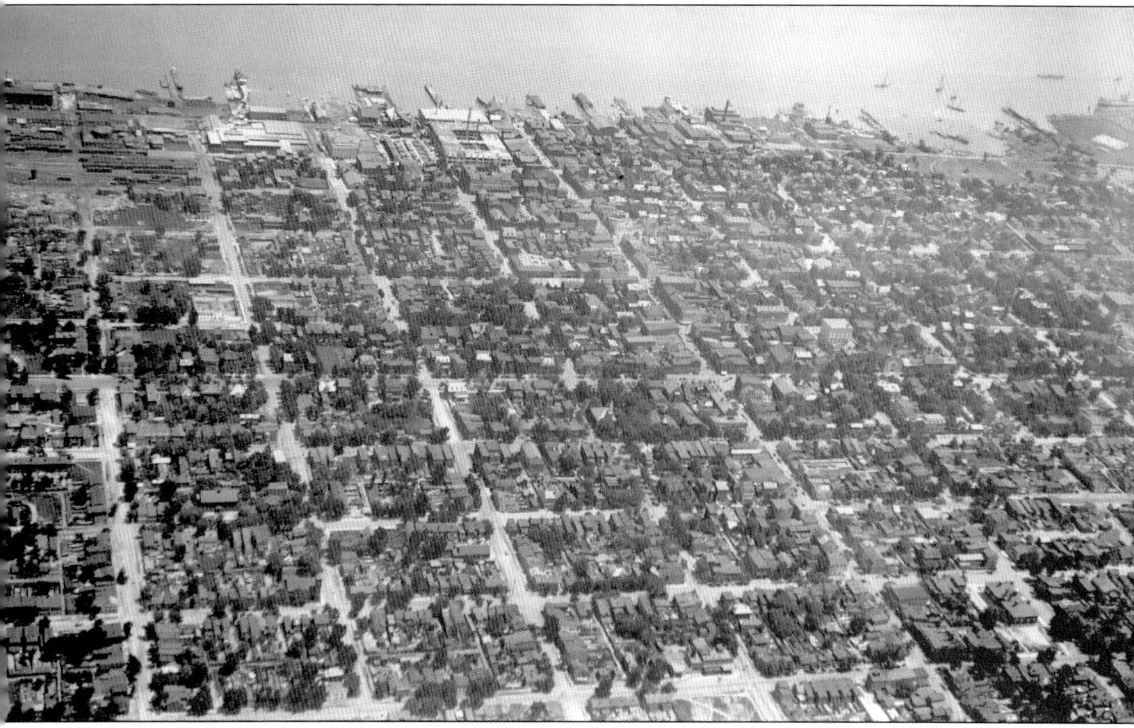

For many years the Alexandria, Loudoun & Hampshire Railroad and its successors carried agricultural goods to the port of Alexandria. The yards of the Alexandria, Loudoun & Hampshire Railroad, the Southern Railway at the time this photograph was taken (1919), were located at upper left below the large gas tanks. The corresponding map shows: (1) Rich A. Wattle's Corn and Feed Mill. (2) Norfolk-Washington Steam Ship Line wharf. (3) US Naval torpedo station. (4) Alexandria Fertilizer & Chemical Company. (5) Alexandria Gas, 1891, later City Gas Works, 1921. (6) Alexandria Fertilizer & Chemical Company. (7) Southern Railway freight station. (8) Southern Railway passenger station (original Alexandria, Loudoun & Hampshire Railroad station). (Above, courtesy of Library of Congress.)

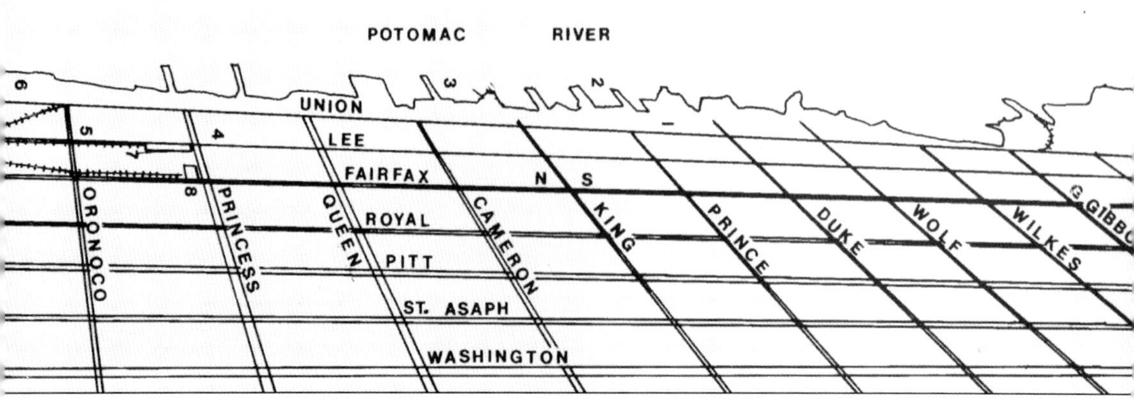

Six

Locomotive Details

This chapter presents a cross-section of locomotives used on the W&OD's system from steam to electric to diesel-electric.

The GF&OD bought three Forney-type steam locomotives from the Manhattan Elevated Railway of New York City to supplement the trolleys when traffic was heavy. The one surviving Forney locomotive, which was used on the Lake Street Elevated Railway of Chicago, rests in the St. Louis Museum of Transportation in Kirkwood, Missouri. For all practical purposes, this locomotive is identical to those the GF&OD purchased.

The Iowa Traction Railway still operates the W&OD's Baldwin-Westinghouse Class B locomotive No. 50 as its No. 50. It was shipped to the W&OD in February 1921. The following series of photographs includes pictures of Iowa Traction Railway's Class B No. 51 as it is being rebuilt for continued service. No. 51 was shipped in December 1923. For a short time in the early 1940s, W&OD Baldwin-Westinghouse locomotives were used to help trains on the steep grades out of Rosslyn to Glebe Road and from Bluemont Junction to Glebe Road.

In 1941, the railroad was short of cash, and the electrical system required rehabilitation, so the railroad decided to convert to diesel power. Joseph Weyraugh, an electrical engineer who frequently worked with the railroad, suggested that they purchase a General Electric 44-ton diesel-electric freight locomotive. George Baggett, W&OD vice president and general manager, obtained money for the down payment on the first 44-ton locomotive from the Southern Railway by promising to turn over the electrical equipment and wire on the Bluemont Branch once the railroad was operating with diesel locomotives. No. 47, purchased in 1941, was the first W&OD diesel locomotive. While seldom used, it is still in running order as Burlington Junction Railway's No. 44. No. 47 and its sister 44-ton locomotives were sold when freight traffic demanded larger locomotives.

The last locomotive pictured, an ALCO (American Locomotive Works Company) switcher locomotive owned by the Toledo, Lake Erie & Western Railway and Museum, is very similar to those the W&OD leased from the Chesapeake & Ohio Railway to handle heavier trains. It represents the heaviest locomotives used on the railroad.

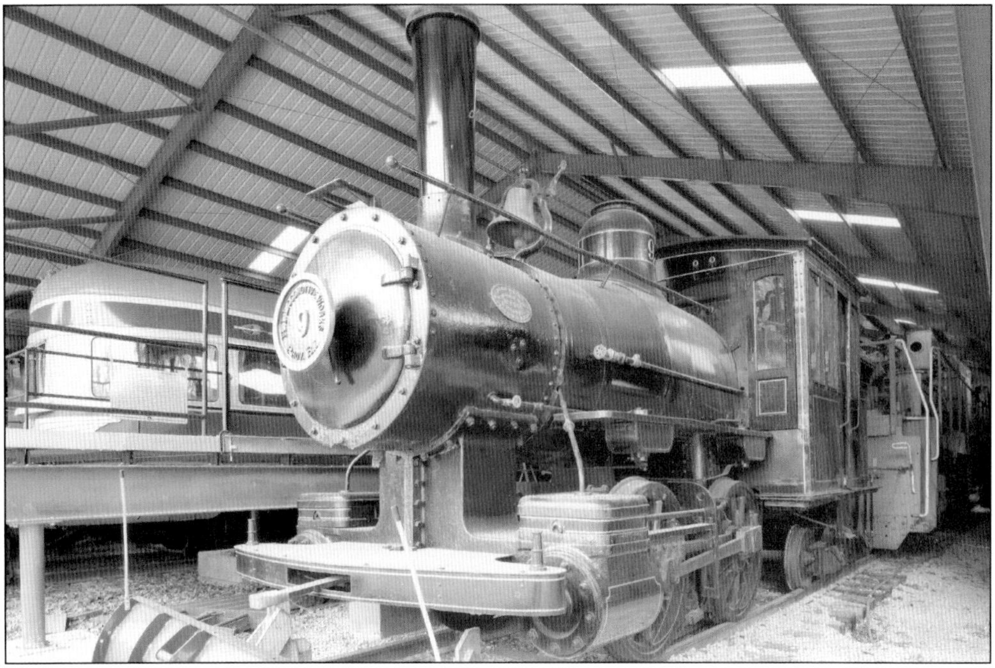

The *Charles H.* is a Forney locomotive; it has a single frame with four driving wheels and a single four-wheel truck under the rear. John H. White Jr., a railroad historian, called them "Spunky Little Devils." They generally pulled trains of five or six coaches back and forth for hours each day, running both boiler-first and tank-first. Needless to say, the locomotives had to be very reliable.

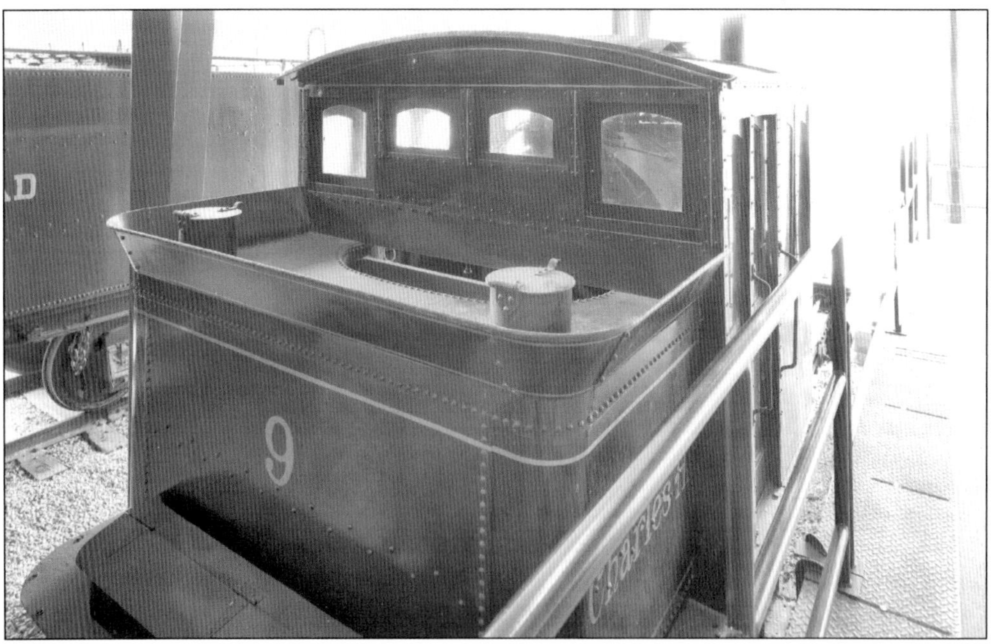

The *Charles H.* resides at the St. Louis Museum of Transportation in Kirkwood, Missouri. This rear view, taken on August 7, 2015, shows the water tank hatches and the small coal bin. Boards placed across the bin's front were removed as the fireman fed the fire. The low tender allowed the engineer to see over it and drive the train easily in both directions.

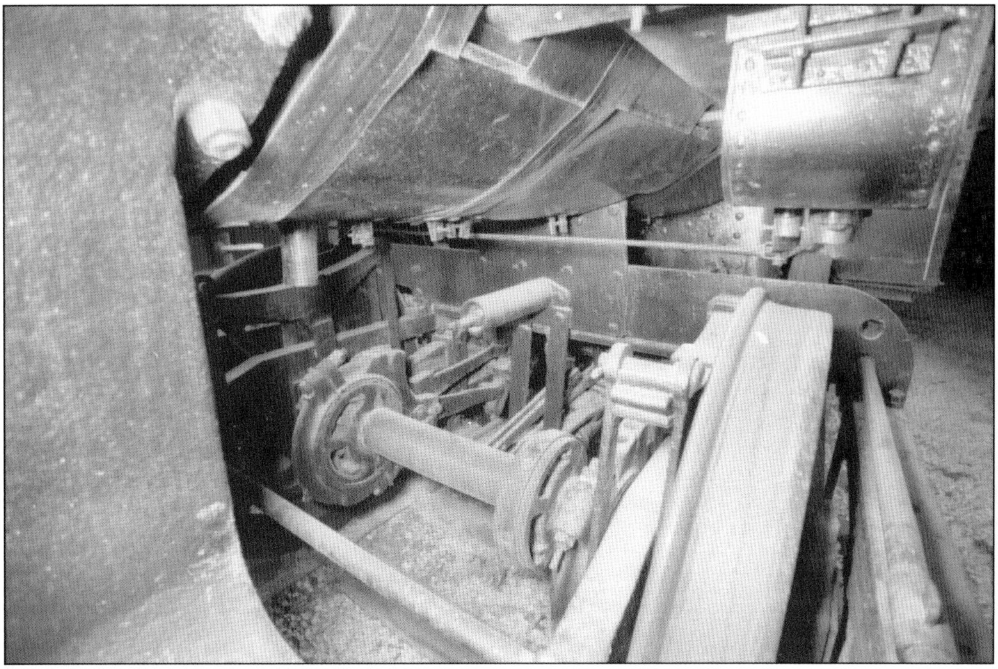

This picture looks under the boiler on the fireman's side at the levers that control the steam valves leading to the cylinders. Two levers on each side, mounted on offset circles ("eccentrics") at either end of the front axle, force the valves on each side back and forth via rods outside the wheels, such as the one at far right. (Courtesy of the St. Louis Museum of Transportation.)

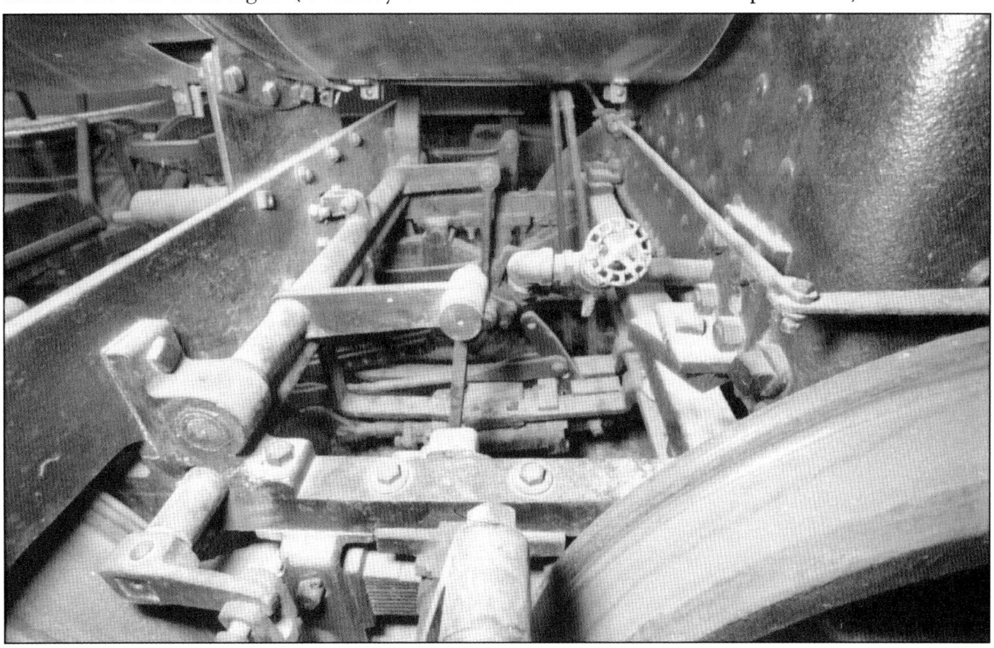

This view looks down between the axles of the driving wheels at the linkages controlled by the engineer to make the locomotive go forward or reverse and faster or slower. The front of the firebox is at right. Setting the timing of the valve gear required getting into cramped spaces and working from a pit below the locomotive. (Courtesy of the St. Louis Museum of Transportation.)

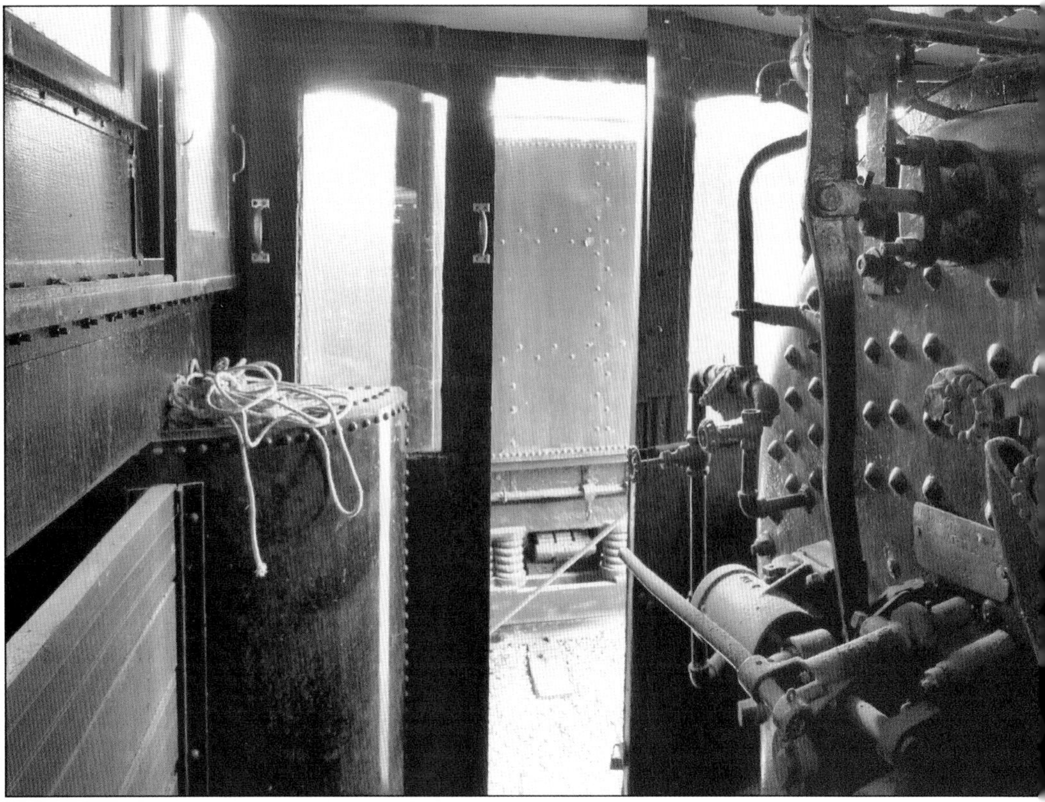

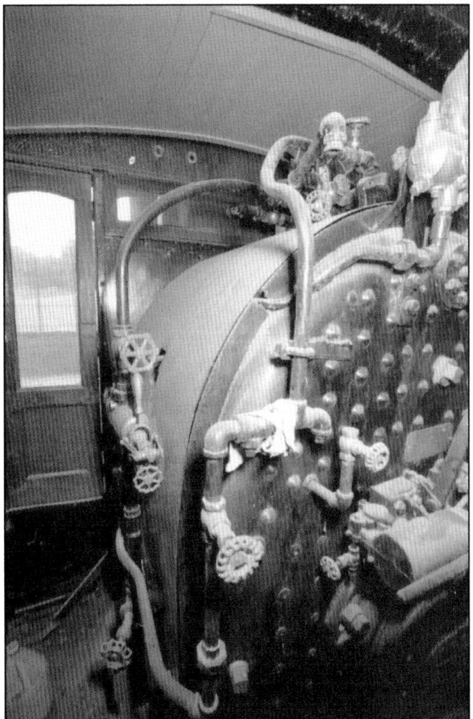

The engineer's controls are on the right. The train's vacuum brakes were controlled by the handle silhouetted in the window. The vacuum was created by a steam ejector that allowed atmospheric pressure to apply the brakes. The throttle is above the boiler at right center. The engineer had to stand between the boiler at his front and the cab side at his rear, not a pleasant position during Washington, DC, summers or winters.

It is a little difficult to get a true feeling of how cramped the cab is without being in it. The fireman probably had to use a very short-handled shovel to feed the boiler, as there was no more than two feet between the back of the boiler and the front of the coal bin.

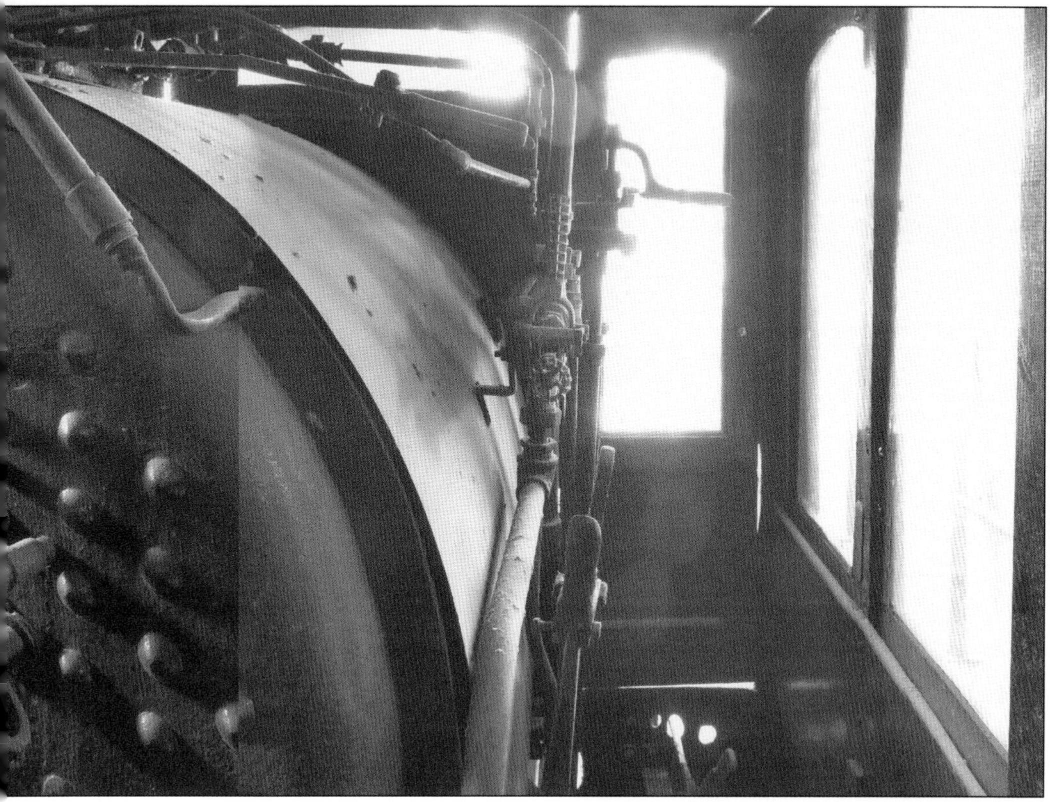

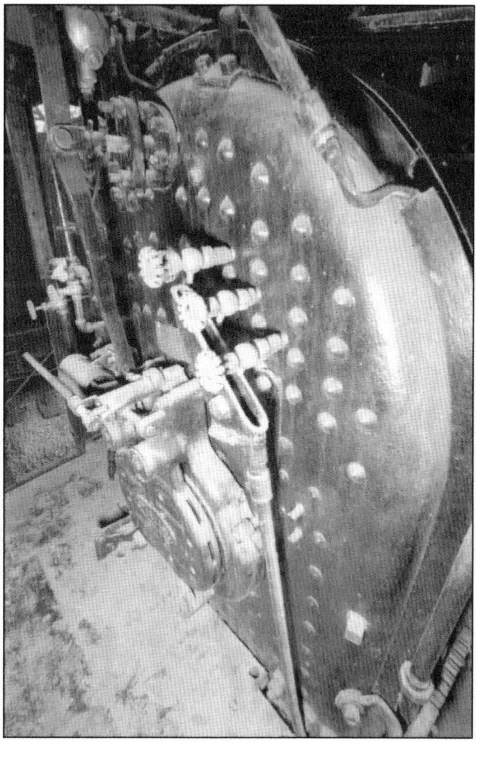

This view looks from the engineer's corner at the back of the boiler. The door to the firebox is at the bottom. The three spigots may have been used to check the level of water in the boiler. The tall lever in the center of the boiler back was attached at the top to the throttle control arm and at the middle to a rod leading to the steam dome.

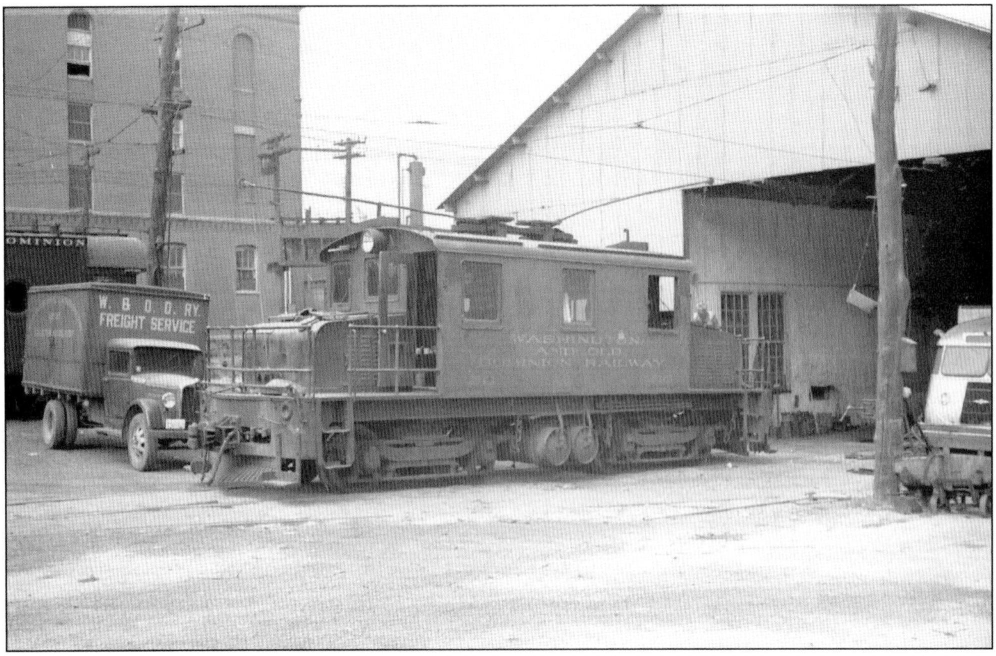

Baldwin-Westinghouse electric locomotive No. 50 is at the Rosslyn roundhouse. One of the railroad mechanics, possibly Carl Crosen or John King, is checking the air compressor or air blower inside the low hood. The blower, by providing a flow of cool air, allows the motors to work more efficiently and provide more power. This photograph was taken by John F. Burns on September 7, 1940.

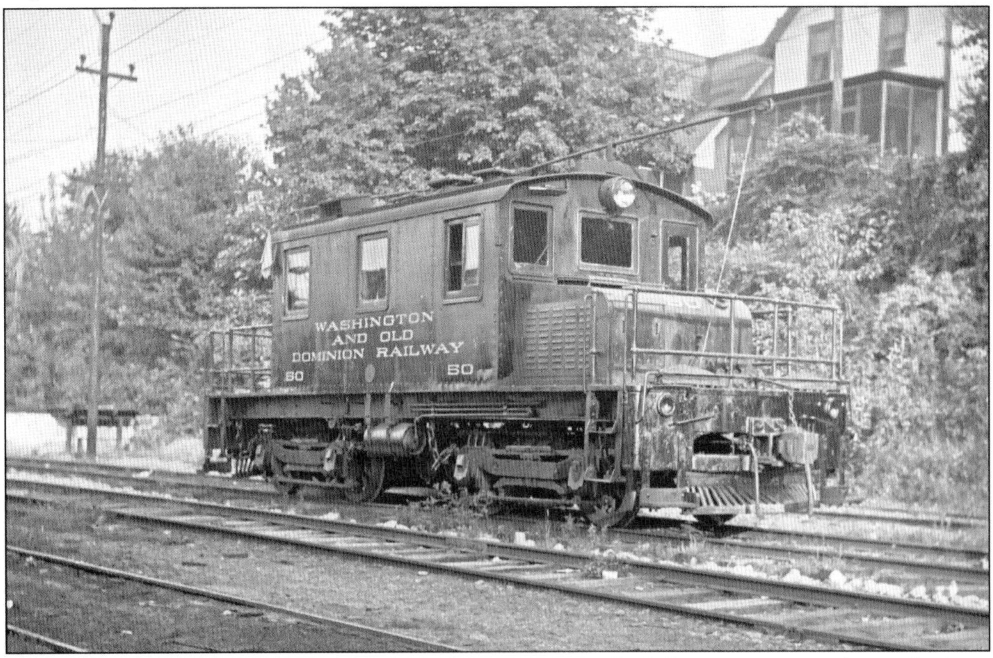

Gerald Cunningham caught No. 50 in Rosslyn on August 17, 1941, resting across the tracks from the Rosslyn freight station. Just to the left of the air tank, the taut chain leads from the brake wheel in the cab to the brake system under the cab.

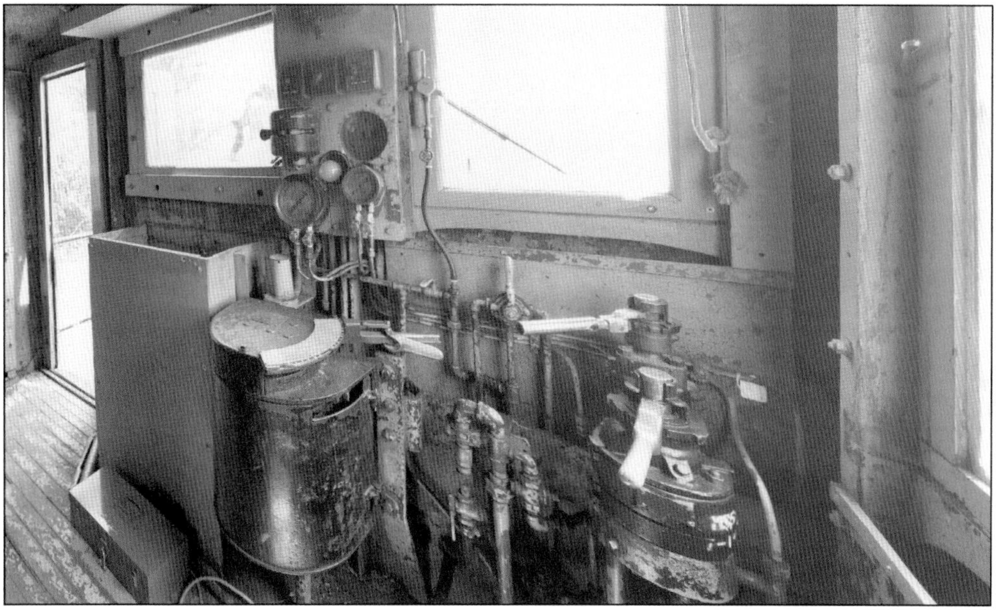

The bell seen through the window on August 4, 2015, indicates that this is the front of the locomotive. Speed is controlled with the lever in the center, attached to the top of the master controller. The engine and train brake controls are on the right. Fresh hoses attached to the air-pressure gauges indicate recent maintenance.

In this July 28, 2014, view, the burning light bulb in the center of the gauge board indicates that the locomotive is receiving electric power from the overhead wires. The box above the gauges houses the control and reset switch. The lever in the can-like fixture near the gauges is the headlight control. Moving the lever to the right dims the headlight, while the center position is off.

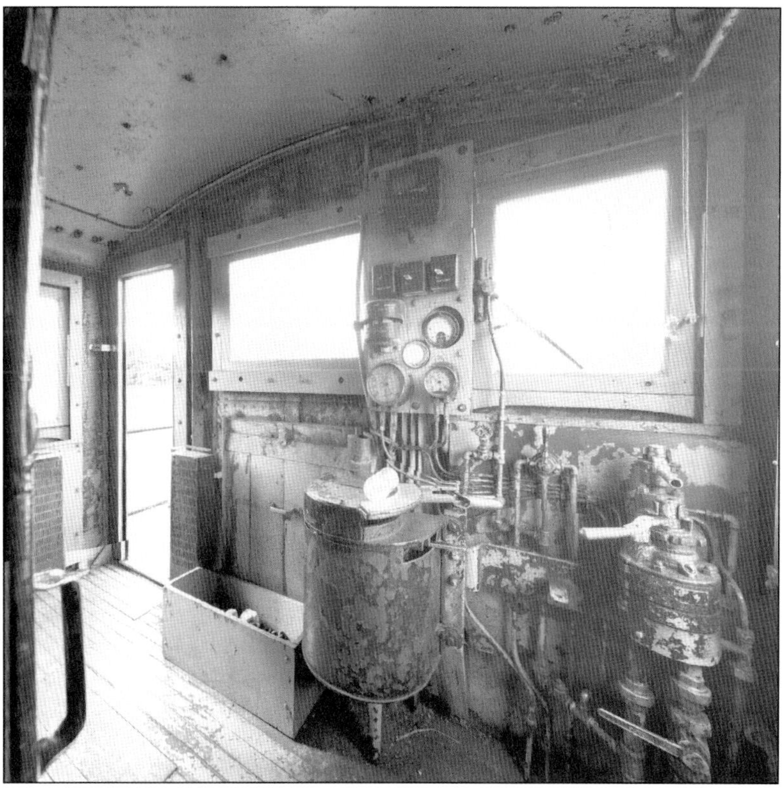

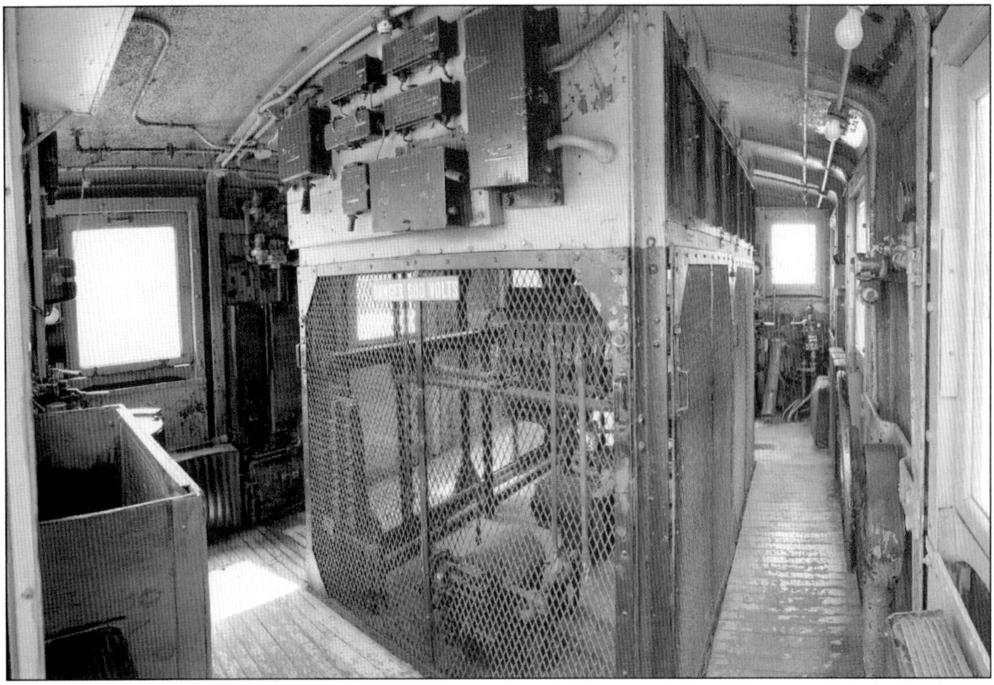

The upper cage wall of the front cab of the locomotive has switch boxes to control the different apparatus, such as the air compressor, heaters, and motor blowers. The locomotive's hand brake wheel and gear housing are at the outer wall at right. The chipped paint might be original, dating to February 1921, when the locomotive was shipped to the W&OD.

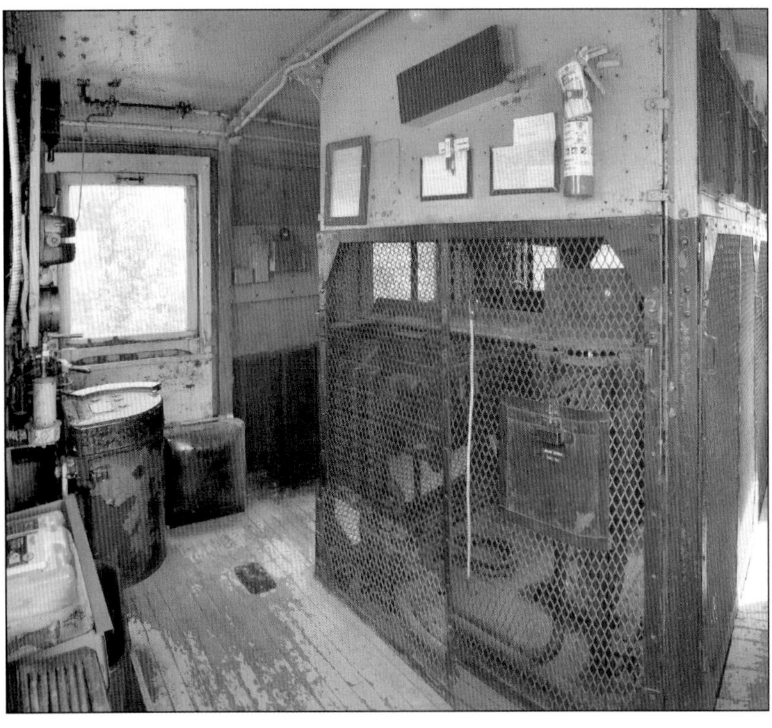

The master controller, with 12 speed steps, controls the locomotive's speed through 12 unit switches that in turn connect the electrical power through grid resistors to the motors, varying the speed of the motors. The resistors are located inside the safety cage at its top. The unit switches are below the resistors. On the floor are the motor cut-out switches and the reverser.

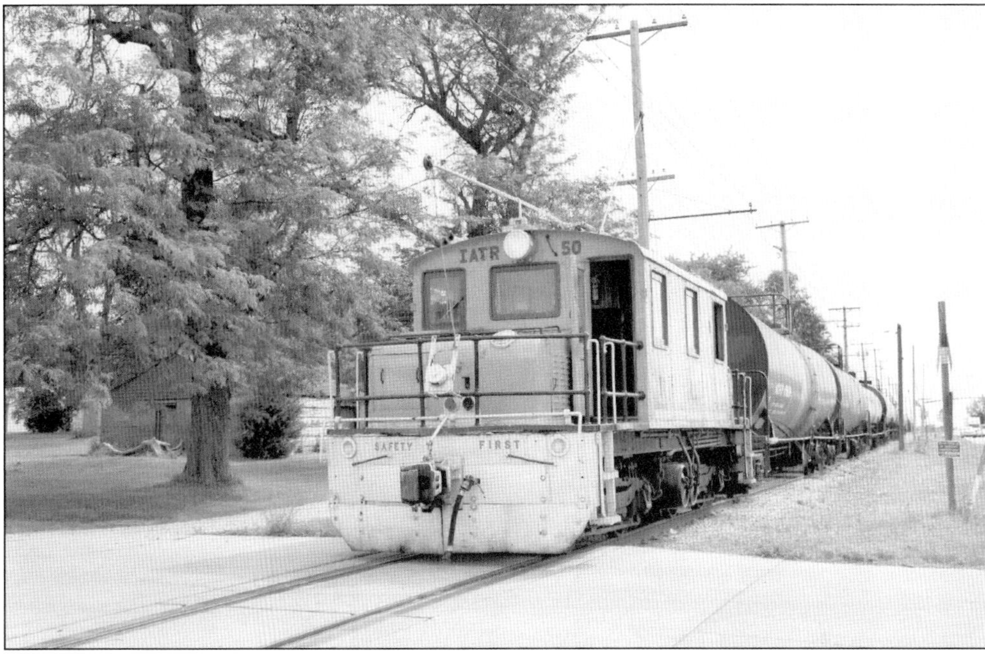

Iowa Traction Railway No. 50 is working along 255th Street, west of Mason City, Iowa, on August 4, 2015. The train, with glowing headlight and trolley pole against the wire, is blowing its rather flat-sounding horn for the road crossing. No. 50 once pulled a train of six heavyweight Pullman passenger cars to a Shriners convention in Leesburg up 1.5-percent grades without any apparent effort.

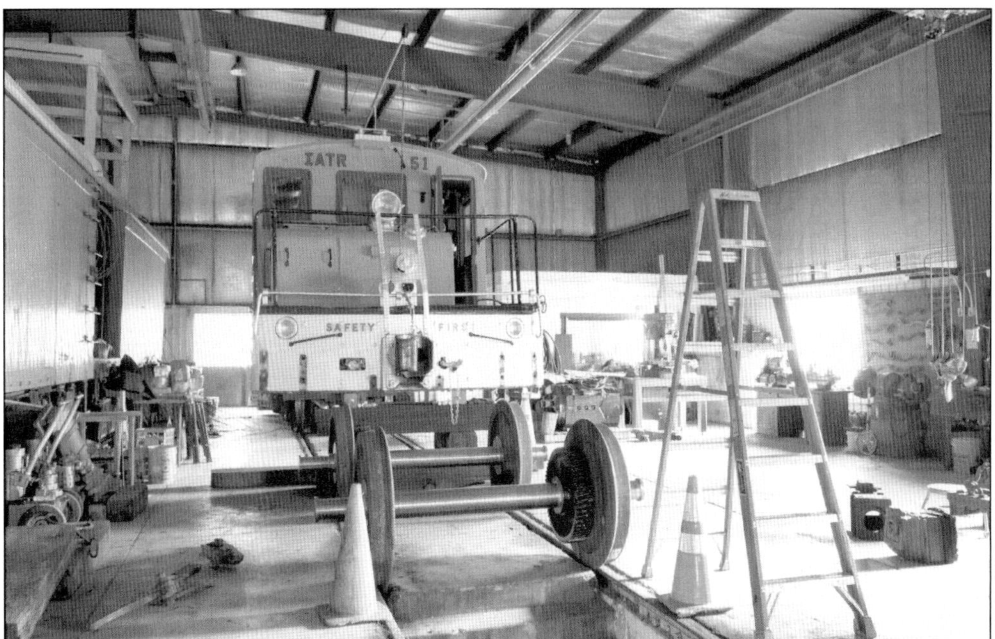

The wheels of Iowa Traction Railway No. 51, an identical Baldwin-Westinghouse electric locomotive, were condemned by a Federal Railroad Administration inspector in 2012 or before for being too thin. On August 4, 2015, the axles of one truck have been returned from Pennsylvania after new wheels had been pressed onto the axles earlier in the year.

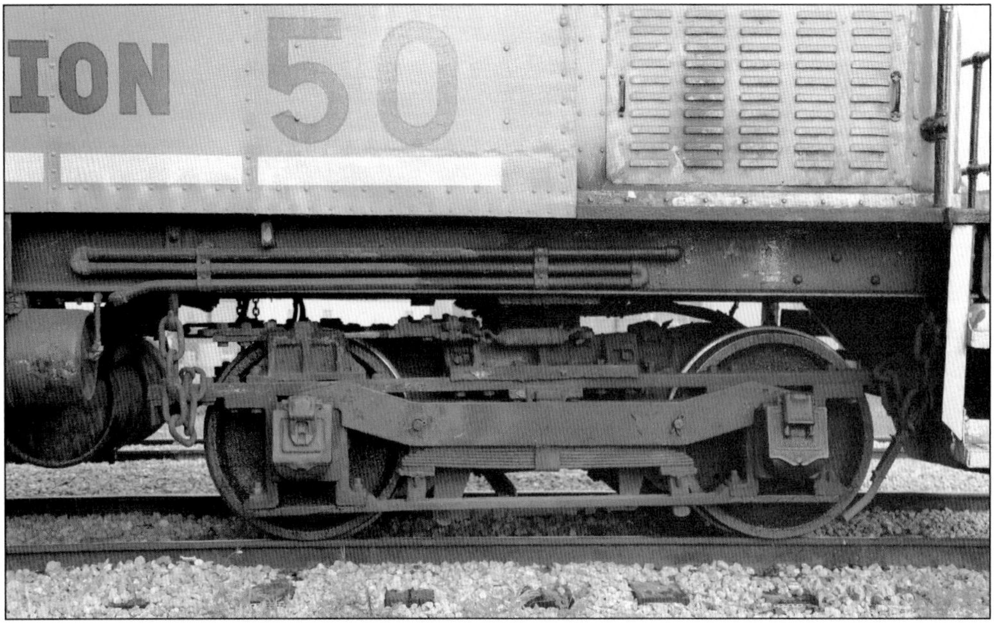

On August 3, 2015, No. 50 is settled down for the night alongside 255th Street in Mason City, Iowa. Here the rear truck of the locomotive is shown in its assembled state. These trucks, manufactured by Baldwin Locomotive Works, are almost identical to those Baldwin used under its steam locomotives. The rectangular support over the left journal box supports the brake linkage.

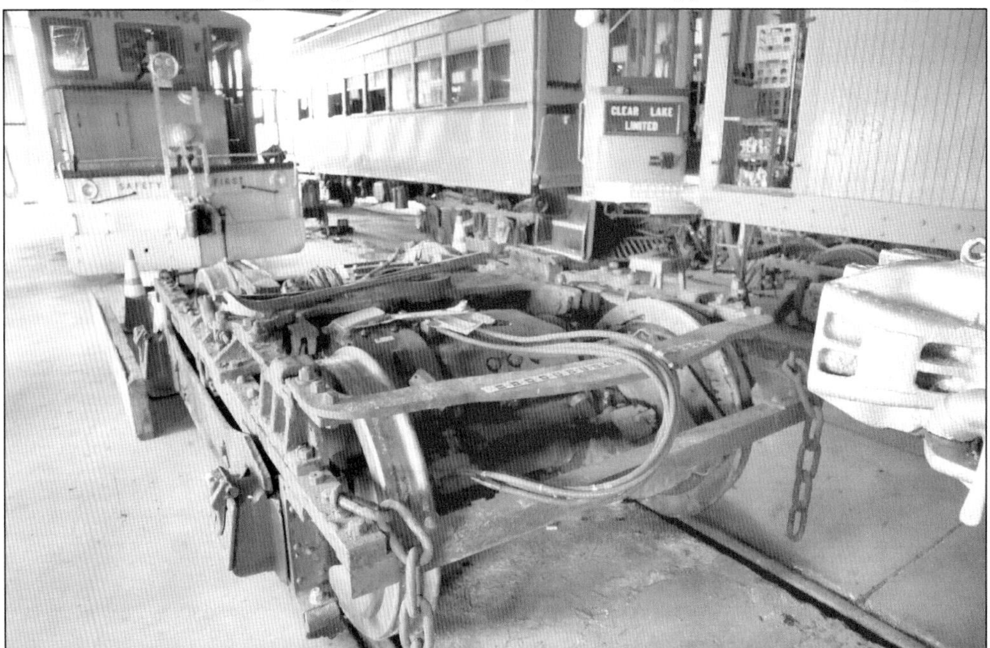

Here, on July 28, 2014, the rear truck of No. 51 has been pulled out from under the locomotive. The ruler rests on the brake linkage mentioned above. The cables connect the truck's motors to the controls. The traction motors still need rehabilitation. The firm of 3-E Motor Works in Des Moines was scheduled to disassemble the motors, re-wind and clean them, and replace worn out parts.

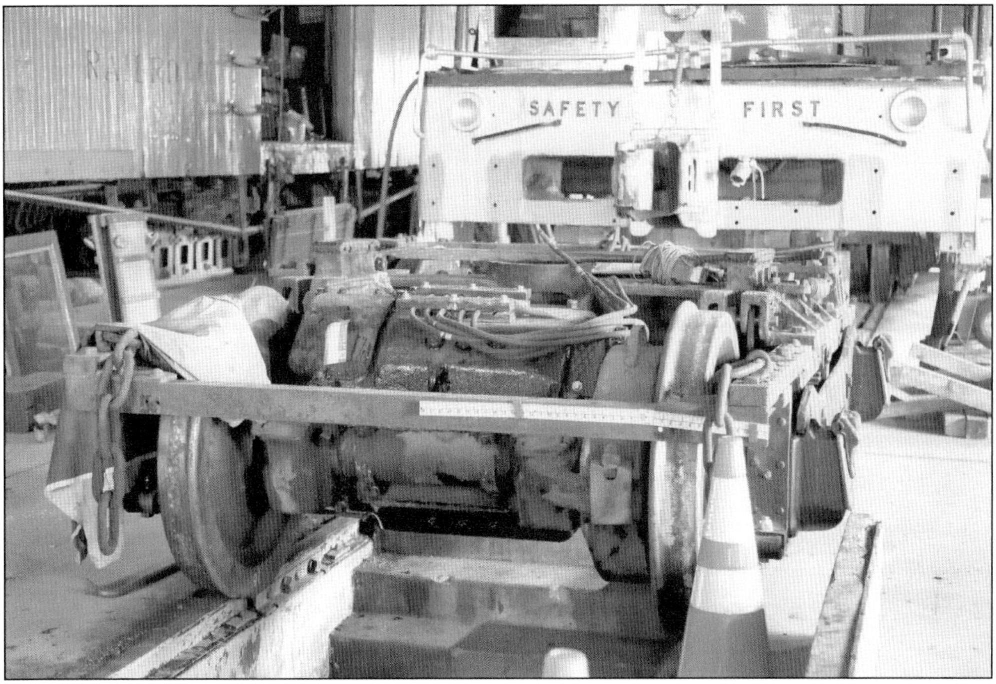

Looking at the same truck from the other direction, steps leading into the locomotive pit can be seen below the truck. Cables for the second motor rest on the motor housing, which is between the wheels of the nearest axle. Each Baldwin-Westinghouse electric locomotive had four 75-horsepower motors. The motors are hung from a central mounting on the bolster and ride on the axle.

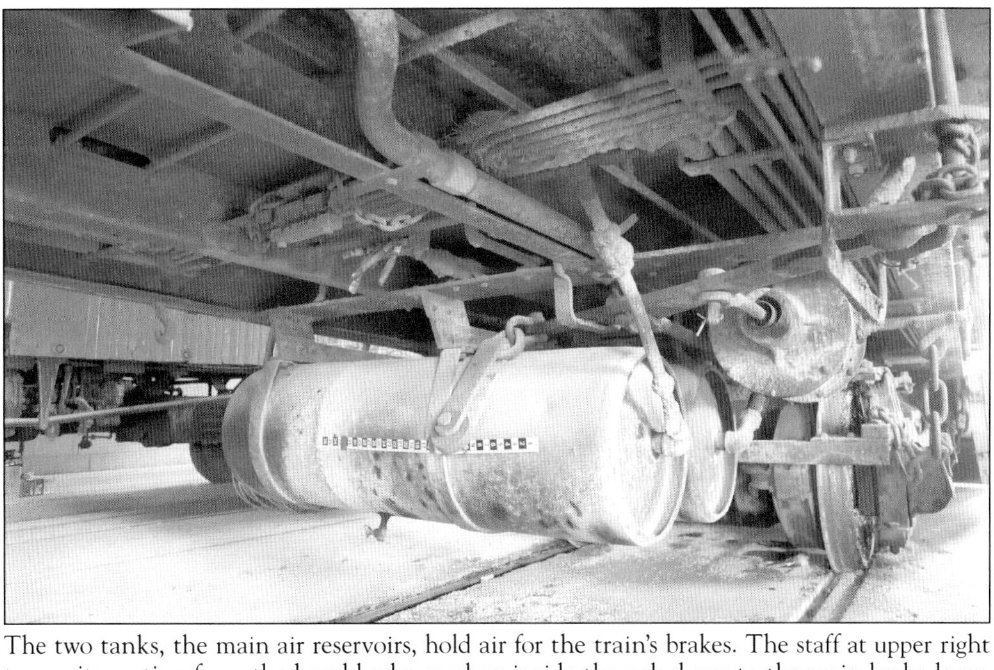

The two tanks, the main air reservoirs, hold air for the train's brakes. The staff at upper right transmits motion from the hand brake gearbox inside the cab down to the main brake lever, which is attached to the brake cylinder rod at right. When this photograph was taken on July 28, 2014, No. 51 had been in the shop for rebuilding since at least 2012.

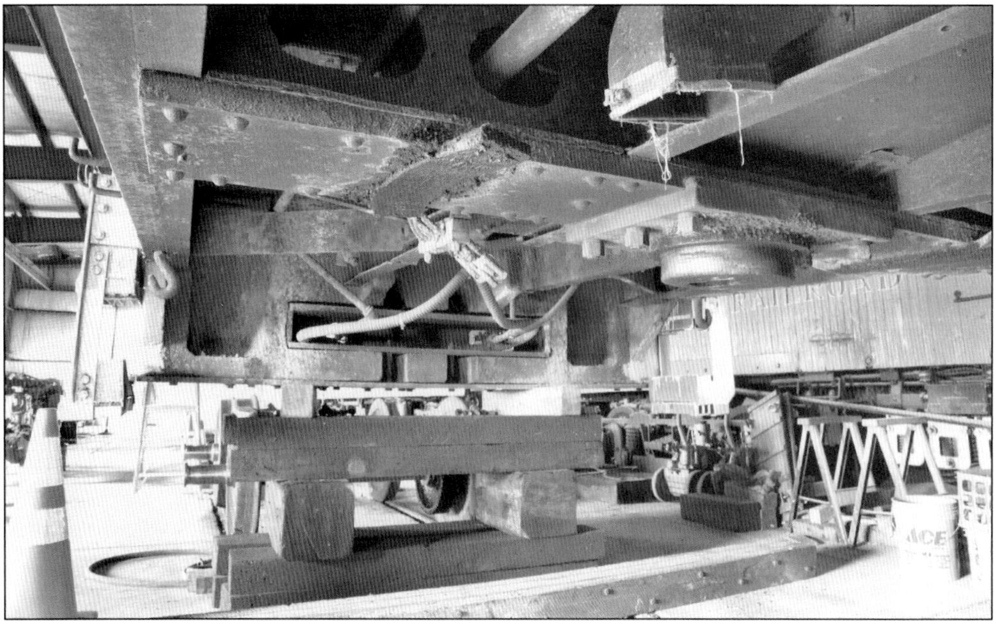

On August 4, 2015, wood blocking is supporting No. 51 while the rear truck is rehabilitated. The truck's bolster mates with the cylindrical plate at right center and is held in position with a center pin. Motor electrical connections are made via the four cables at center. The circular greased bearing plate keeps the locomotive from rocking left and right when running.

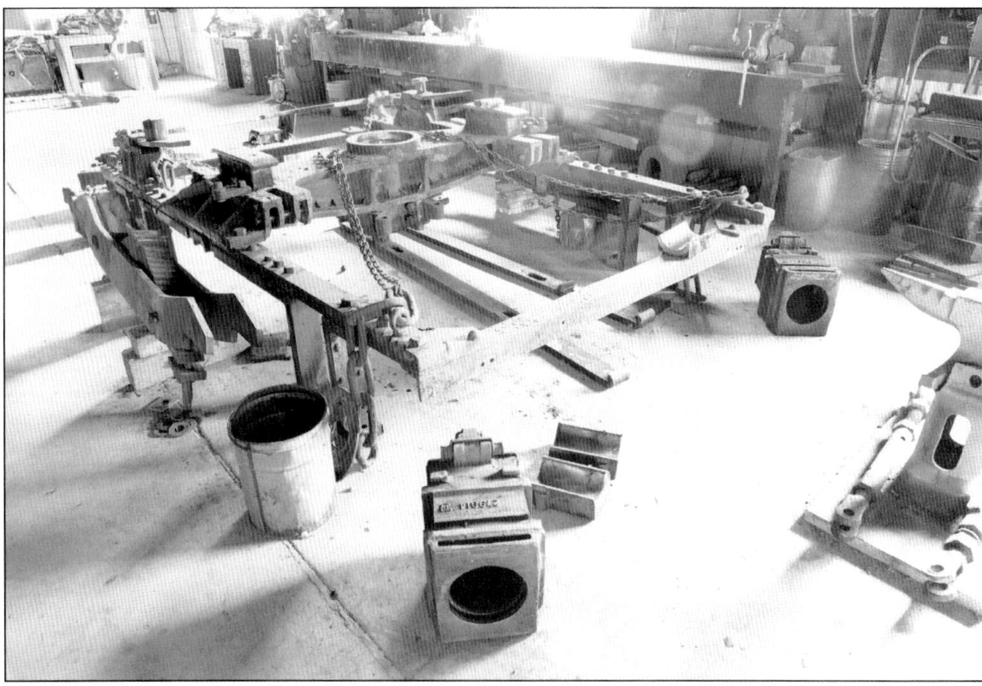

As seen on August 4, 2015, the brake rigging has been disassembled and checked for worn parts. Brake rigging bushings were totally worn out; round holes in the rigging had become elliptical. The holes were to be welded up and re-bored to make them round again. At the bowl for the center pin of the truck, the brass plating had to be replaced.

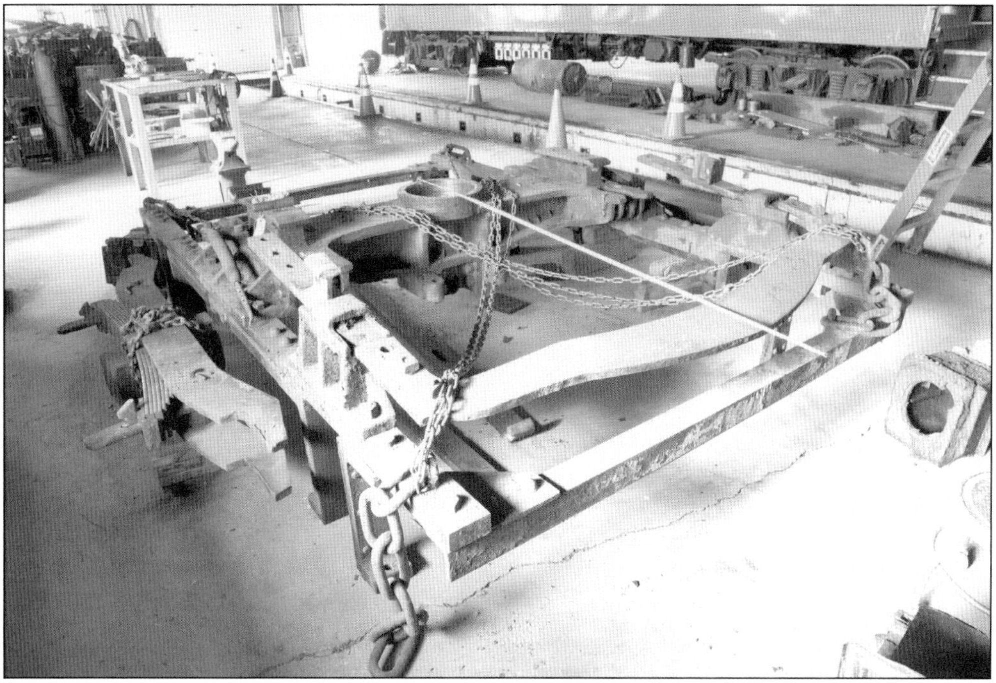

The railroad replaced the wooden seals on the friction bearings where the axles leave the oil boxes. The brake linkage is still attached at the top of the truck frame. The white line from the center of the truck toward and onto the brake linkage is a ruler that is six feet, nine inches overall.

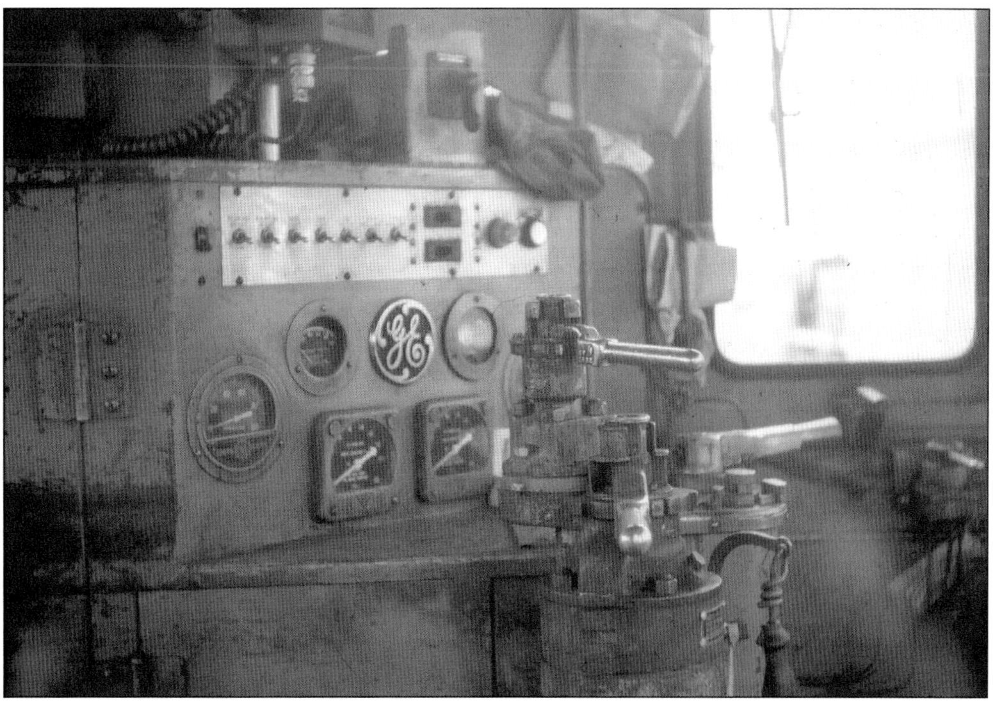

This August 1968 photograph shows the interior of GE 70-ton locomotive No. 57, parked at the engine house in Alexandria, Virginia, next to Slaters Lane, not far from US Route 1.

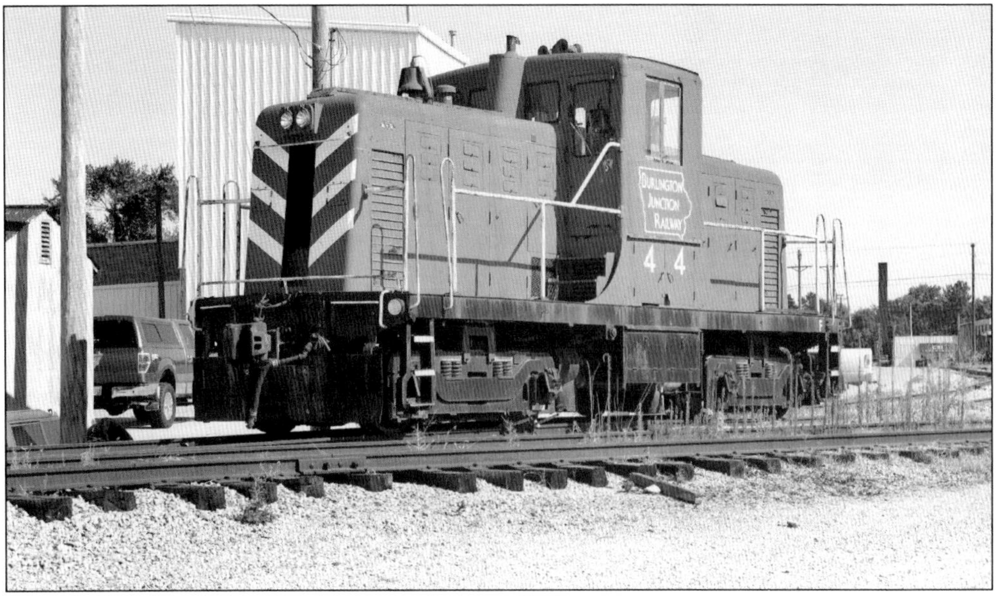

Burlington Junction Railway locomotive No. 44 was purchased new by the W&OD in 1941 as its No. 47. It is seen here on industrial tracks in Burlington, Iowa, on August 4, 2015. The railway uses No. 44 about four or five times a year. Doug Lee said No. 47 was used to pull car No. 46 because it had better speed than the other two 44-ton locomotives bought in 1942.

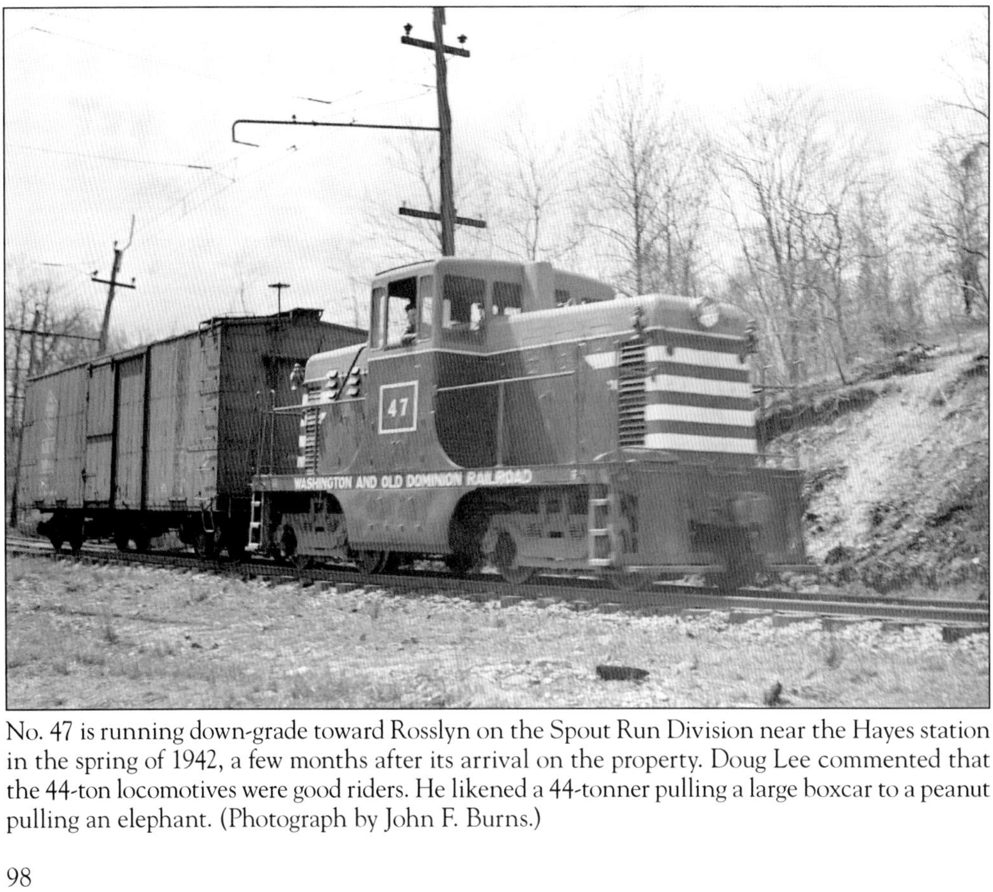

No. 47 is running down-grade toward Rosslyn on the Spout Run Division near the Hayes station in the spring of 1942, a few months after its arrival on the property. Doug Lee commented that the 44-ton locomotives were good riders. He likened a 44-tonner pulling a large boxcar to a peanut pulling an elephant. (Photograph by John F. Burns.)

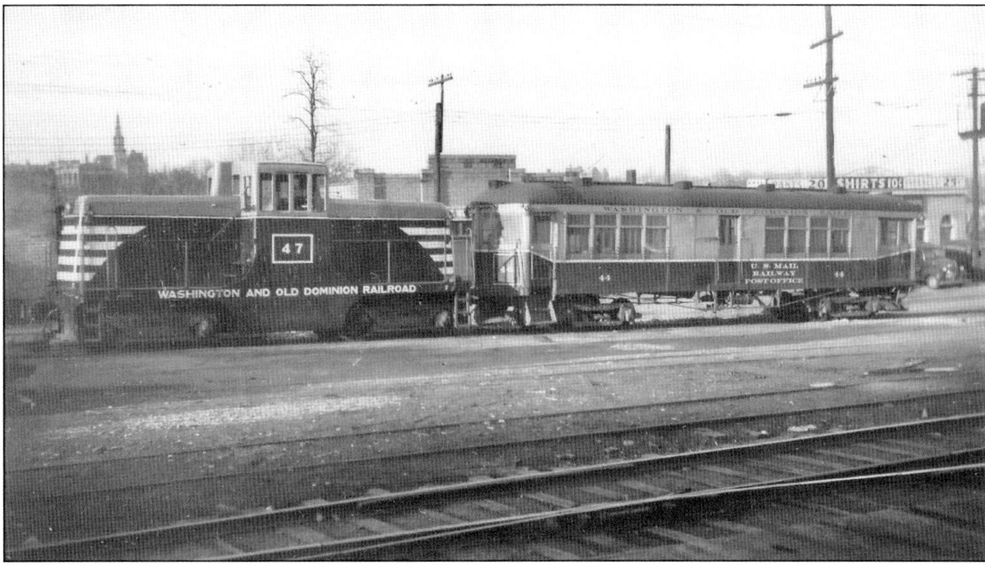

Charles M. Wagner caught No. 47 coupled to Railway Post Office car No. 44 in Rosslyn at the end of a day in 1943 on the back track. No. 44 is seeing its last days as an operating car. Later, when gas-electric combination passenger-express-mail car No. 46's motor broke down, No. 47 pulled it back and forth to Leesburg. (Courtesy of Gerald Cunningham.)

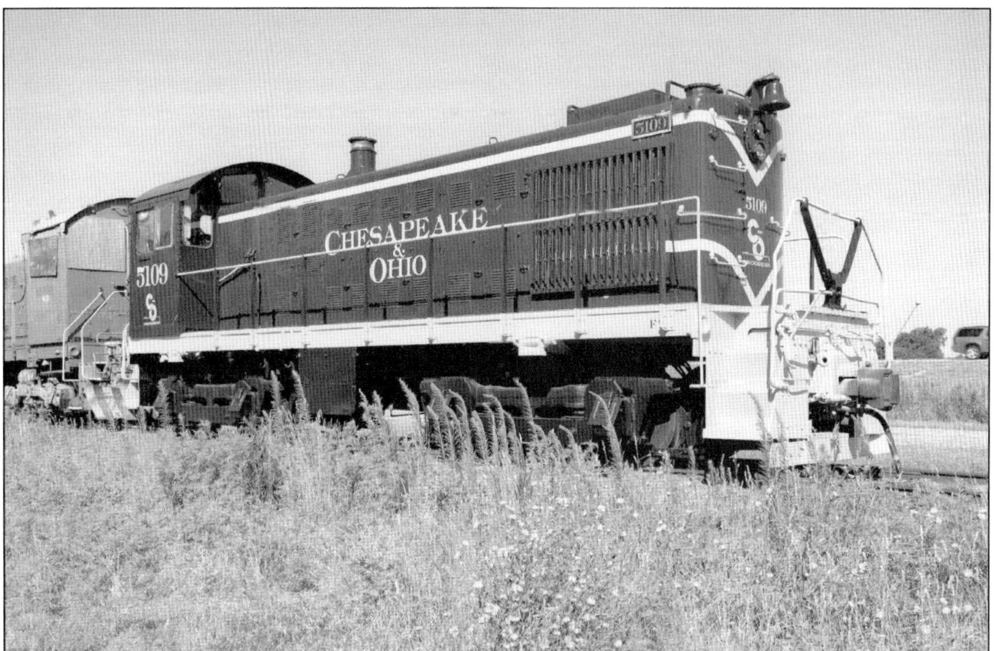

The Toledo, Lake Erie & Western Railway and Museum of Grand Rapids, Ohio, used this 1,000-horsepower locomotive to pull tourist trains over its short line. C&O locomotive No. 5109, seen on July 24, 2014, built by ALCO as a model S-2 switcher, was very similar to locomotives the W&OD leased from the C&O.

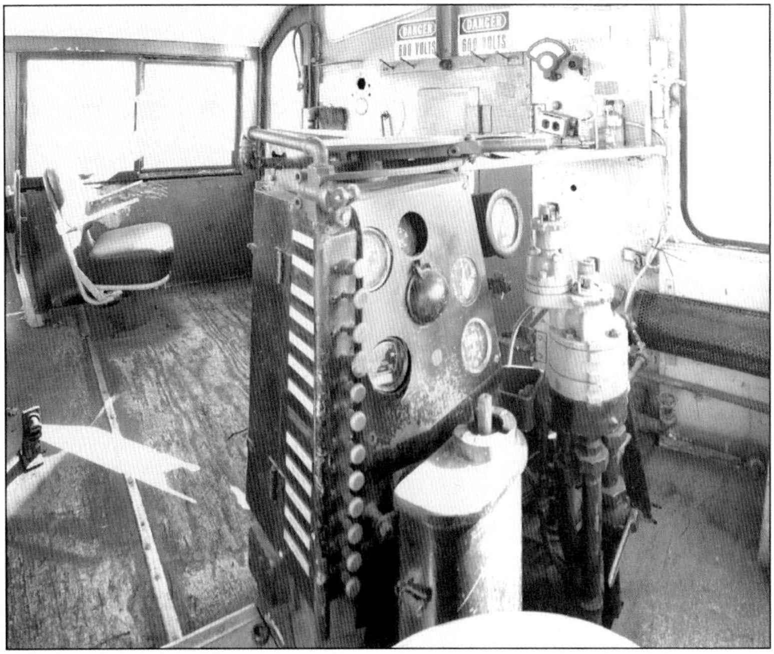

The control handles have been removed from No. 5109 while the locomotive is in storage. The throttle is at top. Directly below the throttle is the controller—it has three positions for forward and three positions for reverse running. To the right of the controller is the brake stand, with the engine brake on the top and the train brake below.

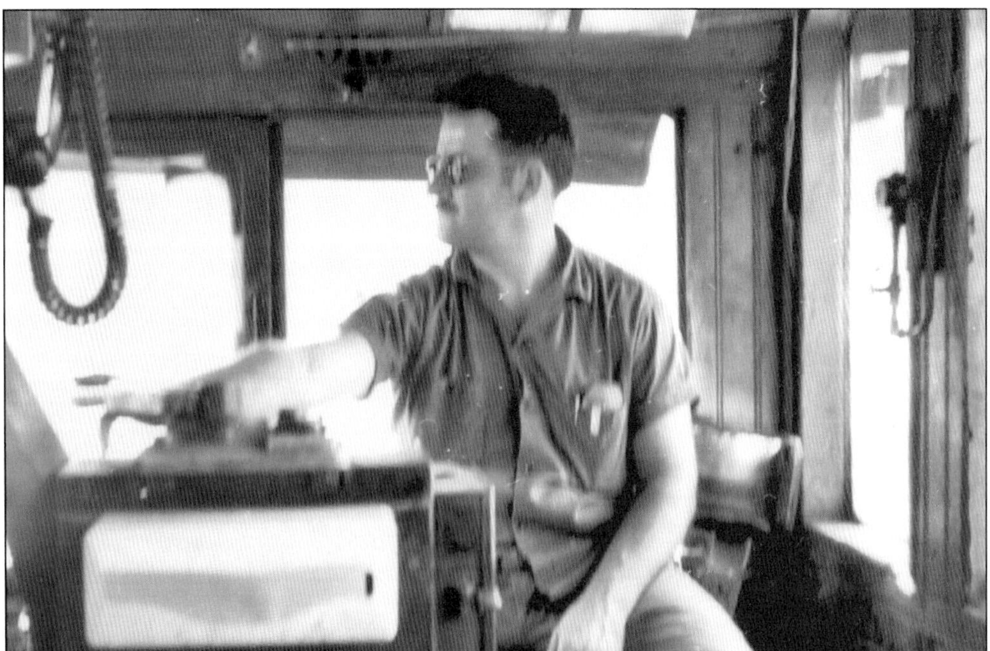

Ames Williams caught engineer Doug Lee at the controls of an ALCO switching locomotive in August 1960. Doug Lee told the author that the locomotive rode rough and that the seats were no more comfortable to sit on than a five-gallon paint bucket. (Courtesy of the Alexandria Library, Special Collections.)

Seven

Maintaining the Right of Way

Right of way maintenance, as shown in the following pictures, includes activities required by normal wear and tear, rain and floods, and broken rails and rotten ties. Doug Lee recalled a passenger being asked how he would know if the train derailed. The passenger replied that the ride would be smoother. Torrential rains on May 31, 1889, (the same rains that caused the Johnstown, Pennsylvania, floods) washed out portions of the railroad, leaving Purcellville without service for several days. During Hurricane Hazel in 1955, the train crew had to deal with seven downed trees on their return trip east to Alexandria. The C&O purchased the W&OD in 1956, anticipating the construction of a coal-fired power plant. The C&O instituted an upgrading program, replacing bridges and ties to prepare for the expected coal traffic. The W&OD's Burro crane played an important role in right of way maintenance and the bridge rebuilding program.

The Burro crane was named after the pack animal of the Old West. Burro cranes are small cranes mounted on a four-wheel chassis. Burro Crane Inc. made two models: Model 30, with a 7.5-ton capacity, and the somewhat larger Model 40, with a 12.5 ton capacity. Burro Crane shipped the W&OD's Model 30 crane, serial number 30-326, in October 1949. It was powered by a gasoline engine. Like the burro, this crane could carry many different types of material. The boom could be fitted with a roller to lay welded rail, a standard hook to lift various objects, rail tongs, tie tongs, a clamshell to move loose bulk materials, an electromagnetic disk to move iron and steel, and other tools. One of its key features was its short tail swing, which allowed it to work on one track without interfering with operations on an adjacent track. Throughout all these maintenance and rebuilding activities, the Burro crane provided needed muscle and reach. What the Burro crane could not do, the railroad's crews had to do manually. For example, cribbing of ties or large timbers placed by hand was used to form embankments after washouts, provide platforms to support car jacks while cars were put back on the tracks, and as a means of moving bridge girders up and down during bridge rebuilding projects.

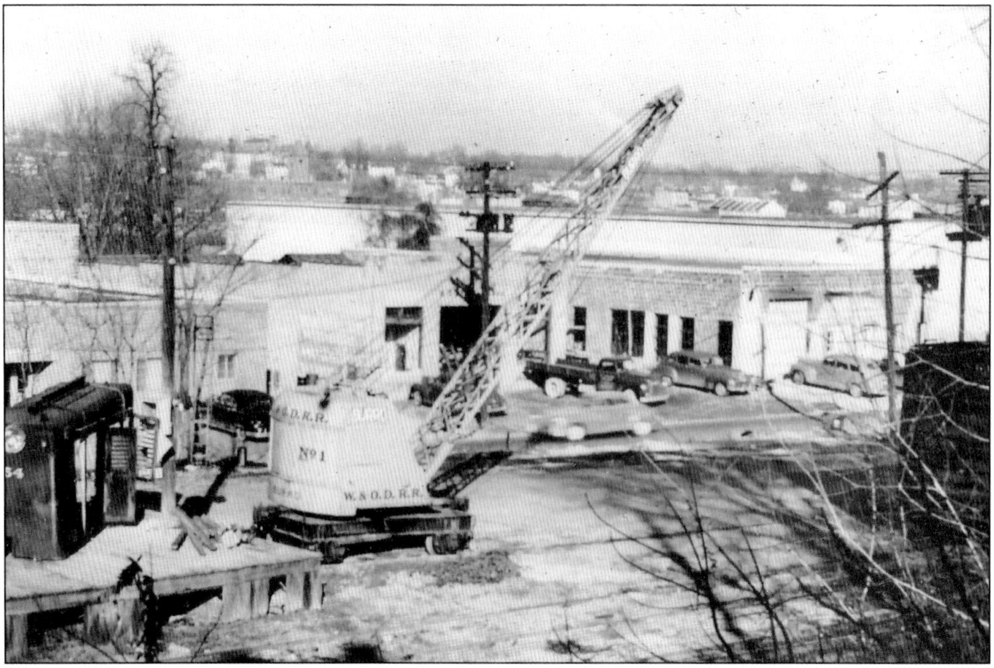

John F. Burns photographed the Burro crane in Rosslyn adjacent to the freight house in November 1949. The Capital Traction Company carbarn is visible above the Potomac River in the background above the crane. The hood of Whitcomb locomotive No. 54 sits on the platform.

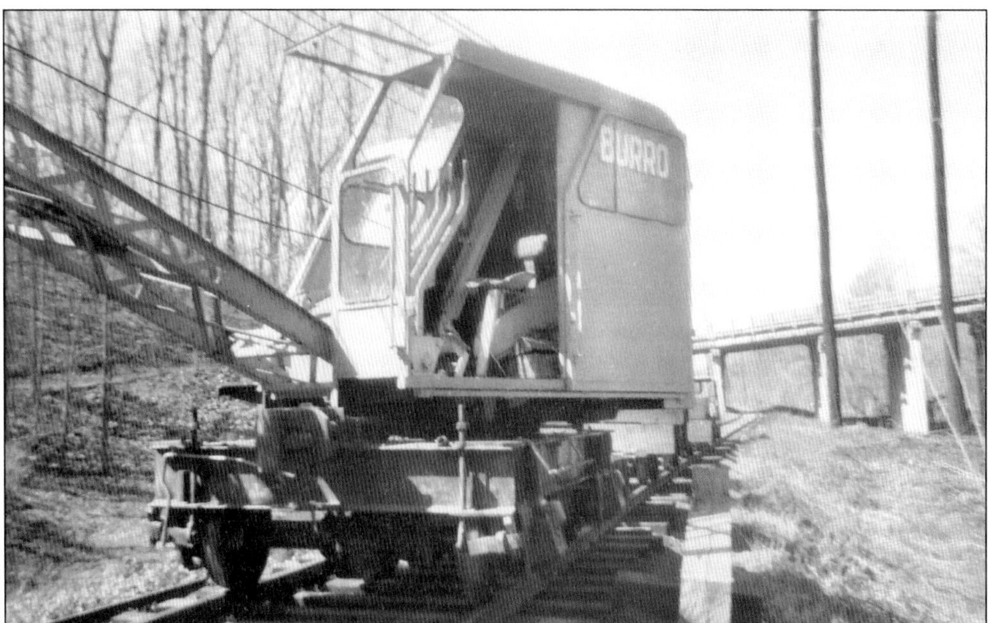

From left to right, the operator control handles are the boom hoist clutch lever, the hoisting or closing line drum clutch lever, the propelling clutch lever, the holding drum clutch lever, and the swinger clutch lever. Each lever had an independent friction clutch to allow quick operation of the different controls. (Courtesy of NOVA Parks.)

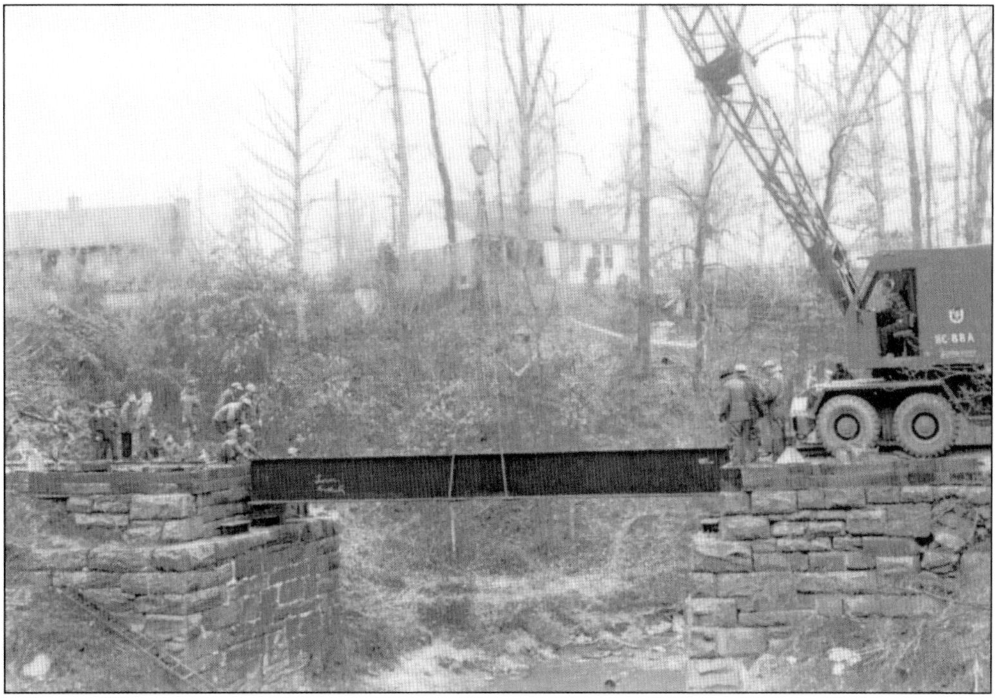

David Marcham photographed a rented crane installing new steel bridge girders sometime in the late 1950s. This bridge was a little east of Bluemont Junction and Wilson Boulevard in the Four Mile Run valley. The bridge carried the railroad over a tributary of Four Mile Run. (Courtesy of David Marcham.)

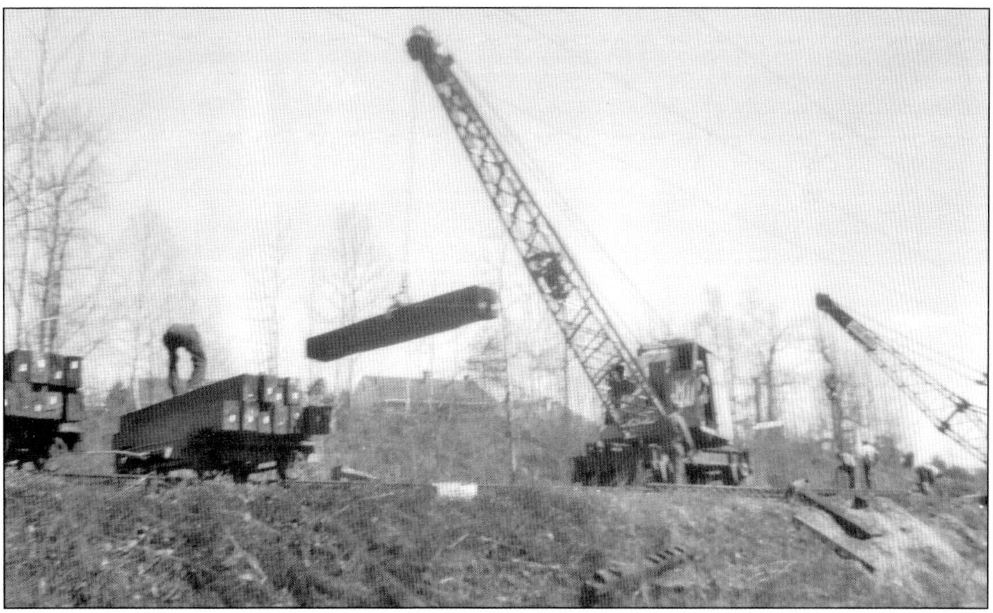

In this photograph by David Marcham, the bridge girders have been placed and the track gang is replacing the ties. The Burro crane is using tie tongs to carry two bridge ties from the small track crew trailer to the bridge, swinging around and backing up at the same time. Bridge ties are notched on the bottom to keep them in place on bridge girders. (Courtesy of David Marcham.)

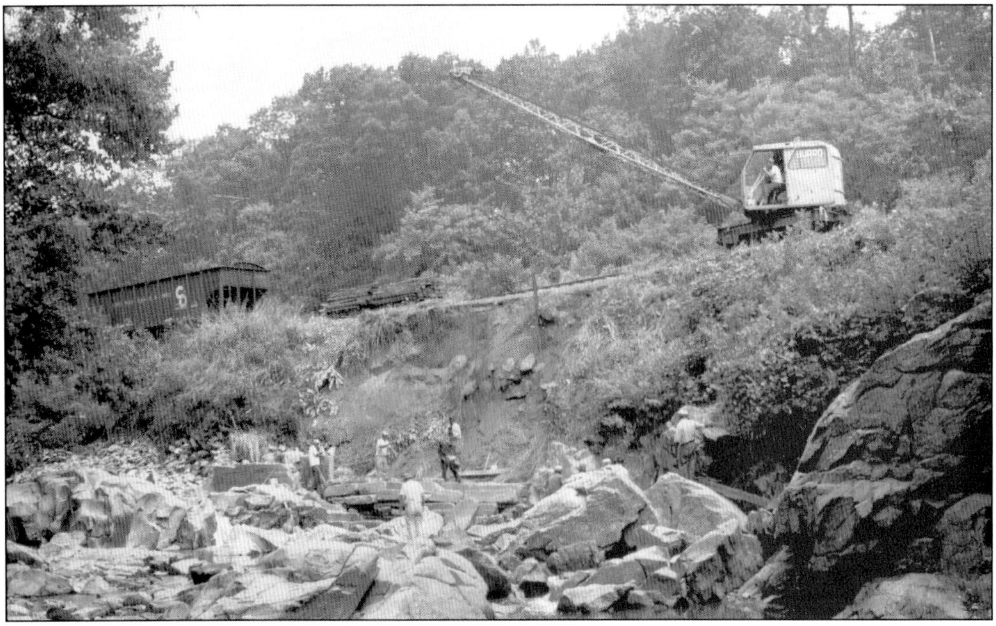

The railroad suffered a washout alongside Four Mile Run between Columbia Pike and Arlington Boulevard. Ames Williams captured the worker in the dark shirt positioning the crane's tie tongs to help move some of the stones on August 24, 1963. (Courtesy of the Alexandria Library, Special Collections.)

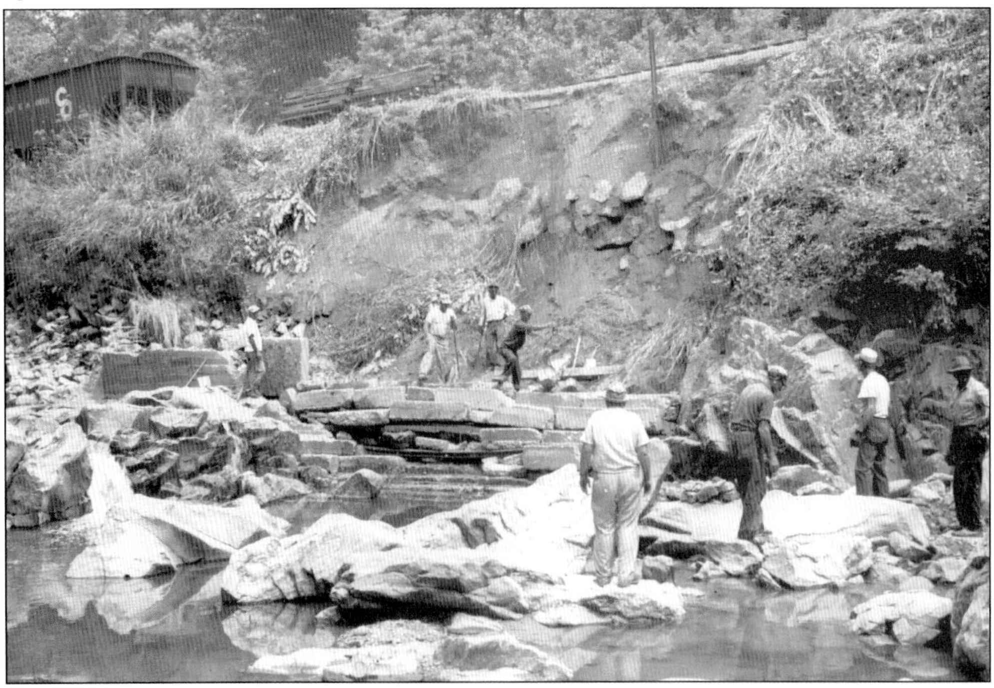

Ever resourceful, the railroad is using tie tongs to move rocks. The worker in the dark shirt is directing the tongs to help build up a wall of old concrete pieces at the base of the washout. This photograph was taken by Ames Williams on August 24, 1963. (Courtesy of the Alexandria Library, Special Collections.)

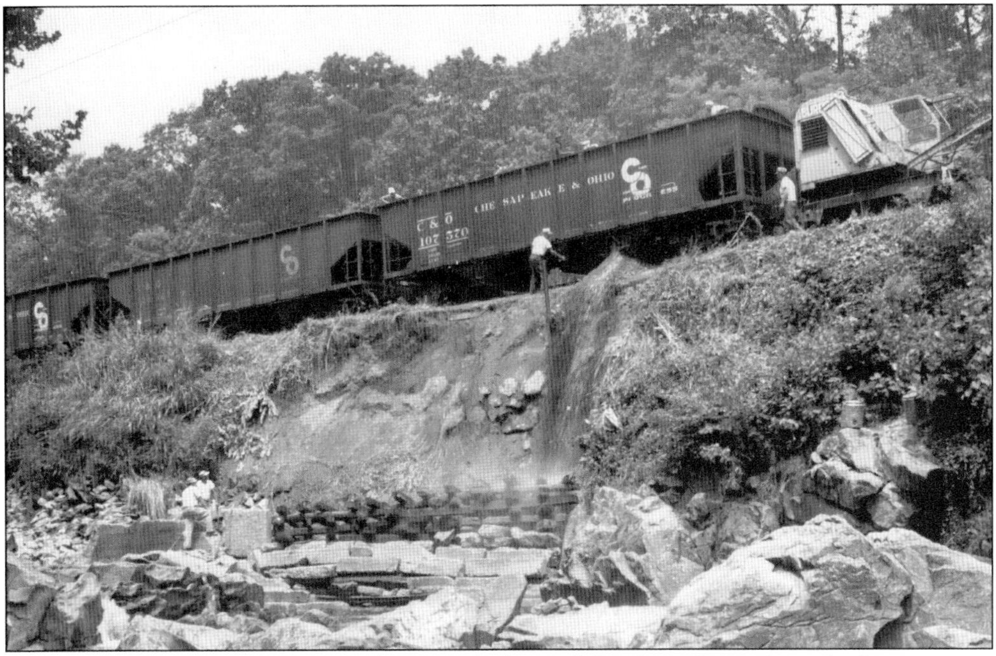

Later, wood tie cribbing has been placed at the base of the slope. Stone from the hopper car is being poured into the cribbing spaces. The Burro Crane has couplers at each end to allow it to move freight cars. This photograph was taken by Ames Williams on August 24, 1963. (Courtesy of the Alexandria Library, Special Collections.)

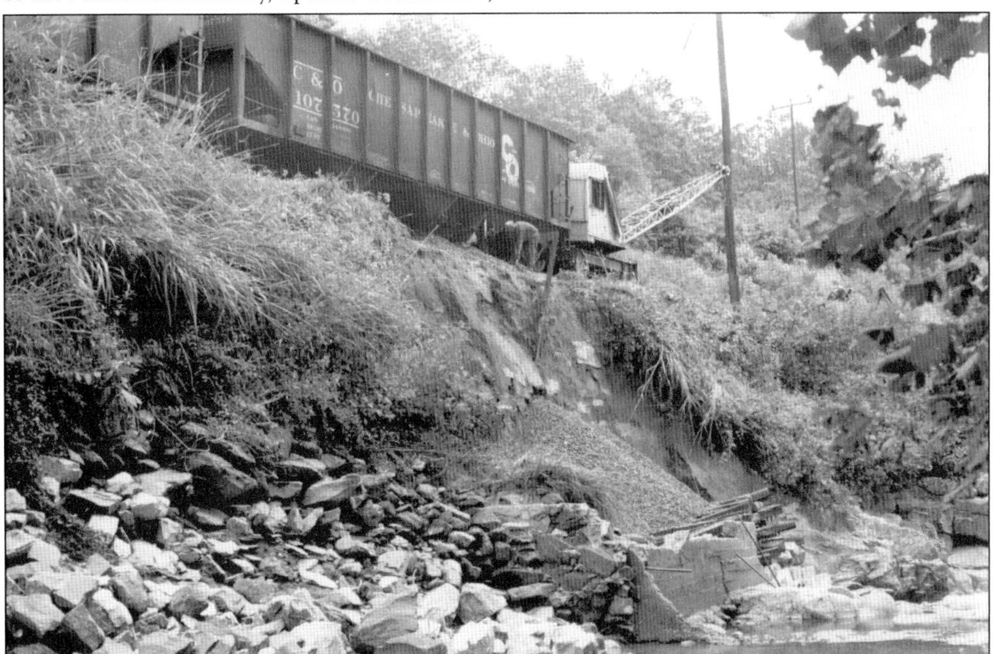

Another view shows the filling process on August 24, 1963. The train crew member may be closing the one hopper door so that the car can be moved to position the next hopper door. (Courtesy of the Alexandria Library, Special Collections.)

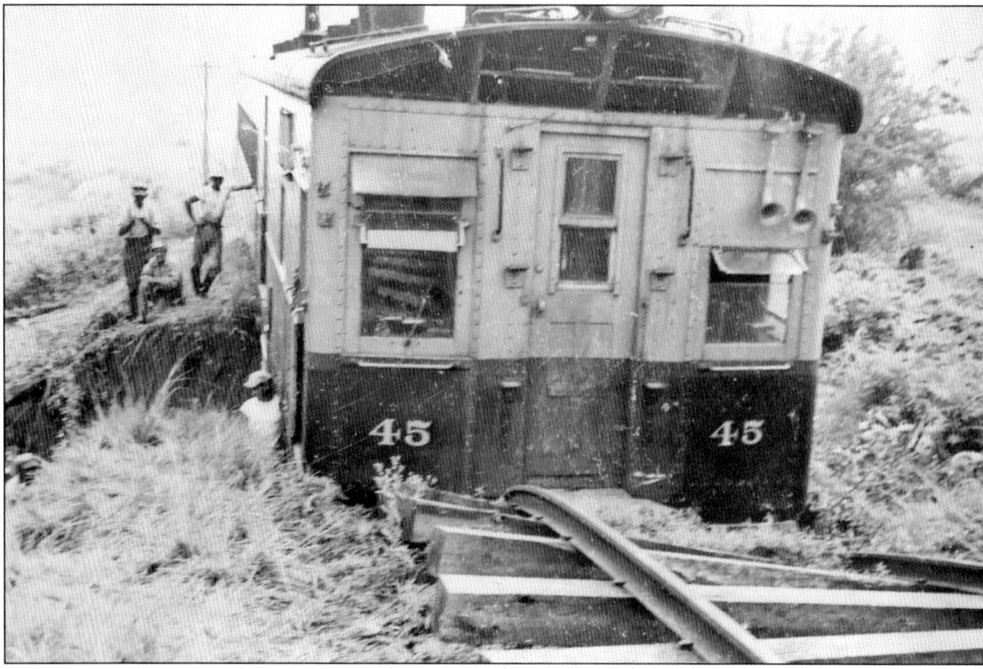

Engineer Dolph N. Cunningham and conductor Doug Lee were running train No. 3 westbound to tie down for the night at Leesburg in 1949 when they met train No. 8 in Sterling. No. 8's engineer, Foster Ormsby, told them that there was dirt on the track near the Lawson station, two miles east of Leesburg. Anticipating a washed out roadbed, engineer Cunningham came around the curve slowly, accounting for the minimal damage to the car. Herbert Cunningham took both photographs. (Above, courtesy of NOVA Parks; below, courtesy of the Fairfax County Public Library Photographic Archive.)

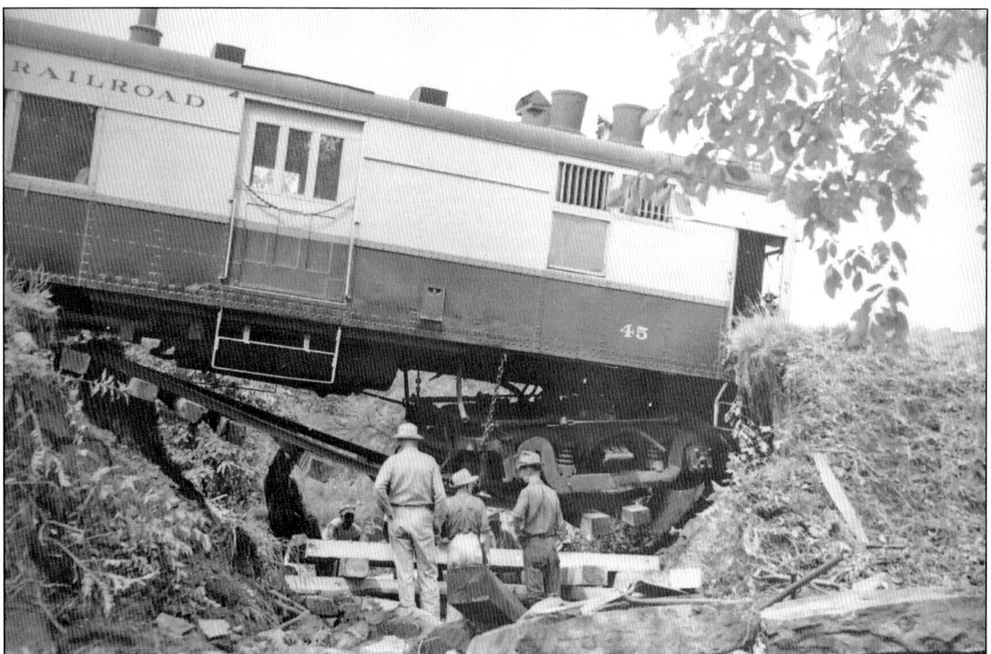

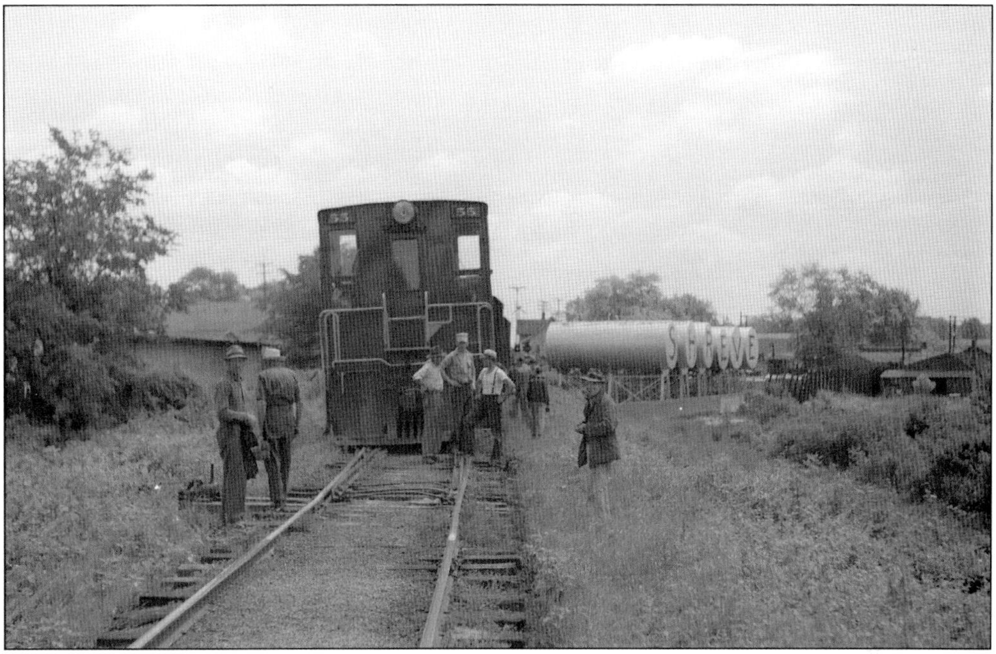

The Robert Shreve Fuel Company was south of the tracks and just west of the East Falls Church station. The company's office was at 6875 Lee Highway just north of the Falls Church City line. John F. Burns photographed the derailment and its repair activity on May 30, 1951.

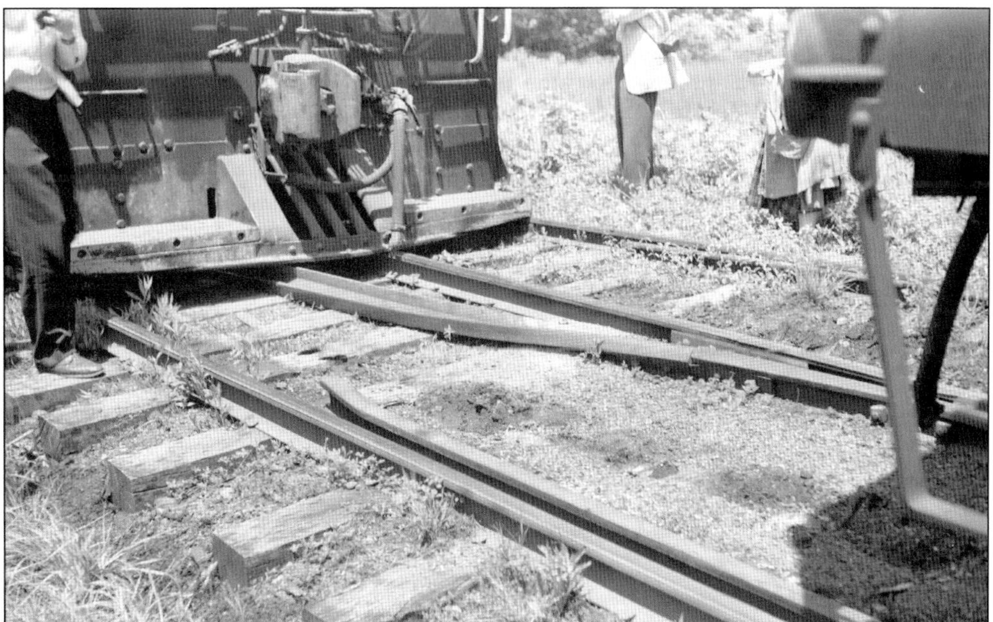

Locomotive No. 55 twisted the broken rail as it went on the ground. Here, Locomotive No. 55 has separated from the hopper car at right and is being put back on the tracks. The locomotive can move itself on the ground, it just needs careful guidance from track crews. John F. Burns captured the event on May 30, 1951.

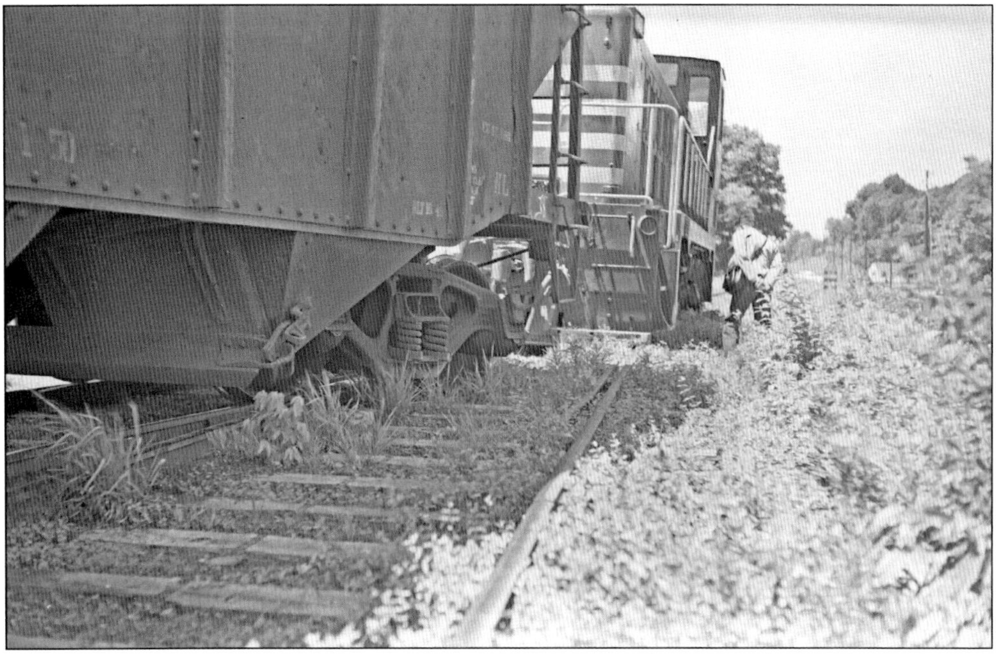

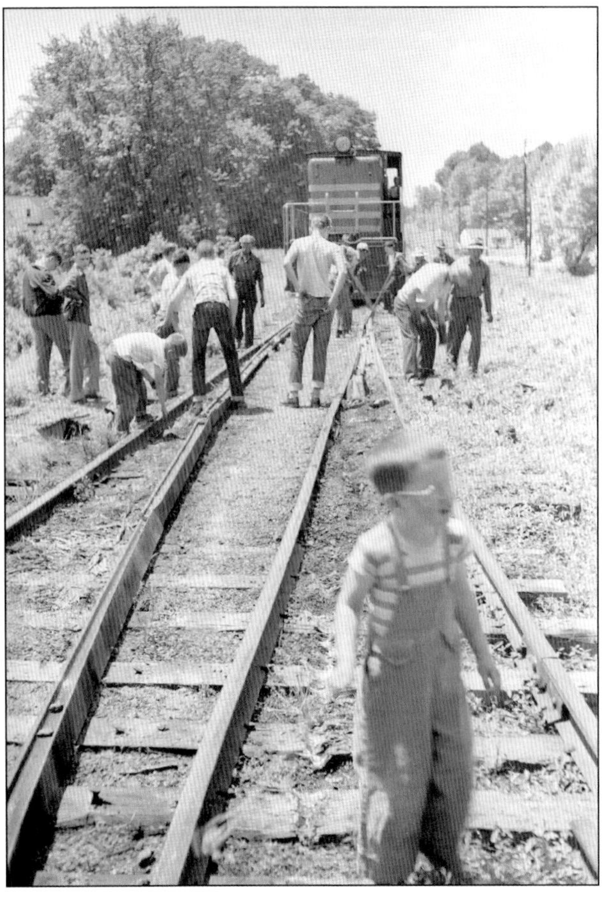

The west end of the hopper car, carrying stone, also went on the ground. Little Falls Street is at the rear. Car No. 45 is barely visible at the right shoulder of the railfan examining No. 55. (Photograph by John F. Burns.)

The track crew is working on the switch points to get them back in order. Meanwhile, grounded passengers of No. 45 are inspecting the broken rail. The photograph was taken by John F. Burns on May 30, 1951.

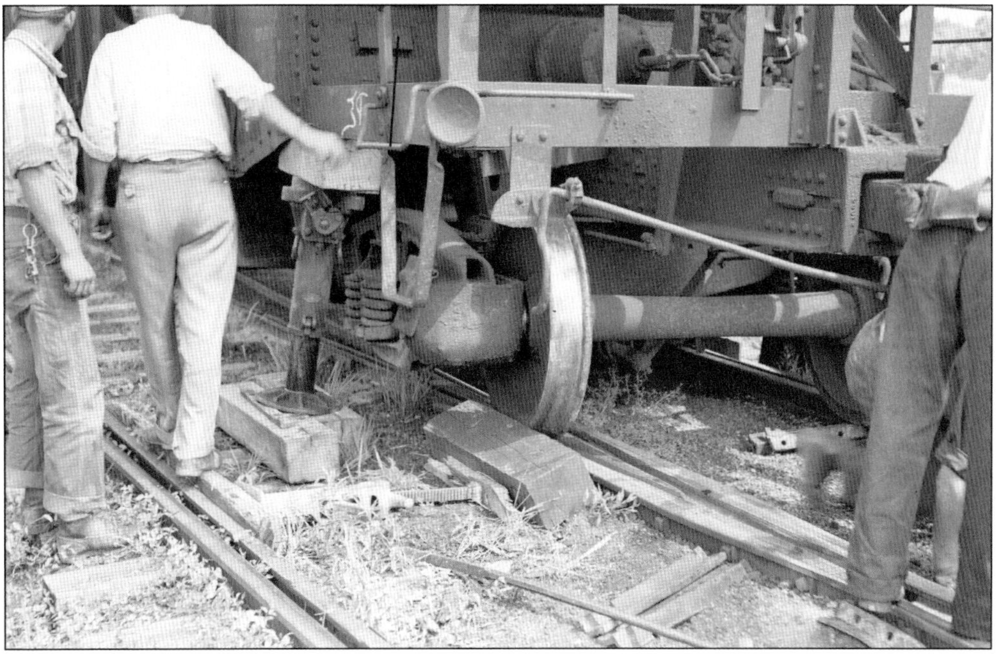

Joint bars abound in this picture. Several are on the ground at right to support the wheel as it is skidded over and up onto that rail. Another bar is under the large jack that is supporting the car end. A smaller track jack is on the ground, pushing the block of wood and the wheel back onto the rail. The photograph is by John F. Burns.

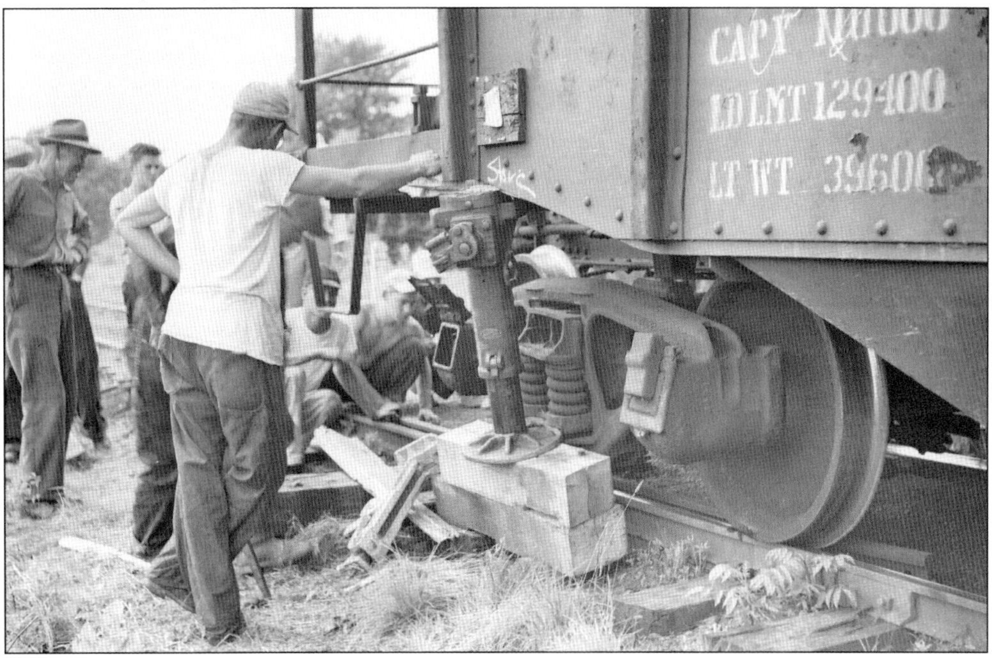

Viewing the hopper car from the other side, a second large jack is helping to lift the car up while the truck wheels are placed back on the rails. One track crew member was jacking up the car when the jack slipped. He said, "Enough to make a man swear when they come down like that. You'd think something would break." The photograph is by John F. Burns.

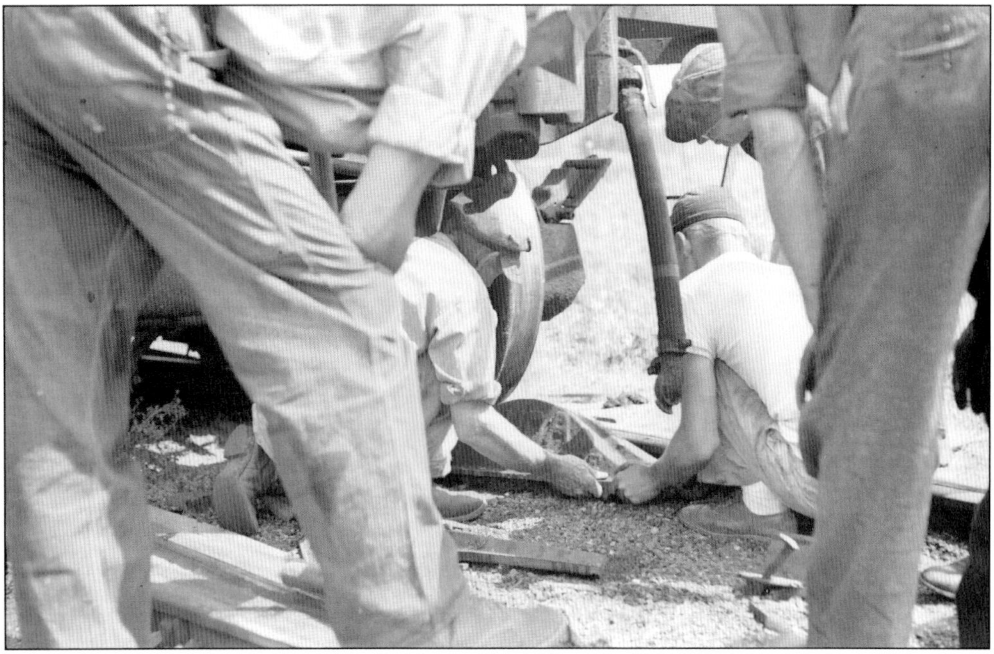

Two track crew members are positioning a Buda butterfly re-railer against the rail. In a few minutes, they will use rail spikes hammered into the ties to hold the re-railer in place, as seen in the next photograph. The photograph is by John F. Burns.

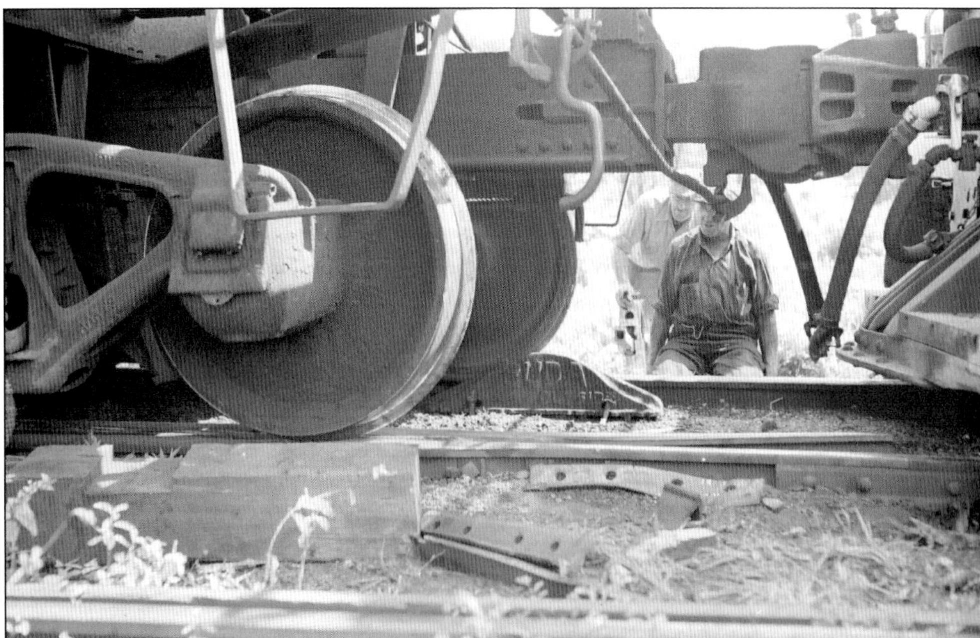

The locomotive was put back on the tracks earlier. Coupled to the hopper car, the locomotive is pulling it back onto the rails under the watchful eyes of the track crew. One track crew member is holding a track jack. The square hole in the end is where a bar is inserted to pump the jack up. The photograph is by John F. Burns.

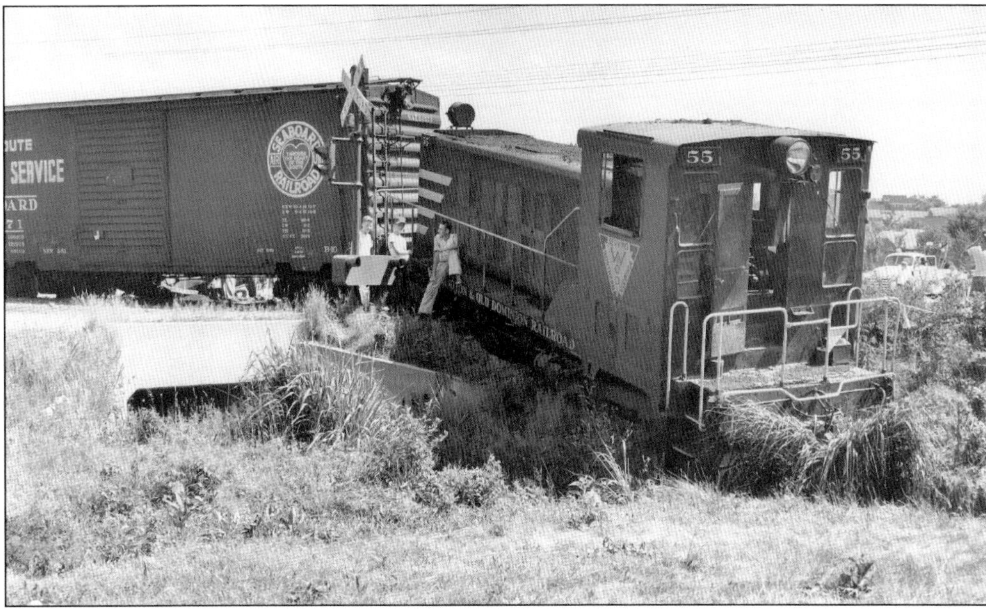

The impact between an asphalt truck and No. 55 on June 26, 1952, knocked the locomotive off the tracks. The impact drove the engine's crankshaft and generator out of alignment. The railroad broke three crank shafts before it had No. 55's diesel engine running again. Doug Lee recalled that asphalt from the truck's load went everywhere and slightly burned the engineer, W.H. Fox. (Courtesy of NOVA Parks.)

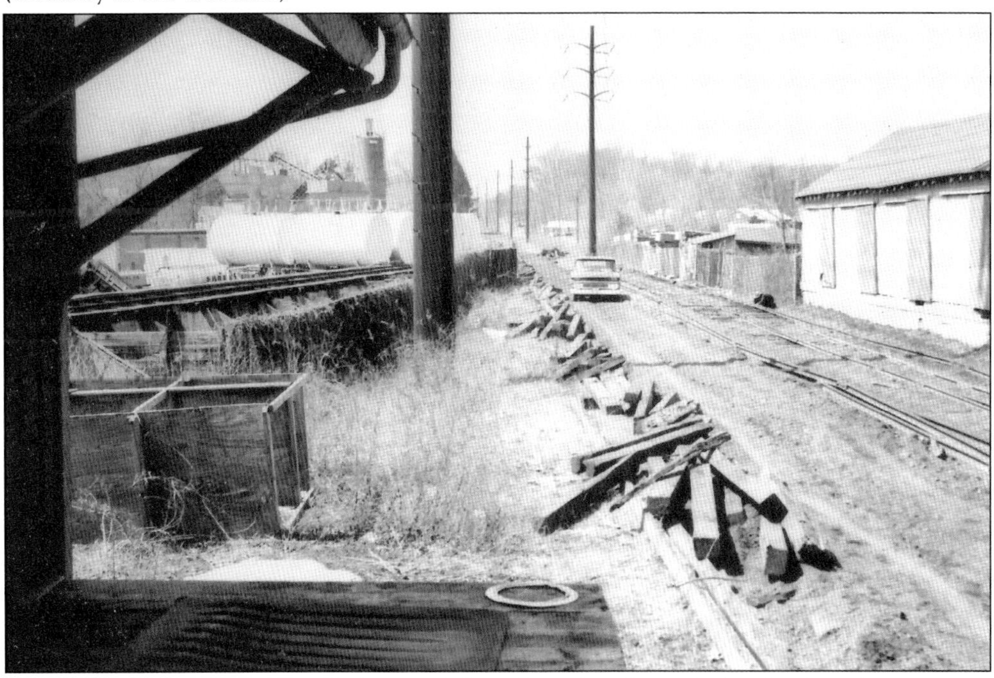

The ties and rails have been pulled up and aligned, ready to be picked up by the salvage crew in this view looking west from the platform of the East Falls Church station. John F. Burns took his last pictures of the railroad on April 11, 1969, in East Falls Church. He rode the trolleys to Great Falls, the interurbans to Bluemont, and the gas-electrics to Purcellville.

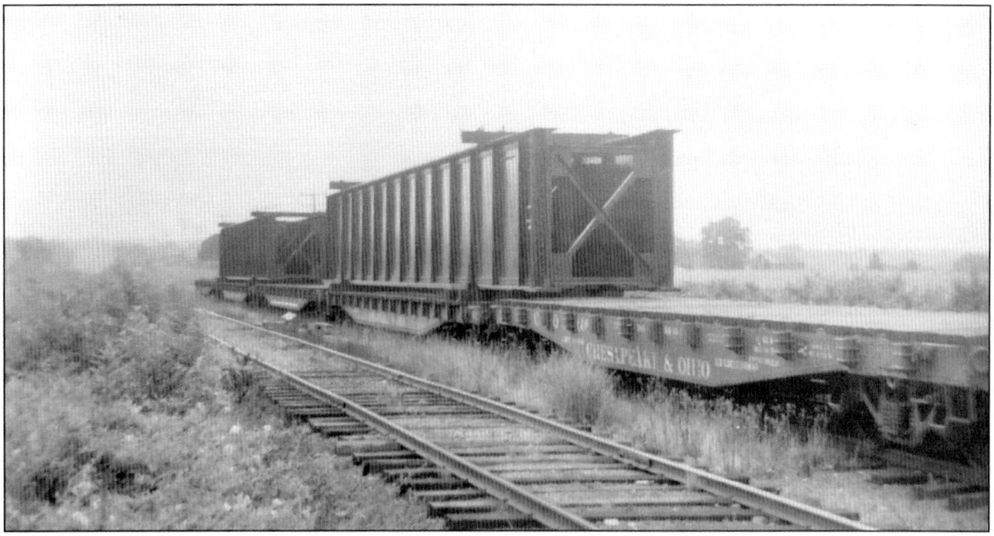

Photographed by W. Burton Barber in the spring of 1958, the two deck girder spans for the replacement Broad Run bridge are resting on flatcars. Five cars were necessary to carry the two 70-foot-long girders so that they could overlap the ends of the flatcars. The cars are parked on a siding west of today's Route 28. (Courtesy of W. Burton Barber.)

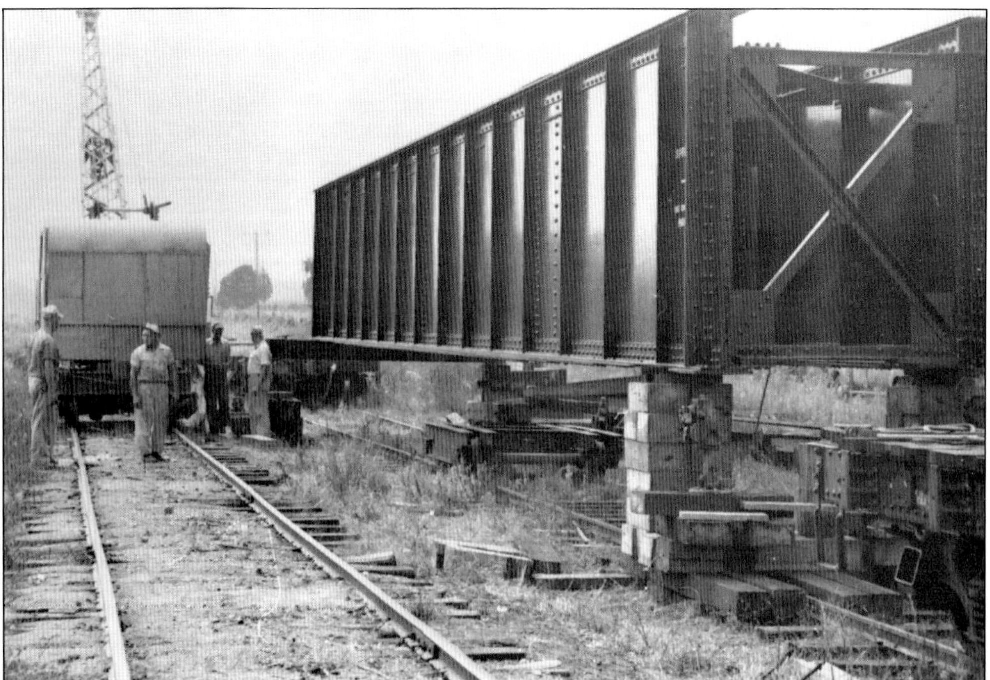

The bridge span was placed on blocks so that the flatcar could be removed and the dolly placed underneath it. The crew will shortly lower the girder onto the dolly, the base of a Burro crane. The bridge crew replaced the bridge in two weekends. (Courtesy of W. Burton Barber.)

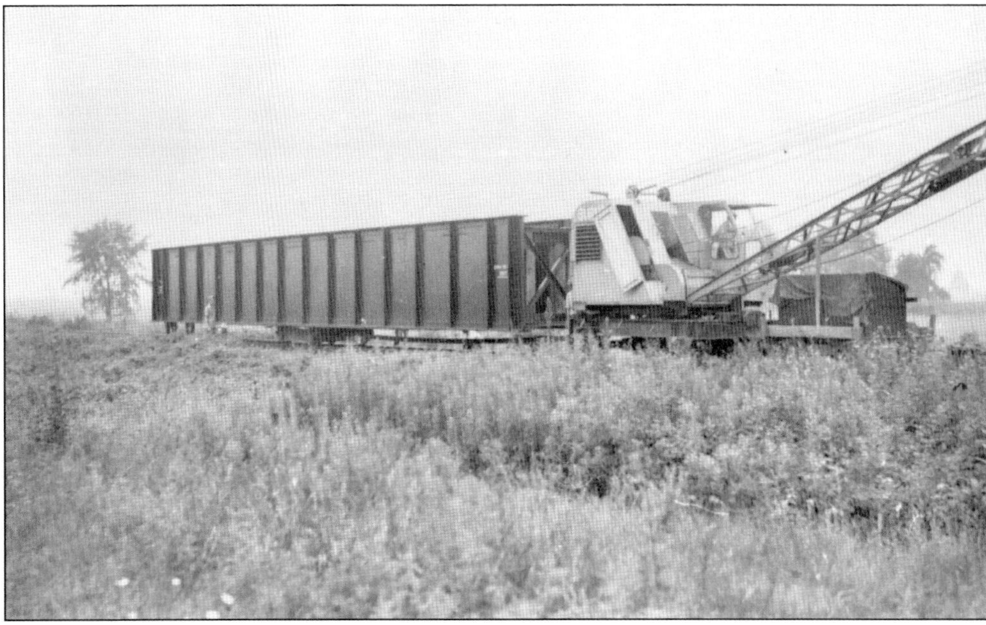

With the girder on the dolly, the Burro crane is pulling it down to the bridge. Bridge gang members on all sides are checking to make sure everything goes smoothly. W. Burton Barber remarked that "when you didn't know how to do something, ask a mountain man." The five-man bridge crew supervised by Ike Isaac had four mountain men. (Courtesy of W. Burton Barber.)

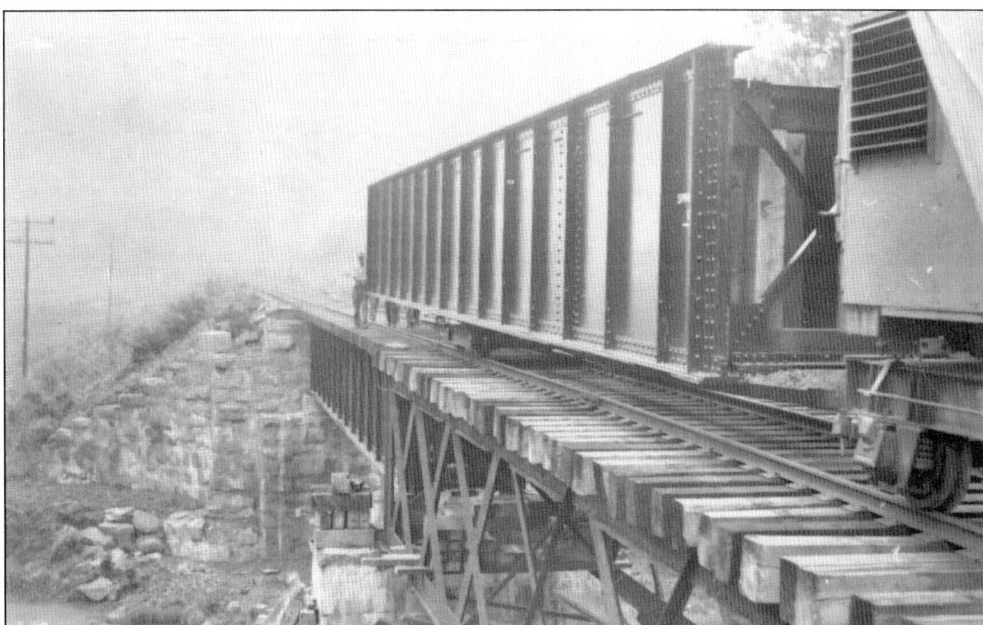

Here the crane is pulling the second span into place. The rails on both spans were kept serviceable so that trains could keep running. W. Burton Barber let the freight train pass Saturday morning before putting the bridge crew to work. (Courtesy of W. Burton Barber.)

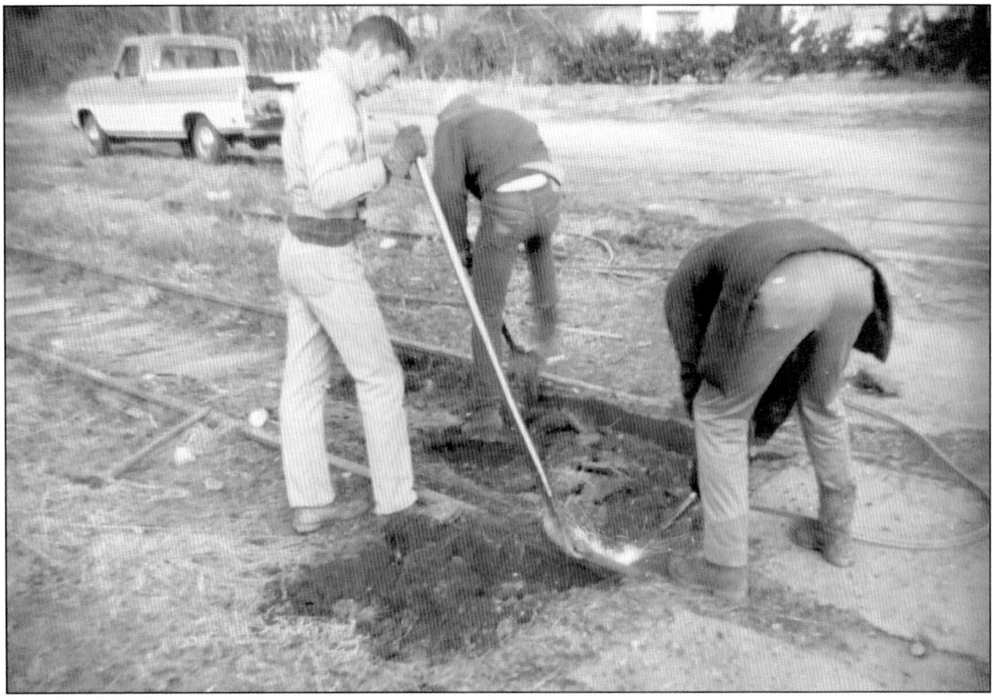

The salvage crew is cutting the rail off at the side of the road where it exits the pavement. There were 108 grade crossings on the line from Alexandria to Purcellville that the salvage crew had to cut. Henry H. Douglas photographed the activity on February 17, 1969, at Grove Avenue in West Falls Church. (Courtesy of the Fairfax County Public Library Photographic Archive.)

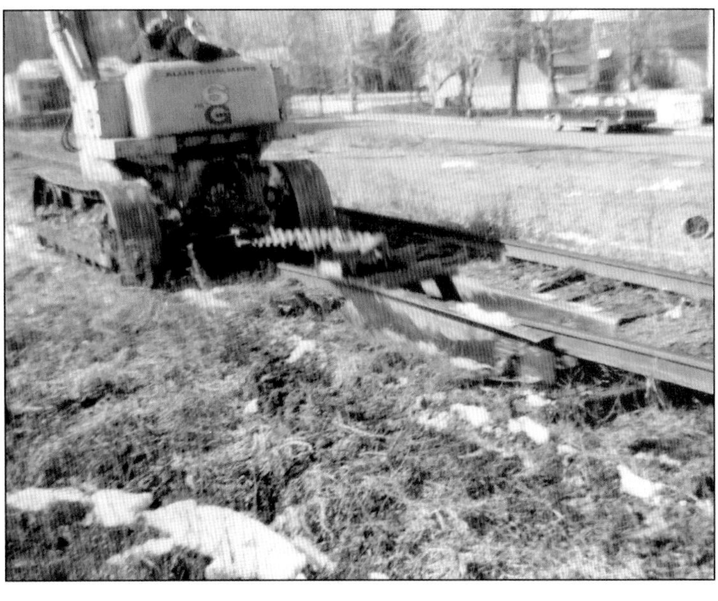

After the rails were cut at grade crossings, the rails had to be separated from the ties. The tractor is pushing a sled under the rails to force the rails from the ties. Henry H. Douglas captured the action in Falls Church on March 7, 1969. (Courtesy of the Fairfax County Public Library Photographic Archive.)

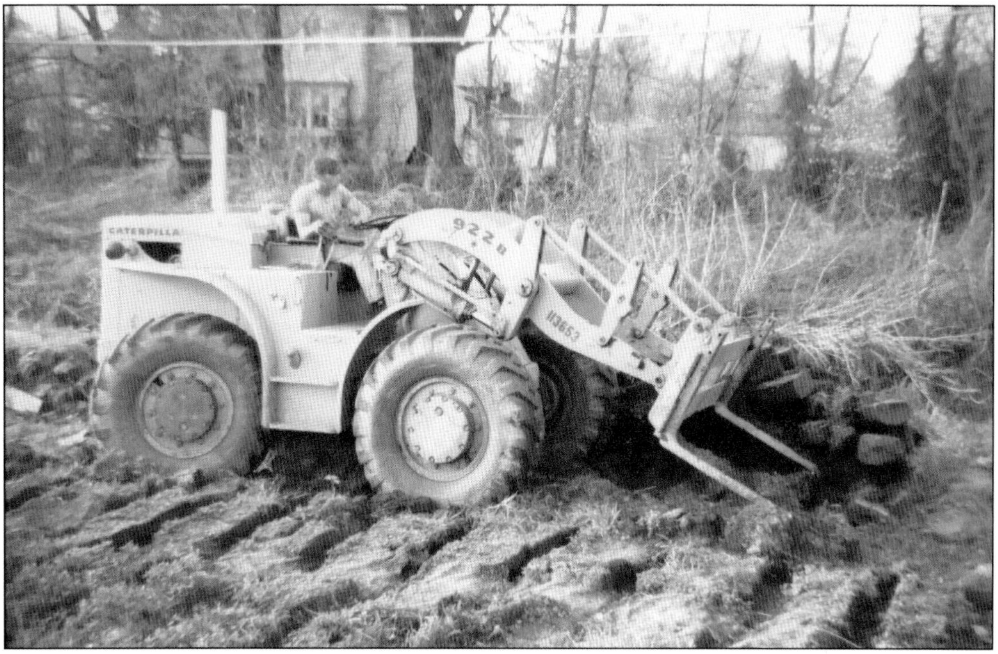

Once the rails have been pulled from the ties, the ties must be removed from the ground. This is a job for a fork truck; the tines are angled down into the earth below the bottoms of the ties, and then the truck is driven forward. This photograph was taken by Henry H. Douglas on April 15, 1969, in Falls Church. (Courtesy of the Fairfax County Public Library Photographic Archive.)

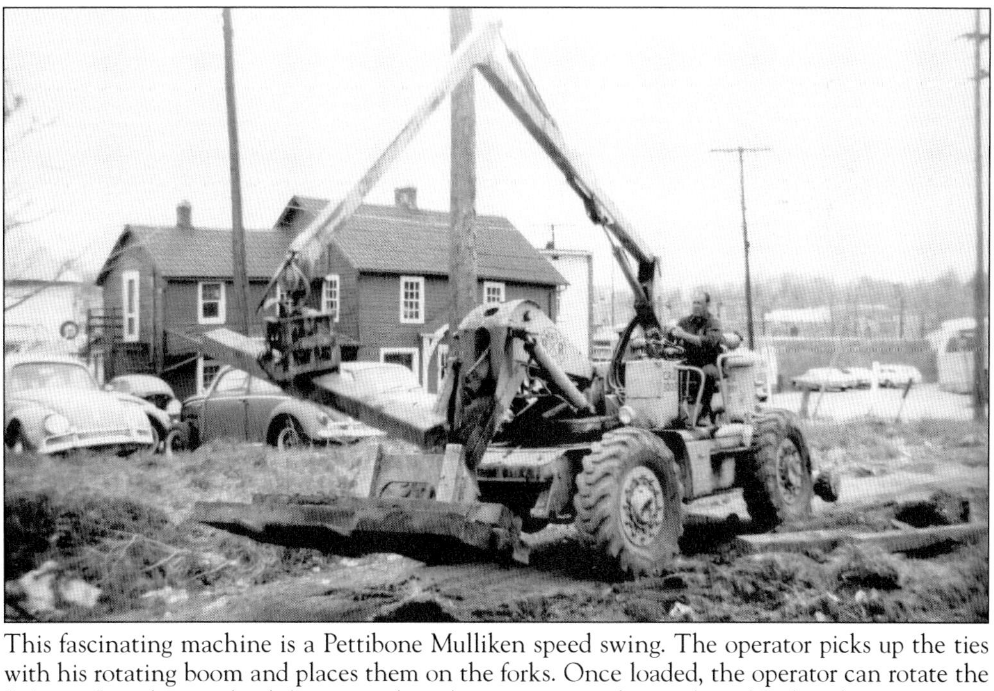

This fascinating machine is a Pettibone Mulliken speed swing. The operator picks up the ties with his rotating boom and places them on the forks. Once loaded, the operator can rotate the forks to the side to unload the ties without having to turn the truck itself. This photograph was taken by Henry H. Douglas on April 15, 1969, in Falls Church. (Courtesy of the Fairfax County Public Library Photographic Archive.)

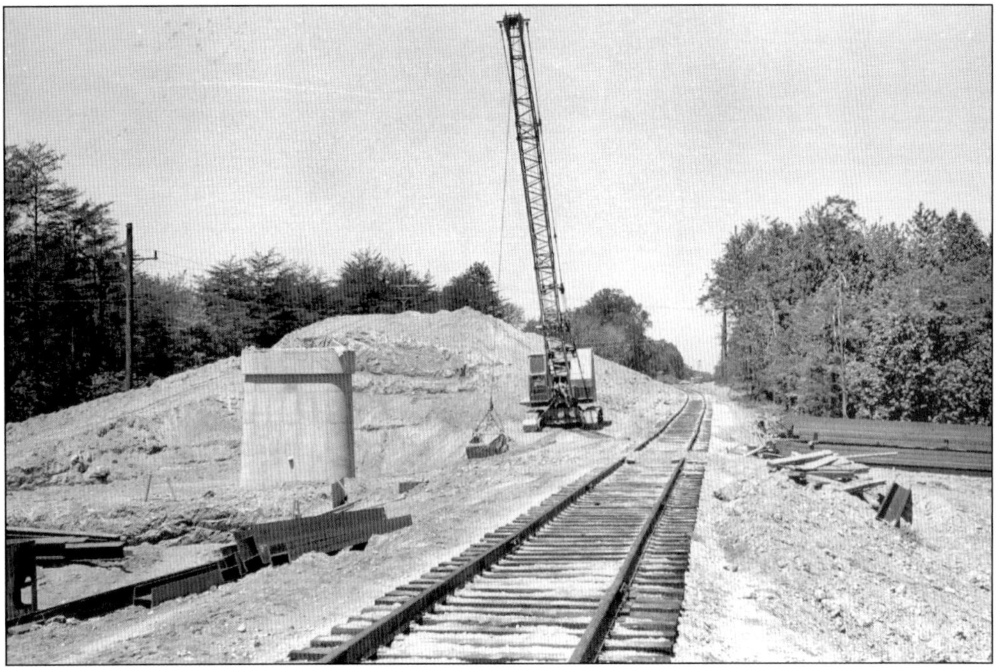

In this scene, the railroad has built a shoo-fly track to bypass the construction area. The pier will become the central pier of the railroad's bridge over the future Interstate 495/Washington Beltway. The crane is pulling a dragline bucket to excavate the soil. Ames Williams took this photograph around October 1961. (Courtesy of the Alexandria Library, Special Collections.)

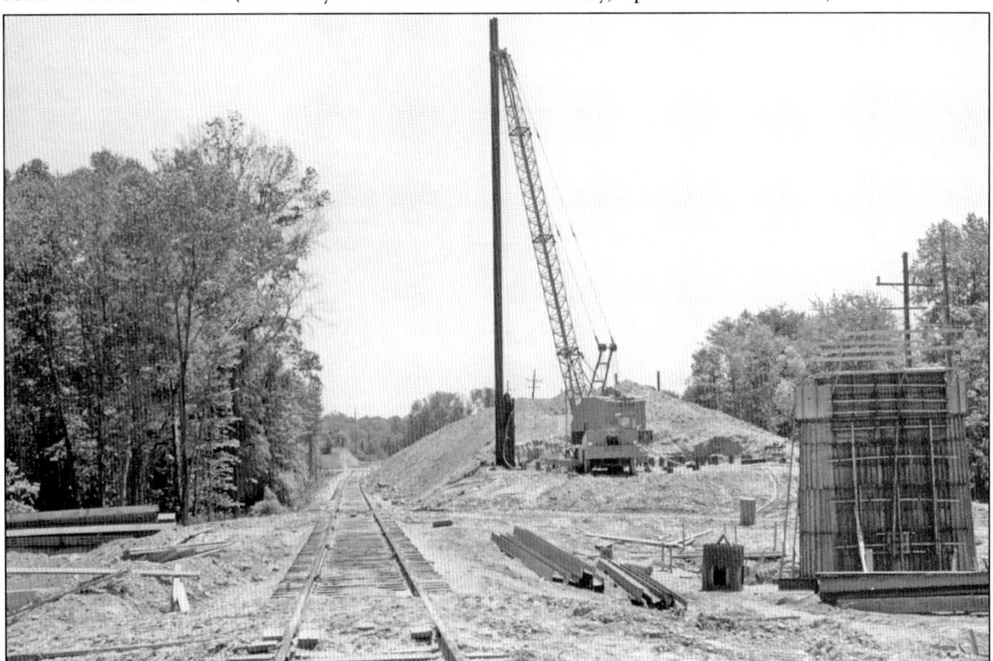

Looking to the east, the crane, now equipped with a pile driver, is preparing the piers for the future bridge over Interstate 495. The central pier is right in this photograph, taken by Ames Williams around October 1961. (Courtesy of the Alexandria Library, Special Collections.)

Eight

W&OD Railroad Regional Trail

Long before the W&OD Railroad abandonment was finally approved by the Interstate Commerce Commission, the railroad ownership negotiated to sell pieces of the rail line to others. The Virginia Department of Highways and Transportation, now Virginia Department of Transportation (VDOT), coveted the rail spur that ran from Bluemont Junction to Rosslyn as a route for a new highway—Interstate 66. Virginia Electric and Power Company (VEPCO), now Dominion Virginia Power, wanted ownership of the rest of the right of way to protect its electric transmission lines and to add new ones.

Others saw potential in the corridor for different uses. Some wanted it to become a high-speed bus route for commuters, while others saw its greatest use as a multi-jurisdictional trail. In fact, once the tracks were gone, people began using the property to hike and bicycle.

By 1978, the Northern Virginia Regional Park Authority negotiated to purchase the W&OD Railroad property from VEPCO and began building a multiuse trail along the 45-mile-long corridor. A 32-mile separate horse trail was also built. By 1988, the trail was complete from the Alexandria city line to the town of Purcellville in western Loudoun County.

Originally, the W&OD Trail was envisioned as a place for exercise and recreation. But just as the W&OD Railroad connected communities and towns, the trail today does the same for people walking and cycling. Local residents use the trail to travel to work and as a route to one of the many schools, shopping areas, and community centers next to the W&OD, taking many cars off the congested roads of Northern Virginia.

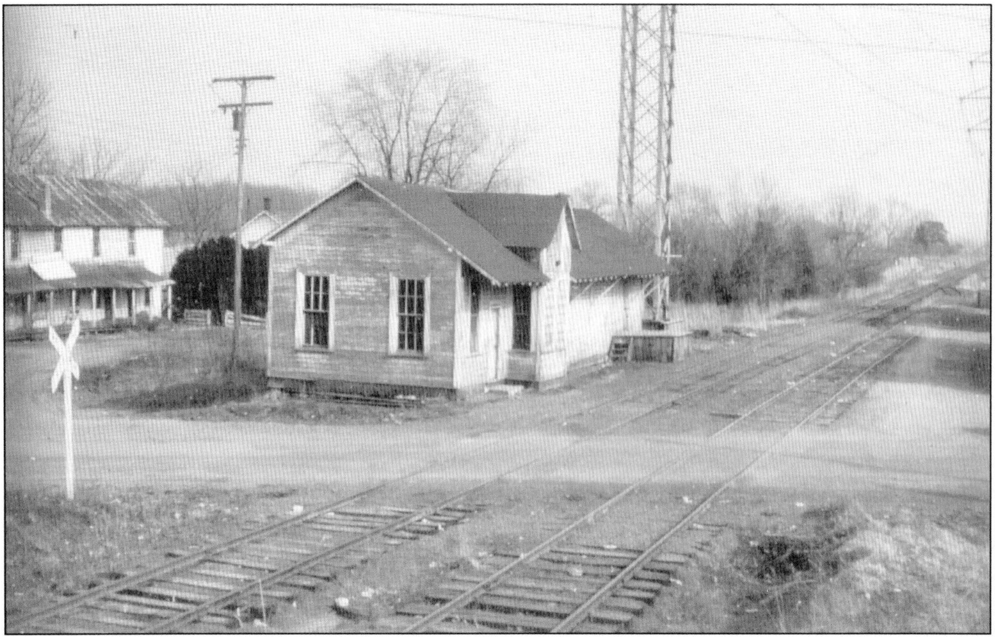

For many years, VEPCO held easements along the W&OD Railroad for its electric transmission and distribution lines, as VEPCO found the rail right of way to be an easy path for moving power through Northern Virginia. The company's purchase of the W&OD in 1968 kept the main line intact and led to its use as a trail 10 years later. The Ashburn station was photographed in 1966 by Paul Dolkos. (Courtesy of NOVA Parks.)

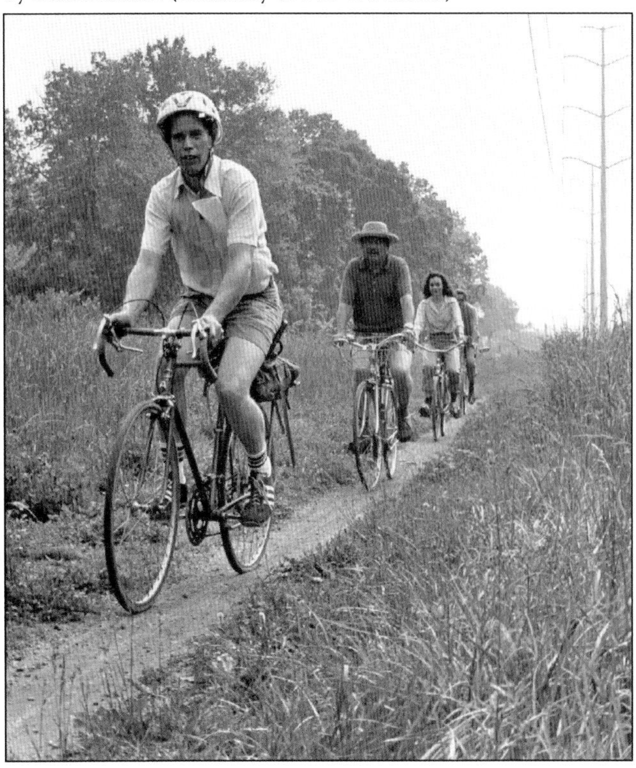

Before being turned over to the new owners, the rail line was stripped of anything salvageable: rails, ties, and even ballast. This left a dirt and sometimes gravel path where the tracks formerly ran. Local residents immediately began using the empty right of way for cycling and hiking and called for the creation of a park with an improved trail on the W&OD right of way. (Courtesy of NOVA Parks.)

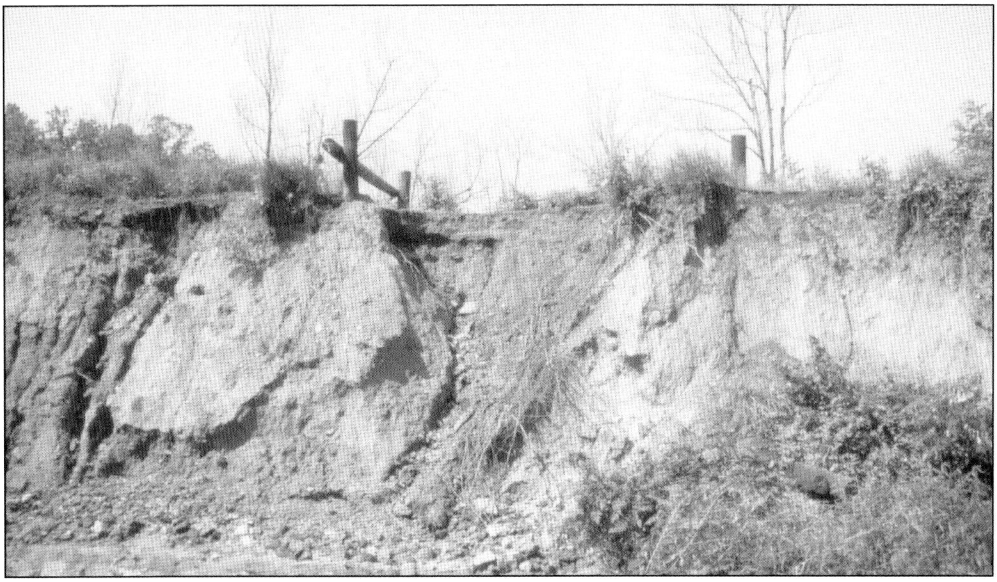

In 1977, after a long negotiation, VEPCO sold the property to the Northern Virginia Regional Park Authority (now known as NOVA Parks), a park agency with jurisdiction all along the W&OD. One of the obstacles to building a formal trail was the deterioration that had occurred both before and after the abandonment. Numerous cuts and fills along the roadbed had eroded and in some cases collapsed. (Courtesy of NOVA Parks.)

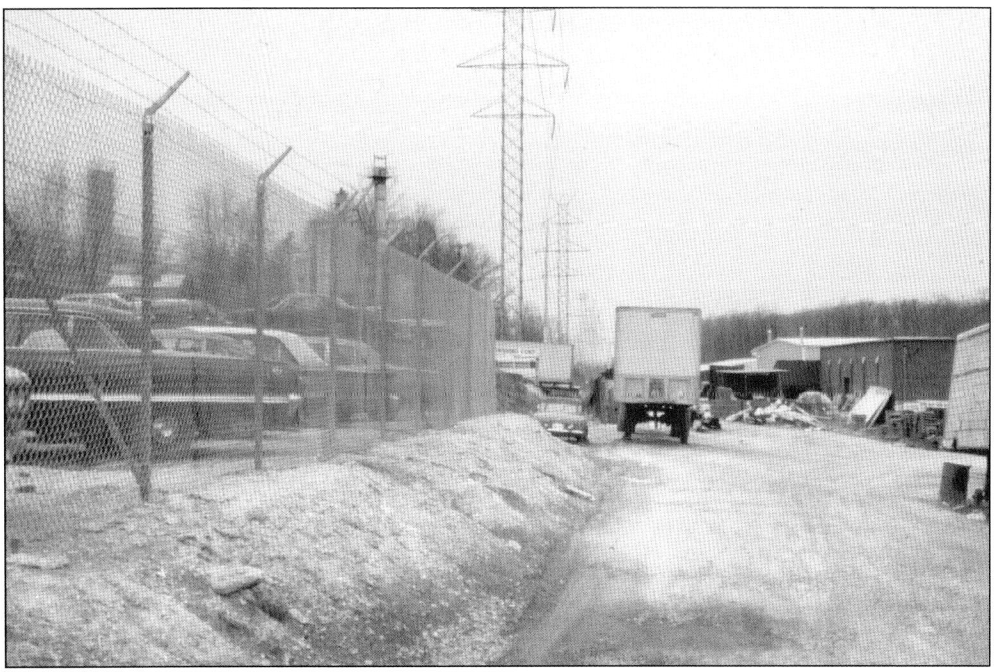

Another impediment to building a trail was that a number of businesses had encroached on the old trackbed with parking lots, storage lots, and even buildings. Some had done so under license from VEPCO, while others took over without authorization. NOVA Parks allowed some to stay alongside the trail as a way to benefit business while providing a revenue stream for the new park. (Courtesy of NOVA Parks.)

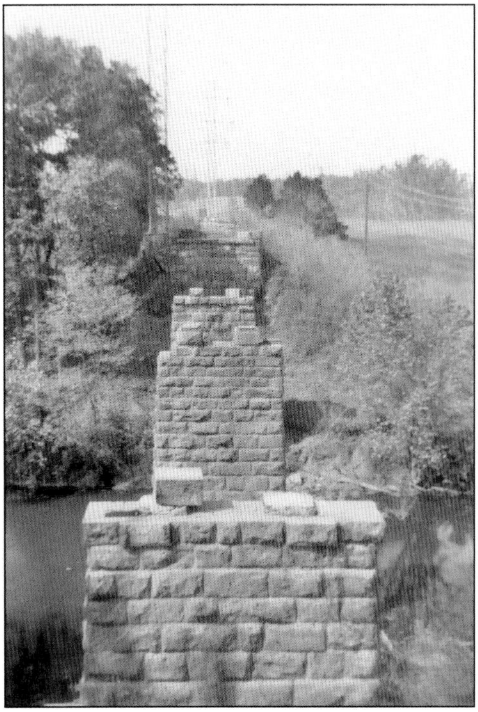

The owners of the W&OD Railroad also looked to the bridges for materials they could sell for salvage. Rails, ties, and structural steel were stripped from the bridges and sold. Most of the stone piers and abutments that were left, and which dated to before the Civil War, were in good shape and mostly just needed repointing with mortar. Larry Crosen photographed the piers at Goose Creek after 1969. (Courtesy of NOVA Parks.)

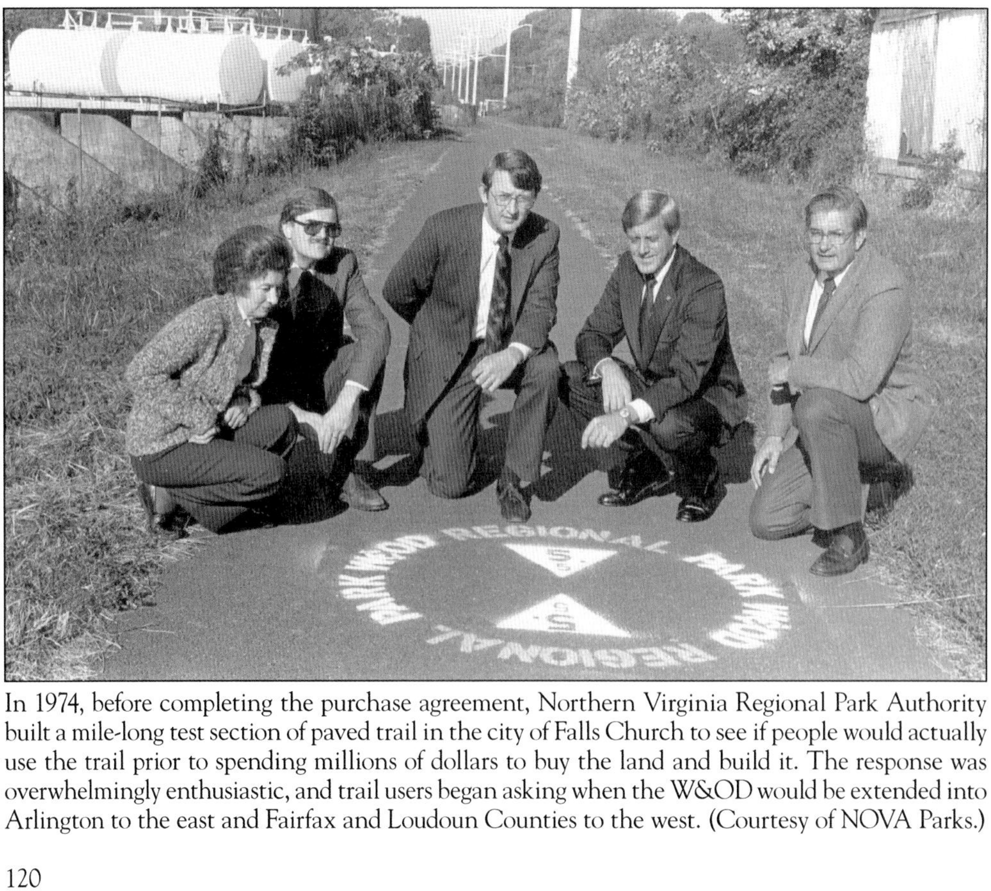

In 1974, before completing the purchase agreement, Northern Virginia Regional Park Authority built a mile-long test section of paved trail in the city of Falls Church to see if people would actually use the trail prior to spending millions of dollars to buy the land and build it. The response was overwhelmingly enthusiastic, and trail users began asking when the W&OD would be extended into Arlington to the east and Fairfax and Loudoun Counties to the west. (Courtesy of NOVA Parks.)

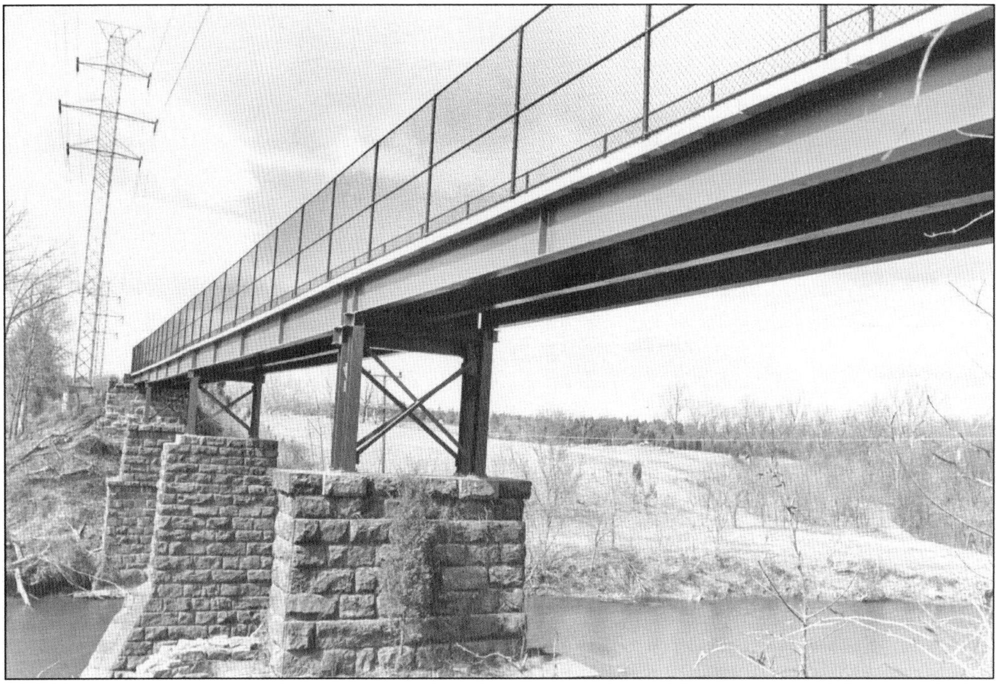

Before new sections of trail could be built, new bridges had to be placed to cross the creeks and roads. The highway department helped by building bridges over Interstate 495 (the Washington Beltway), Interstate 66, and the Clarks Gap/Route 7 Bypass in western Loudoun County. Northern Virginia Regional Park Authority had to build 13 stream bridges and two road overpasses (Broad Street in Falls Church and the Route 7 Bypass on the west side of Leesburg) in order to complete the W&OD Trail construction. (Both, courtesy of NOVA Parks.)

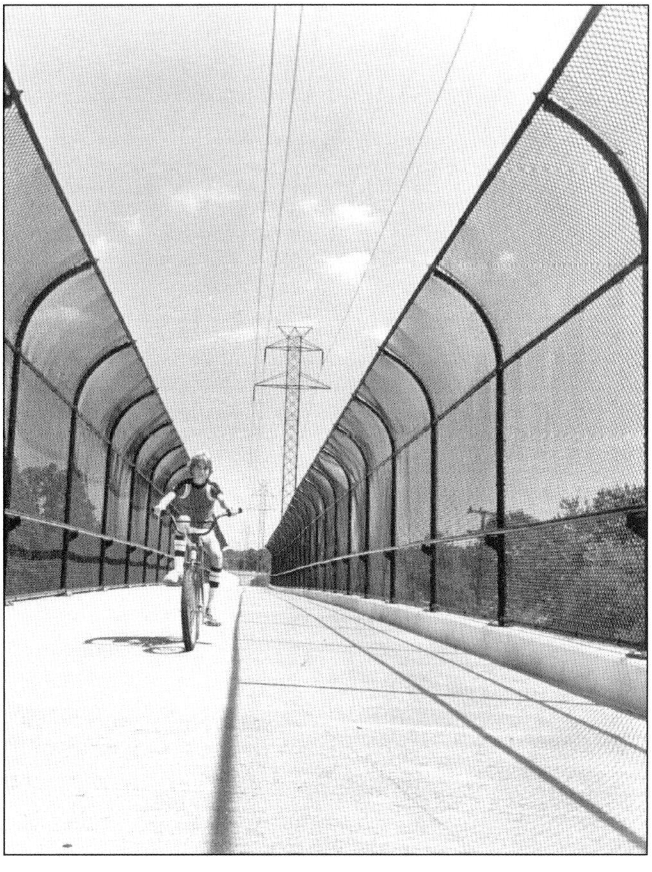

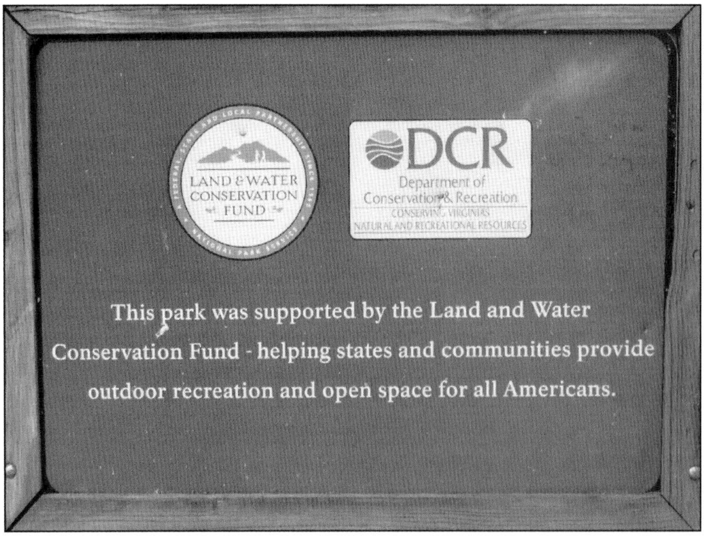

Local money was not enough to both buy the W&OD and develop it as a trail, a combined cost of more than $14 million. Much of the funding came through grants from the Land and Water Conservation Fund, a federal source of recreation and conservation dollars. The grants also provided protection from outside projects that could damage the historic or recreational integrity of the W&OD. (Courtesy of NOVA Parks.)

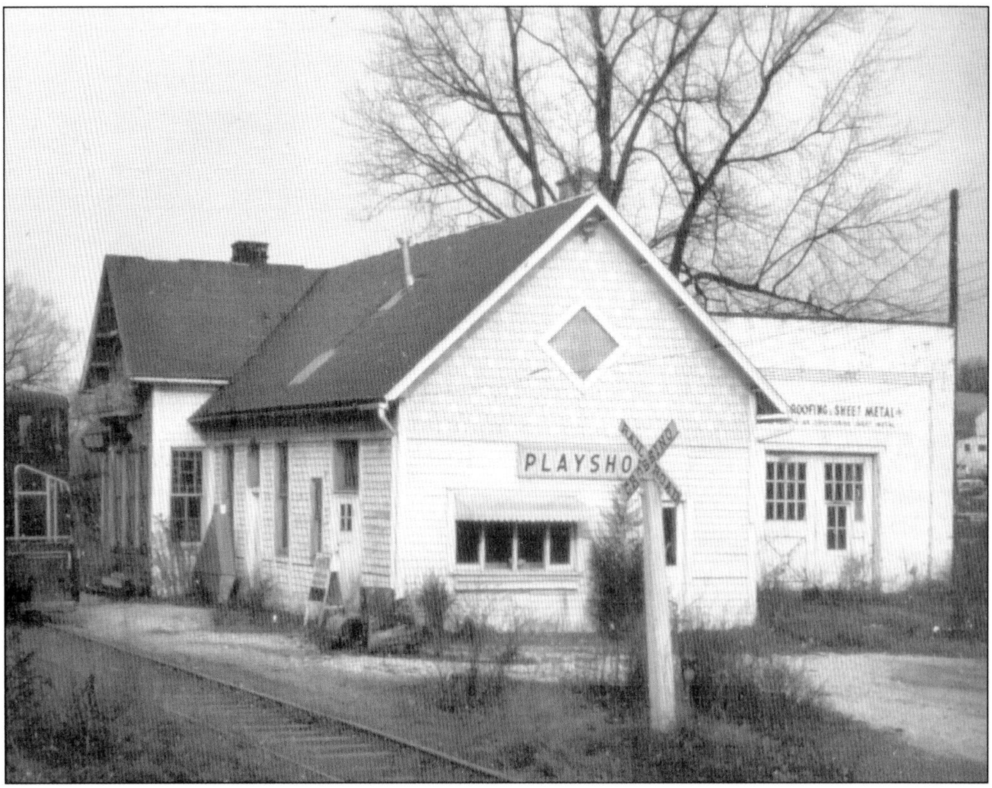

Most of the remaining W&OD stations along the trail were in disrepair and continued to deteriorate as time went on. VEPCO had no need for the structures, and unless another entity agreed to maintain them for public use, they were either demolished or allowed to be moved offsite. The Leesburg passenger station, photographed by Paul Dolkos in 1966, was destroyed. The Vienna, Sunset Hills, Herndon, and Purcellville stations were saved and remain today. The Hamilton station is privately owned. (Courtesy of NOVA Parks.)

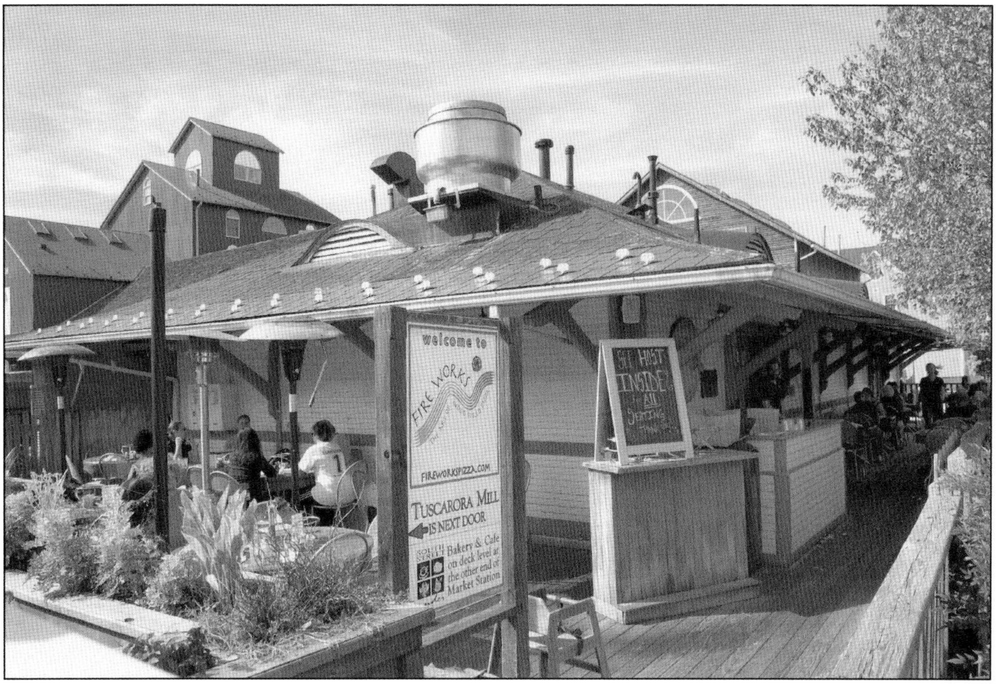

The Leesburg freight depot was moved to become part of the Market Station complex. Other stations finding alternative uses included the two Round Hill stations and the Round Hill substation as homes, the Herndon station housing the town museum, and the Purcellville station as a community meeting space. The Vienna station was leased by the Northern Virginia Model Railroaders, who repaired and renovated the building, turning the freight section into a scale model of a North Carolina railroad. (Both, courtesy of NOVA Parks.)

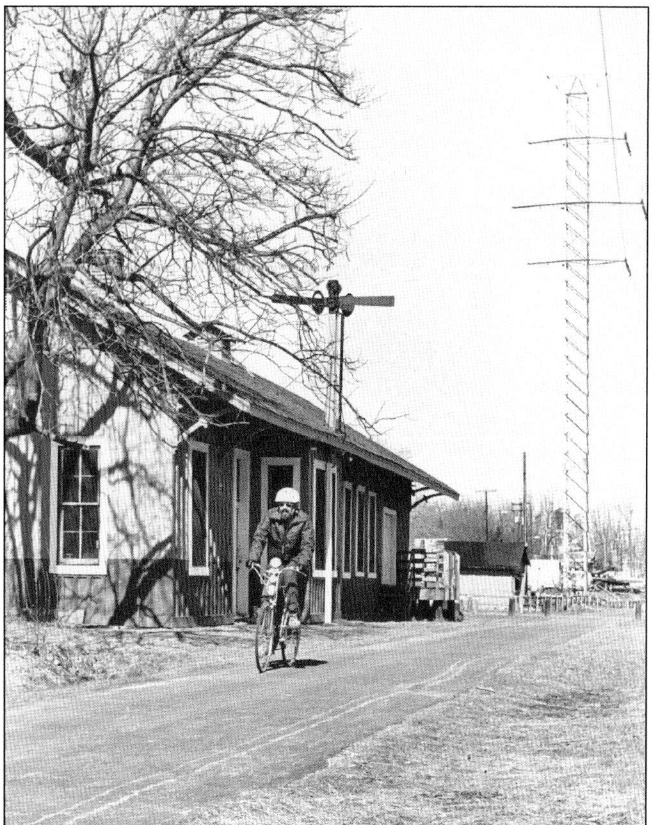

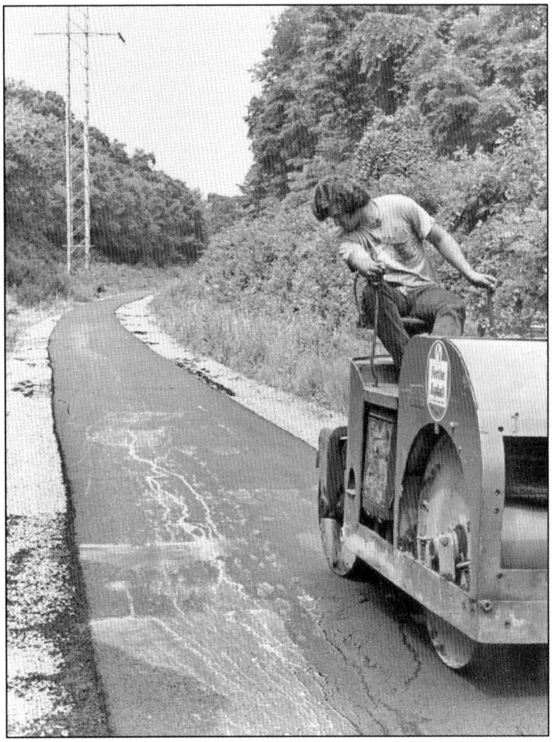

While some called for the new trail to maintain a natural surface, park officials knew that cyclists needed a hard surface for easier and safer riding. An asphalt surface was set as the standard for the multiuse trail to be built primarily on the old roadbed, taking advantage of its flat and relatively straight alignment. Trail users could not wait for the path to be paved and often rode as the work was ongoing. (Both, courtesy of NOVA Parks.)

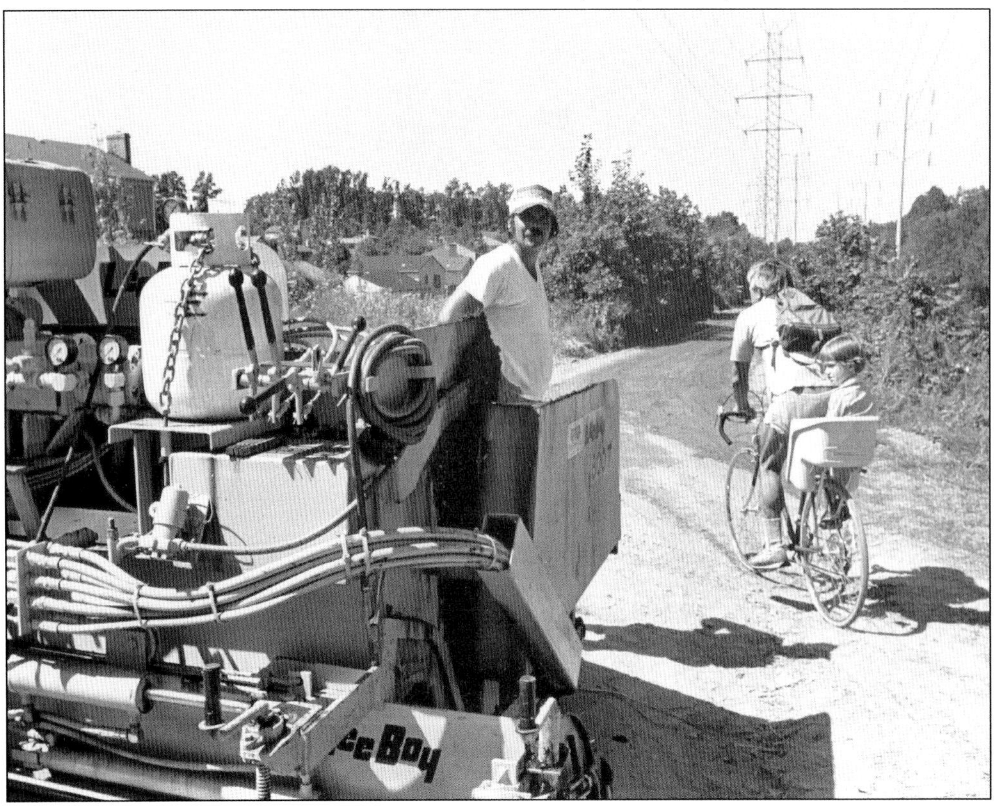

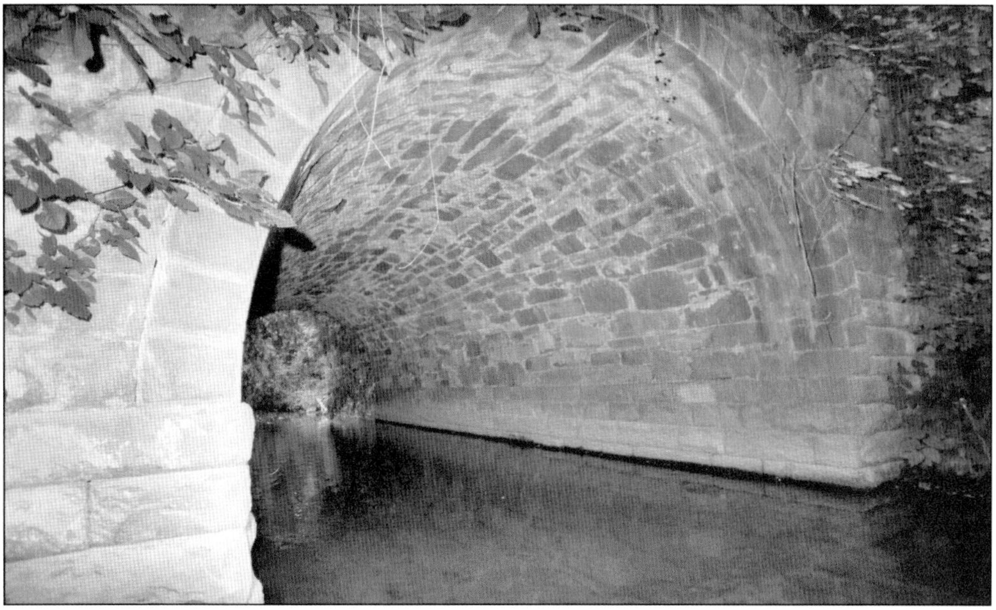

During construction of a trail bridge over the new Fairfax County Parkway, engineers proposed altering the nearby pre–Civil War stone arch carrying Sugarland Run under the old roadbed. Local historians objected, citing the importance of the original railroad structure, and after a study of the railroad history and remaining features, the W&OD Trail was determined to be eligible for the National Register of Historic Places. This protected the original features of the railroad from any project receiving federal funding.

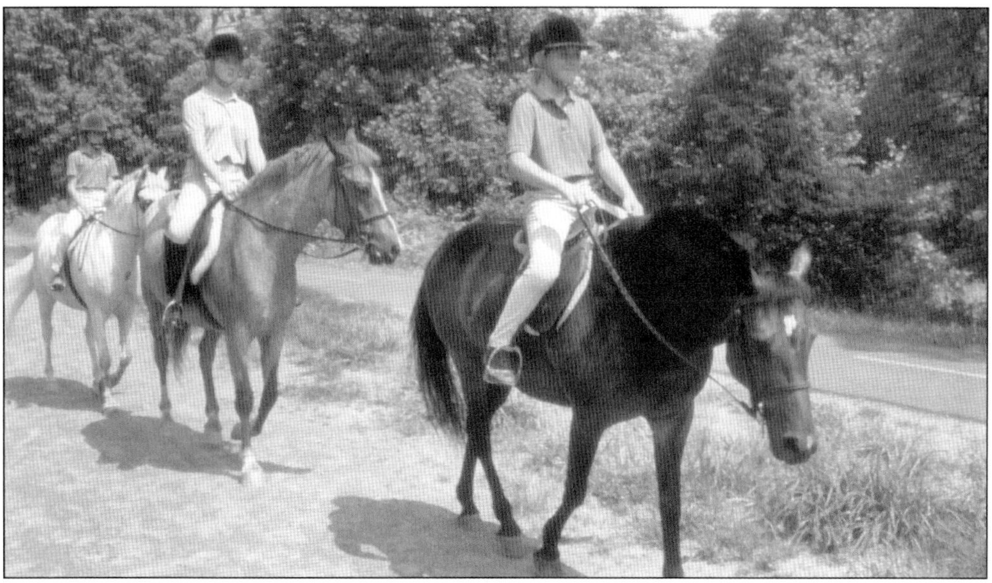

Horseback riders became concerned about sharing a trail with bicycles. Northern Virginia Regional Park Authority then planned a separate horse trail and asked the equestrian community to help choose surface standards. During one memorable meeting held to choose a bridge surface, a horse owner pulled out a sack of severed horse legs borrowed from a veterinary teacher and proceeded to drag the hooves with different horseshoes across the concrete samples until she found one with satisfactory traction. (Courtesy of NOVA Parks.)

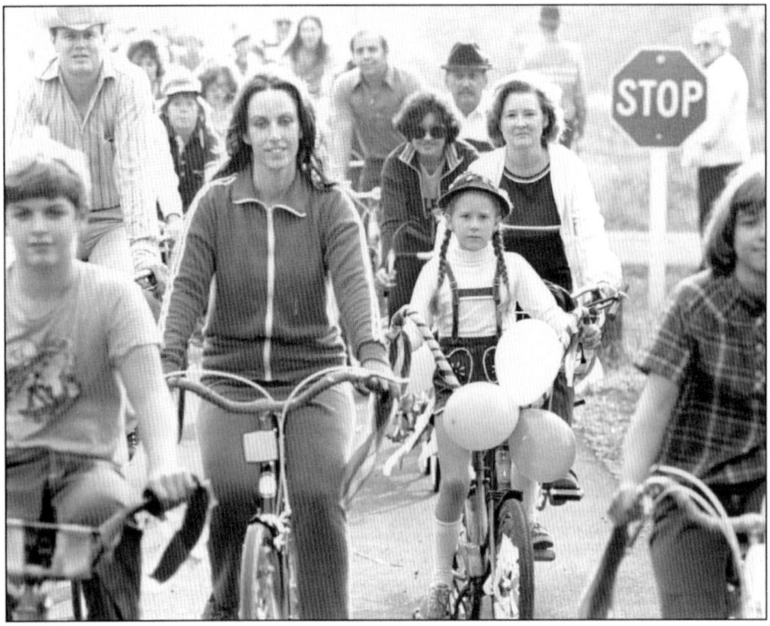

Once the first section of trail was built and for each section afterwards, Northern Virginia Regional Park Authority held a dedication to celebrate and let people know that the trail was open. At this dedication in Vienna, hundreds of people turned out for clowns, pony rides, speeches, and at the end, a group ride on the trail. (Courtesy of NOVA Parks.)

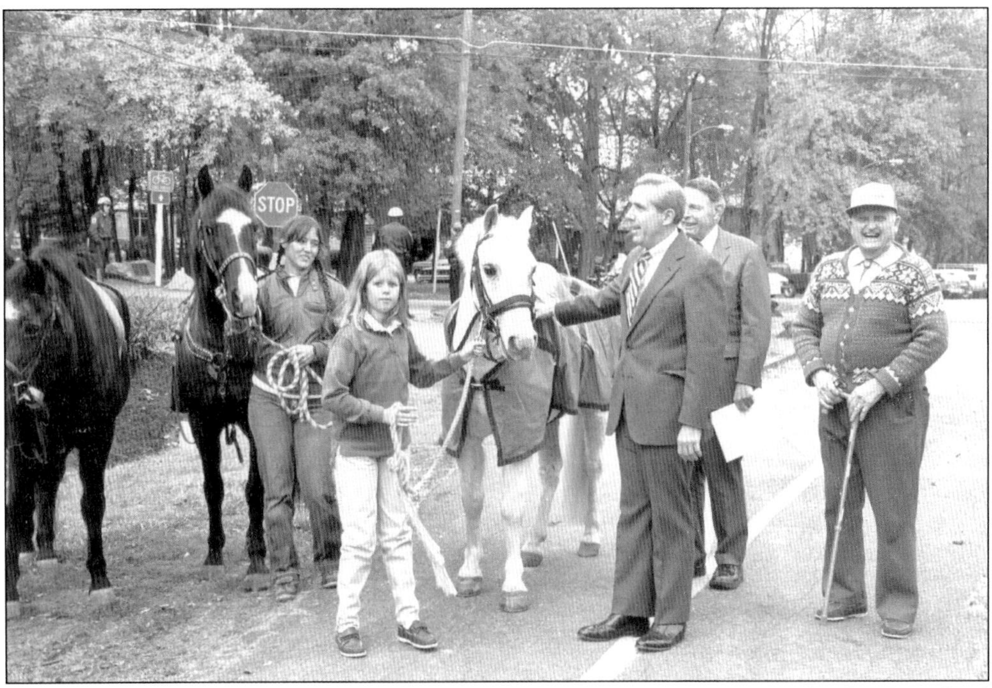

The W&OD Trail experienced such a great success from the beginning that park officials realized the six-foot-wide asphalt trail would not be wide enough. Later sections would be built at eight and 10 feet in width. Some sections, such as along the busy Reston Town Center area, were reconstructed to 12 feet to handle the daily traffic. (Courtesy of NOVA Parks.)

The W&OD Trail also attracted uses that were not imagined when it was first proposed. Cross-country skiers used the trail right after snow fell, lovers of inline skating found the W&OD to be an ideal place to exercise, and groups planning fun runs, walkathons, and fundraisers of all sorts came to the trail as a safer alternative to the streets. (Courtesy of NOVA Parks.)

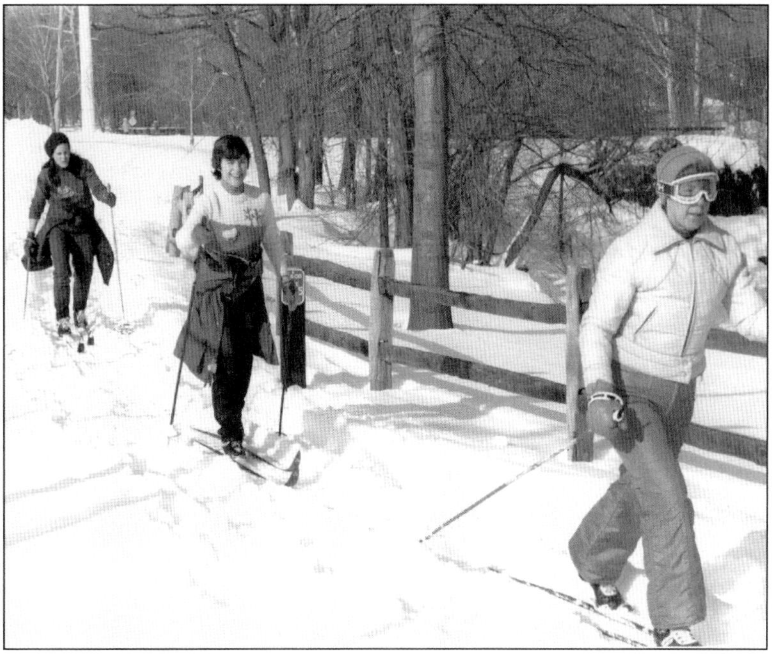

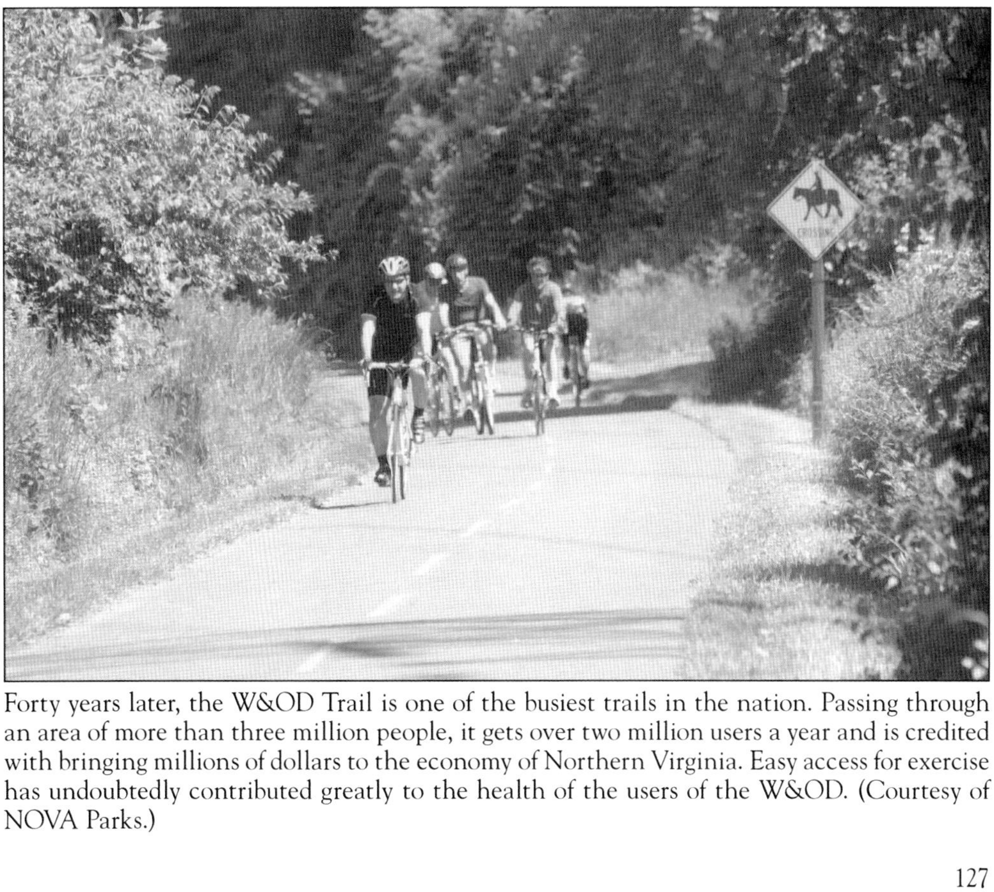

Forty years later, the W&OD Trail is one of the busiest trails in the nation. Passing through an area of more than three million people, it gets over two million users a year and is credited with bringing millions of dollars to the economy of Northern Virginia. Easy access for exercise has undoubtedly contributed greatly to the health of the users of the W&OD. (Courtesy of NOVA Parks.)

Consistent with our mission to preserve history on a local level, this book was printed in South Carolina on American-made paper and manufactured entirely in the United States. Products carrying the accredited Forest Stewardship Council (FSC) label are printed on 100 percent FSC-certified paper.

MADE IN THE USA